D0523892

GBC

GOVERNMENT BEYOND THE CENTRE

SERIES EDITORS: GERRY STOKER & STEVE LEACH

The world of sub-central government and administration – including local authorities, quasi-governmental bodies and the agencies of public-private partnerships – has seen massive changes in recent years and is at the heart of the current restructuring of government in the United Kingdom and other Western democracies.

The intention of the *Government Beyond the Centre* series is to bring the study of this often-neglected world into the mainstream of social science research, applying the spotlight of critical analysis to what has traditionally been the preserve of institutional public administration approaches.

Its focus is on the agenda of change currently being faced by sub-central government, the economic, political and ideological forces that underlie it, and the structures of power and influence that are emerging. Its objective is to provide up-to-date and informative accounts of the new forms of government, management and administration that are emerging.

The series will be of interest to students and practitioners of politics, public and social administration, and all those interested in the reshaping of the governmental institutions which have a daily and major impact on our lives.

Government Beyond the Centre

Series Editors: Gerry Stoker and Steve Leach

Published

Wendy Ball and John Solomos (eds)
Race and Local Politics

Richard Batley and Gerry Stoker (eds)
Local Government in Europe

Clive Gray
Government Beyond the Centre

John Gyford
Citizens, Consumers and Councils

Richard Kerley
Managing in Local Government

Steve Leach, John Stewart and Kieron Walsh
The Changing Organisation and Management of Local Government

Yvonne Rydin
The British Planning System

John Stewart and Gerry Stoker (eds)
Local Government in the 1990s

David Wilson and Chris Game with Gerry Stoker and Steve Leach
An Introduction to Local Government

Series Standing Order

If you would like to receive future titles in this series as they are published, you can make use of our standing order facility. To place a standing order please contact your bookseller or, in case of difficulty,write to us at the address below with your name and address and the name of the series. Please state with which title you wish to begin your standing order. (If you live outside the United Kingdom we may not have the rights for your area, in which case we will forward your order to the publisher concerned.)

Customer Services Department, Macmillan Distribution Ltd
Houndmills, Basingstoke, Hampshire RG21 2XS, England

Citizens, Consumers and Councils

Local Government and the Public

John Gyford

MACMILLAN

First published 1991 by
THE MACMILLAN PRESS LTD
Houndmills, Basingstoke, Hampshire RG21 2XS
and London
Companies and representatives
throughout the world

ISBN 0–333–52534–5 hardcover
ISBN 0–333–52535–3 paperback

A catalogue record for this book is available
from the British Library.

Reprinted 1994

Printed in China

In memory of my parents

Contents

Preface

The basic challenges facing contemporary local government have
been summed up as follows: 'Local authorities have to become
closer to their public as customer and citizen [and] resources have
to be managed to achieve value in service...' (Clarke and Stewart,
1989, p.v). In this book I am concerned with the first of these
challenges, becoming closer to the public, rather than with the
second, managing resources, although of course the two are not
unrelated.

I have attempted to provide an illustrative, rather than a
definitive, account of the ways in which local authorities have
been trying to get closer to their public: the pages which follow
represent an essay in reconnaissance rather than research in a
field of rapidly developing activity. It has not been possible to
refer to every single initiative currently taking place but I hope
that those discussed will give a fair idea of the range of ventures
that are under way. To those local authorities which provided me
with access to officers, members, documents and publications I
am extremely grateful. I also acknowledge with great thanks the
assistance of the Nuffield Foundation, whose award of a grant
helped considerably in the preparation of this book. I am also
indebted to Steven Kennedy, Steve Leach and Gerry Stoker for
some sound editorial advice and to Layla Buzinin for converting
my handwriting into a typescript.

The purpose of what follows is not to provide a manual of
good practice, for such documents are now readily available from
the former Local Government Training Board (now the Local
Government Management Board), the Audit Commission and the
Institute of Local Government Studies. Instead I have attempted
to link the development of such good practice with the context

from which it emerged and with recent debates about 'the proper place of local government in our society' (Ridley, 1988, p.5). Any shortcomings in this attempt are of course my own.

JOHN GYFORD

1 Local Government and the Public

[T]he public: this is the heterogeneous amalgam of actors, a
diversity of behaviours.

> Fagence, 1977, p. 141; emphasis in original.

Social groups

As our opening quotation suggests, attempting to define a local
authority's public is not as simple as it may at first appear. One
shire district for example, in the summer of 1989, circulated an
internal document which defined its public as those who 'live, work
and play within the district'. The outcome of subsequent discussions amongst officers and councillors however was a decision that
a primary duty was owed to those who lived locally, within the
district; debate about the council's objectives was thereafter
couched in terms of that particular definition of the public.

On occasion such debates may spill over into the wider arena of
local electoral politics. Smith (1967) for example records how a
Residents' and Ratepayers' Association enjoyed some political
success in Torquay by articulating the views of those who resented
the council's enthusiasm for catering to the needs of visiting
holidaymakers at the expense, as they saw it, of actual residents
of the locality.

In practice many local authorities will be providing facilities
which are used by visitors and employees from outside the area.
Such people may well of course be paying for these facilities as well
as using them, for example through car parking tickets or

admission charges to sports centres. The reality of this multiple public was recognised in the arrangements for the Revenue Support Grant introduced under the community charge legislation. Provision was made in the formula for the calculation of the Standard Spending Assessment for each authority for the inclusion within the population figures not only of local residents but also of visitors and of those who travelled into the area to work. Such an attempt to accommodate the reality of multiple publics does not however exhaust the problem of definition: there are for example other ways in which the issue of the relevance of locality presents itself over and above the division between resident and non-resident publics. For example there may be divisions of interest which can be broadly grouped under the description of 'the locals versus the newcomers'.

Particularly dramatic instances of such divisions have arisen in those localities where the newcomers were in fact a not yet arrived future population in whose prospective interests existing localities were to be developed or re-developed. New towns, expanding towns and most recently the London Docklands have been the scenes of conflict between those committed to defending the interests of an existing local public and those promoting the cause of 'tomorrow's' incoming public or of what Dennis (1970, p. 339) describes as 'the benefit of posterity'. Thus for example in 1984 the London Borough of Tower Hamlets expressed its concern to the London Docklands Development Corporation about the danger that 'the needs and aspirations of local people are set aside "for the time being" as having a less immediate or substantiated claim on the future' (quoted in Ambrose, 1986, p. 248). The borough feared that once 'set aside' the interests of local people would remain forever in the background.

Another version of this sort of problem can arise in respect of conflicts not between existing and future publics but between local and national publics. The long saga of the search for a site for the third London Airport shows a number of instances of local authorities fretting anxiously over the problem of balancing the competing claims of the two publics (McKie, 1973). A similar analysis can also be made of the conflict in the London Docklands where Ambrose (1986, p. 252) talks of the 'mismatch between clearly and democratically expressed *local* needs and the "new right" government's perception of *national* needs' (his emphasis).

Clashes between an existing local public and a new or future incoming public are not peculiar to areas of planned development or redevelopment. Piecemeal population movements can produce similar divergences of interest. The arrival of the professional middle classes in rural villages has been seen as the source of just such divergences, with farmers and other locals labelling them 'urban newcomers' and 'challenging the legitimacy of their viewpoint and their right to have a say on what happens in the area' (Buller and Lowe, 1982, p. 25). The professional middle classes have of course not confined themselves to discovering and settling in rural England; they have sometimes brought about substantial changes in the nature of the inner city public through the process of gentrification. Sometimes such changes have also been compounded by shifts in the ethnic composition of the local population.

Goss (1988) for example gives a graphic account of the way in which the changing nature of the public affected the local politics of Southwark from the 1950s onwards. Following the industrial struggles of the pre-1914 era there emerged a local political culture based on a proud self-awareness amongst a dominant working class in a community where over 90 per cent of employed males were manual workers. Service provision was largely geared to the needs of a public within which the norm was the nuclear family headed and supported by the male, white manual worker as breadwinner. From the 1950s onwards however economic and social changes undermined first the numerical and then the political dominance of this particular form of white working class public. It came under increasing pressure from new arrivals, gentrifiers, single parents, blacks and the homeless among them, all gradually making demands for representation and service provision. These demands could not always be accommodated easily under the rules of access that had evolved to meet the needs of the established local community. The resulting conflicts were sometimes sharp as the 'old' public began to see itself as increasingly displaced whilst the 'new' fought to overcome what they perceived as their exclusion from access to services and to power.

Changes such as Goss records in Southwark relate to rather different categories of public from those referred to earlier on. In particular the example of Southwark opens up the question of publics who may be defined primarily on the basis of fundamental social categories such as class, race and gender.

The notion that the public embraces members of different social classes is of course commonplace, at least amongst those who accept the reality of class as a feature of social stratification. Moreover at the local level the historical pattern of urban and industrial development, under the impact of the policies and preferences of local authorities, developers and building societies, has often produced a social geography marked by significant degrees of class segregation. As a result individual wards, even entire local authorities as in the case of Southwark, may at a certain point in history constitute a public with a clearly dominant class. Local authorities in turn may respond very directly in order to preserve the character and interests of such local class based publics. Thus Glassberg (1981, p. 46) found that in the 1970s Tower Hamlets was seeking to retain its working class character by preventing the development of new private housing whilst Bromley sought 'to stay predominantly middle- and upper-class by preventing any significant increase in the amount of public housing'. As we have seen, in the 1980s Tower Hamlet's aspirations in this respect were to be thwarted by a Docklands Development Corporation attuned to the interests of well-to-do middle class newcomers moving in from outside the borough.

So long as class remained a major feature of social stratification and also a major factor in determining political loyalty then some authorities were clearly dominated by the linkages of public-class-party. Goss for example shows how at one time Southwark was characterised by a series of inter-connections: people, class, unions, party and council were all interwoven in different ways. There is perhaps some sort of similarity here to the links which were noted in Conservative Croydon by Saunders (1980, pp. 310, 313). In Croydon 'the organizations in which town centre businessmen became involved are those in which local authority members and officers are also to be found'. The result was the existence of 'a relatively dense and cohesive network of business and Conservative political activists, interacting regularly and relatively informally in a variety of institutional contexts'. In both cases, in Southwark and in Croydon, we thus see clear examples of class based institutions providing the social stage on which local politics was enacted.

There are of course those who have denied the relevance of class to an understanding of politics, or at least have deplored the idea that it should become a factor in politics at the local level. The local press for example have long preferred to celebrate the 'good of the town' rather than to interpret the locality as an appropriate arena for class based politics and this is a view which has commanded much support on the right of politics. Yet the success of the suburban middle class in Croydon in defending property values, low rates and educational privilege led Saunders (idem, p. 271) to comment on the paradox that 'the very people who tend to deny the relevance of class divisions . . . are also those who mobilize most strongly in defence of their economic interests'. Nonetheless, if we cannot reasonably discount class as the basis of one important division within the general public, it has been joined in that role during the past decade or more by other social categories, most notably those of gender and race. More specifically there have emerged demands for the recognition and effective representation of female and black publics.

In one respect the relationship between women and local government, especially in earlier times, has been chronicled in some detail by Hollis (1987). She concentrates however on those women who were elected to local office as councillors, as members of school boards or as Poor Law Guardians. These 'ladies elect' as Hollis calls them, often concerned themselves with issues of special importance to women and in doing so took the demands of a female public directly into council chambers and committee meetings. Even so it was not until 1928 that the local government franchises for men and women were assimilated to put them on an equal footing. As for the election of women to local office, they still account for barely a quarter of all councillors despite an increase in their number over the past twenty years. Moreover despite the efforts of generations of women who did succeed in obtaining local political office it was all too easy for their more numerous male colleagues to marginalise them and their concerns. The problem has been clearly stated by Button (1984, p. 4):

Women constitute more than half the electorate, but when they are not invisible they are seen as a minority political interest. They are constantly identified by reference to their husbands, fathers, children or their employment. Very rarely is gender accepted as a valid basis for analysis of needs or responses to policy proposals. Consequently, political agendas are set according to the priorities of the dominant group in society which is

comprised primarily of men. "Women's issues" are largely
organísed out of the public political debate, trivialized, and
relegated as second order issues.

The 'invisibility' of women to which Button refers is clearly evident
in the attempt of John Maud (1937) to sketch the impact of local
government on an ordinary citizen. This citizen is 'municipal man'
whose use of local services and whose eventual emergence through
trade union politics as Labour Mayor of his town is recorded with
only a passing acknowledgement to the existence of women and
then only in their roles as his mother, his wife and the mother of his
son (*sic*). Maud's perceptions were not peculiarly his own. There
are echoes in his sketch of Southwark's 'working-classness [which]
was constructed through male traditions which excluded women's
experience' (Goss, 1988, p. 185).

Such an apparent invisibility of women and the overlooking or
marginalisation of issues important to women have been among the
targets of the women's movement in local government: so too have
been the limited opportunities open to women in both the local
government workforce and in council politics. These concerns have
emerged in the wake of earlier national campaigns in the 1960s on
equal pay and sex discrimination and on abortion and represent
merely one strand in the wider women's liberation movement. In
some authorities specific initiatives were taken in the early 1980s to
address these concerns, notably through the establishment of
women's committees. We shall explore later the nature of these
initiatives.

Initiatives were also being taken at the same time to address the
needs of black people, those whom Bhaduri (1988, p. 22) described
as 'the "invisible" consumers . . . who come from a different race
and culture'. These initiatives included the formation of local
authority race relations committees to articulate black demands.
The particular impetus towards such ventures has been ascribed
variously to political expediency, the desire to court the black
electorate, the pressure of local community relations agencies, the
impact of the 1981 street uprisings, and the determination of a
small number of campaigning individuals (Ouseley, 1984). As was
the case with the demands of the women's movement the issues of
race relations and racial inequality in local government had
antecedents in the 1960s. Thus the report *Colour and Citizenship*

(Rose et al., 1969) drew attention to the difficulties which black people experienced in getting access to housing, education and social services. It also noted that local authorities were loath to employ black workers in professional jobs and had at best a patchy record in respect of black participation in the manual workforce. Although this study was in its way a path-breaking venture some came to see it as flawed through an implicit identification of the black minority as the source of the problem rather than locating the latter in the structures and attitudes of the wider society (Zubaida, 1970). The report did however acknowledge that 'local attitudes affect the policies of local authorities which in turn reinforce the attitudes of their electors' (Rose et al., 1969, pp. 675–6). Breaking down such attitudes became one of the concerns of those councils which addressed themselves to the development of racial equality policies during the 1980s.

We have seen that both women and blacks shared the critique that they were in some way 'invisible' publics to professional and political decision makers, whose assumptions were predominantly those of white males. This critique was expanded by disabled people and by gays and lesbians who complained that those dominant assumptions were also those of the able-bodied and the heterosexual. There were complaints for example that 'people with disabilities are often allowed little control over their own lives and suffer paternalistic attitudes from local authorities' and demands that 'lesbians and gay men should have the option to form households of their choice without having to hide their sexuality' (Dutta and Taylor, 1989, pp. 39 and 33).

The introduction of new social categories based on gender, race, sexuality and disability thus added new publics to those based on class and on aspects of locality. The wisdom and the consequences of accepting such new categories as legitimate varieties of public became a matter of some political debate. Those on the political right, who traditionally had difficulty coping with notions of class, often had even greater problems with social categories originating in gender, sexuality and race. For those on the left the challenge was rather different: the question was one of how to relate the new categories to the left's traditional preoccupation with class as the only truly significant social category. To some extent local councils were forced to accord some recognition to some of the new categories by virtue of the demands of legislation such as the

Race Relations Acts of 1965, 1968 and 1976, the Sex Discrimination Acts 1975 and 1986 and the Disabled Persons (Services, Consultation and Representation) Act 1986. Recognition and action was not however always as wholehearted as some would have wished and charges of tokenism were sometimes levelled: 'an Equal Opportunity logo, a black appointment, a toothless committee, marginal funding for a small project' for example (Liverpool Black Caucus, 1986, p. 137). Nonetheless by the end of the 1980s the claims of these new social categories had been placed firmly on the agenda of local government even if some councils dealt with them in a rather gingerly fashion.

In referring to them as social categories however we do them less than justice, for they are clearly more than elements in a system of social classification. We may also refer to them as social groups, actual or potential. A social group usually has 'at least a rudimentary structure and organization' and also some basis in 'the consciousness of its members': families, villages and political parties are examples. There are also quasi-groups, lacking such structure, organization and consciousness, and typified for instance by social classes, age groups and sex groups. However, 'the frontier between groups and quasi-groups is fluid and variable. Quasi-groups may give rise to organized social groups as, for example, . . . the feminine sex group to feminist associations' (Bottomore, 1975, p. 99). On this basis we may therefore see the appearance of new, often self-defining, categories of the public as also entailing the emergence of new social groups with a potential for articulating their own demands for recognition as components of the general public.

Individual roles

Social groups are not the only forms in which members of the public may present themselves to local government. Individuals also occupy multiple statuses in society as parents, motorists, students, sports players and shoppers for instance. Closely linked to each such status is an appropriate role, 'an expected pattern of conduct' which embraces both 'the expectations and . . . the performance of an individual occupying a particular status' (Gerth and Mills, 1969, p. 83; Smith and Preston, 1977, p. 78). In the context of local government there are three particular roles which have traditionally dominated relations between local authorities and the public: the ratepayer who funds the local services, the client who receives the services and the voter who authorises their provision through the ballot box.

Traditionally the role of ratepayer was one which was accorded a certain degree of privilege. The Municipal Corporations Act 1835 'emphasised not the services which borough councils might give to the people, but their duty to prevent unauthorised expenditure'. As a result councils were seen 'primarily as trustees of public funds . . . [which] justified the exclusion from the franchise of every person who did not directly contribute to the funds of the local authorities' (Keith-Lucas, 1952, pp. 9–10). The electoral public of post-1835 local government was thus initially very modest in size, basing itself on those who paid the rates.

Despite the gradual broadening of the franchise thereafter to the point of universal suffrage there still persisted the view that actual ratepayers stood in a special position in relation to any wider public. Thus the 'Fares Fair' policy of public transport subsidisation introduced by the Greater London Council (GLC) fell foul of just such a view when challenged in the courts in 1983. The House of Lords eventually ruled that the GLC owed a special fiduciary duty – a duty of trust – to the ratepayers, which outweighed its obligations to members of the public who used the transport system or to those who benefited indirectly from the existence of such a system. The reduction of fares under the contested GLC policy was held to constitute 'a thriftless use' of the ratepayers' money. This ruling, as articulated by Lord Diplock, has been criticised for its 'extreme formalism and lack of rigour' (Loughlin, 1986, p. 73) but it stands squarely within a tradition which places the interests of the ratepaying public before those of the service using public.

Indeed this tradition has sometimes gone as far as desiring not merely to promote the interests of the ratepayers but also to curb the rights of service users. This was particularly true in the case of those in receipt of poor relief who were disqualified from voting in local elections until 1918, and who were also disqualified from membership of certain types of local authority until 1948 when the last vestiges of the Poor Law were swept away. This clash of interests between those who were seen as the financial providers of services and those who were seen as the recipients of services was to have a recurring significance in debates about accountability in local government. For example the Green Paper *Paying for Local Government* produced in 1986 referred to the government's concern over the fact that out of 35 million electors only 18 million were liable to pay rates and of the latter only 12 million were liable to pay their rates in full. One consequence was that 'those who receive full relief can vote for higher services without having to pay anything towards them' (idem, para. 137). Furthermore, the non-domestic ratepayers enjoyed no direct electoral representation. As one government minister explained:

> if you take out all the commercial and industrial ratepayers . . . who don't have a vote; and those on supplementary benefit who don't pay rates; those who have a rate rebate; council tenants who don't know they pay rates and those who work for the council then you're left with only a relatively few free standing rate payers. That's hardly taxation with responsibility (quoted in Gyford and James, 1983, p. 174).

The minister's concern for the primacy of the ratepayer's interest as against that of the users of council services is a modern version of that fear expressed by Lord Salisbury in 1886 when contemplating the administration of the Poor Law coming under the control of the non-rate paying common people; it was, he warned, 'rather like leaving the cat in charge of the cream jug' (quoted in Keith-Lucas, 1952, p. 110). The fact that Salisbury's concern related to the Poor Law was not accidental.

> In school board work, those who paid rates, those who voted, and those who benefited from educational services overlapped. As school standards rose and as more lower-middle-class children attended board schools, the overlap strengthened . . . . The reverse was true within the poor law. Those who received poor relief and the increasing number who had medical aid, were automatically disenfranchised. So the concept of accountability was a very ambiguous one. To whom? Paupers? Ratepayers? Working Men? (Hollis, 1987, p. 221).

There has then been particular concern about accountability in respect of those local services which ratepayers saw themselves as providing for others, rather than for themselves. It was moreover a concern predicated upon the proposition that ratepayers were in some way a put-upon minority liable to be taken advantage of by the beneficiaries of the services that they financed.

This ignored of course the fact that some of those who did not individually pay rates might well be contributing through other taxes and then via central government grants to local authority finances. In any event, most individuals who did not pay rates were members of a household that did; indeed in 1986 94 per cent of all electors saw themselves as ratepayers (Widdicombe, 1986a, p. 40). There is moreover no evidence to show that non-ratepaying individuals were more likely to vote at local elections in order to extract advantage from non-voting ratepaying fellow residents. As Miller concluded;

> ratepayers and non-ratepayers were almost equally likely to vote in local elections, with the merest hint of higher turn-out rates amongst ratepayers . . . . Contrary to central government's fears that irresponsible non-ratepayers would take advantage of the opportunity to impose taxes on the ratepayers, the non-rate-payers not only failed to turn out in especially great numbers, they failed even to appreciate that they were non-ratepayers (Miller, 1988, pp. 232–3).

The community charge or poll tax was of course offered as a solution to what the government saw as the lack of an adequate link between taxation and representation. By obliging every individual adult to pay the tax it was hoped to ensure that every voter would also be a taxpayer. This aspiration appeared to ignore the likelihood that in practice the charge would often be paid out of household income rather than individual income, except of course in the case of single people. However the imposition of the community charge on an individual basis, rather than on a property related basis, did have one significant consequence. It completed the process whereby the ratepayer (now the charge-payer) had over the years moved from being conceived of as a member of a particular social category of property owner to that of a role to be enacted, if not enjoyed, by all adult members of the public: whether the burden of that role had been fairly distributed remained of course a matter for vigorous debate.

A similar translation from restricted social category to a universal individual role had been experienced by the local government elector as the franchise was gradually extended through the passage of over thirty Acts of Parliament in the nineteenth and twentieth centuries. The view that 'the right to vote was inherent not in the individual but in the occupation of property' (Keith Lucas, 1952, p. 75) was to succumb gradually to the pressures for universal suffrage: and as local government thereby became more formally democratic, so too its own justification as an institution came to include the claim that it constituted a mechanism through which local services could not only be provided but could also be made accountable to the community as a whole through the ballot box. In the words of the report of the Widdicombe Committee (1986a, p. 56; emphasis in original):

> If . . . local government is strong on the delivery of services but weak in the extent to which it provides for local democratic self-expression it ceases to be sufficiently distinct from local *administration*.

The validity of the democratic claims for local government is one which merits more examination. Any such examination must of course involve us in a consideration of how the public themselves perform their role as voters. First we need to consider whether the public's opportunity to perform its electoral role is either wide-spread or meaningful. The opportunity to vote presumes the existence of contested elections: on this score the modern elector can rarely complain. Ever since the second World War, and especially since the local government reorganisations of the early 1970s, there has been a steady growth in the proportion of contested seats at local elections. The days when an incumbent councillor could survive without challenge over successive elections have now largely disappeared, except in the remoter rural areas. The engine of this advance in electoral competition has been the spread of party politics, for it is the parties which have seized on council elections as arenas not only for contesting for local power but also for keeping the party organisation in fighting shape and for renewing their supporters' voting loyalties.

However, more contested elections might not necessarily signify more meaningful or more politically consequential contests if hitherto unopposed candidates now become regularly re-elected candidates as a result of the local social geography mandating a permanent one-party majority on the council. Thus for example, Dunleavy (1980, ch.5) argued that effective party competition at the local level was the exception rather than the rule: he calculated that three-quarters of the population of England and Wales lived in areas where changes of party control were unlikely to occur at the most important levels of local government, namely the shire counties, the metropolitan districts and the London boroughs. Under such circumstances the role of the individual elector could be seen as one of minimal significance.

For the period up until the 1980s Dunleavy's analysis seemed to contain a ring of truth, for most students of the topic were aware of such seemingly impregnable party strongholds as the Conservative and Labour London boroughs of Richmond-upon-Thames and Tower Hamlets respectively, where leafy suburbs and dockside communities seemed locked into perpetual re-election of their traditional majority parties. Yet in 1986 the then Liberal–SDP Alliance won control of both authorities, with the Liberal Democrats retaining control in both cases in 1990. Similarly the notion of the enduring Conservatism of the shires was widely accepted; but in 1985 twenty-one of the thirty-nine county councils in England became 'hung' authorities with Alliance-led or Labour-led minority administrations taking over in eleven of them. Despite a swing back to the Conservatives in 1989 some twelve counties still remained as hung authorities. It is too early to tell whether such departures from traditional one party domination in some authorities were anything other than a temporary phenomenon, a product particularly of the brief burgeoning of the Alliance in the mid-1980s. They may however have also been a reflection of a wider loosening of party loyalties and a greater volatility amongst the electorate, of which the Alliance was itself a temporary beneficiary, but which may yet express itself in less predictable voting patterns than hitherto and perhaps allow more scope to the electoral role.

Whatever changes may have been under way during the 1980s one phenomenon does seem to have been consistent with previous decades, namely the low turnout at local elections. This is something which has been bemoaned by successive generations of commentators since the 1920s. Britain's low turnout – around 40 per cent during the 1980s – has also been compared unfavourably with that prevailing in other countries. For example the Widdicombe Committee (1986e, p. 146) reported a turnout of roughly 70 per cent in city elections in twelve western nations. In his research into local electoral behaviour Miller (1988, p. 233) concluded that low turn-out 'was produced by intermittent participation rather than by an electorate stratified into consistent voters and consistent abstainers'. However even if most voters do vote at some time or another, with greater or lesser frequency, one persistent concern has been their apparent tendency to vote not on local issues but on the basis of national factors.

Miller's investigations for the Widdicombe Committee (1980d, pp. 158–72) put the proportion of voters who cast their local vote exactly in line with their national party preference at 80 per cent: the remaining 20 per cent either had no consistent national party preference or, if they did, were prepared to ignore it in casting their local vote. If the figure of 20 per cent of votes prepared to cast a 'non-national' vote is an overall average – as indeed it is – then in individual localities the percentage could of course be higher. This in turn could produce those local elections in which the results undoubtedly run counter to the national trend, as observed for example by Jones and Stewart (1982), and in which electors have performed their roles with locally distinctive consequences.

In general however it seems safe to agree with the assessment of Bristow (1982, p. 163) that such local variations exist 'within a pattern whose outline is defined very largely by national considerations': or as Miller puts the same point in a slightly different way; 'clearly local choices are *not totally* dependent upon national choices; equally clearly they are fairly strongly related to national preferences' (Miller, 1988, p. 236, emphasis in original).

In their roles as voters and as ratepayers–chargepayers, members of the public provide local councils with political authorisation and financial resources for the conduct of their activities. In carrying out those activities councils then deal with the public as recipients of their services and in that context the public can be perceived as occupying the role of client. Dictionary definitions of the term 'client' tend to stress either a lay person's relationship with a professional person or a quality of dependence. Both these characteristics have their relevance when considering the client role in relation to local government. Stewart (1986, p. 217) has described local government as an institution dominated by 'managerial professionalism' which 'retains much of the identity of the profession . . . but on an organisational rather than on an individual basis'. Despite the general truth of this account however it is important to note that not all the local authority professions stand in quite the same relationship to the public.

An important distinction is that drawn by Laffin (1986, p. 23). He distinguishes between the 'public service' professions and the 'technobureaucratic' professions. The first group 'are in the front line of service provision' and include social workers, housing managers, teachers and planners. The second group, the techno-bureaucrats, are concerned with managing the organisations within which the public service professions are employed; they include for example local authority administrators and accountants. It is the public service professionals who have the most direct contact with the public. Their attitudes to the public and to the proper relationship between professionals and lay people can be a crucial element in the contacts between councils and their public.

As local government developed its welfare functions, and therefore its greater involvement in the lives of ordinary people, such involvement produced problems in its wake. Hollis (1987, pp. 394–5) records the way in which in the Edwardian era local government viewed from below by the recipients of its attentions looked very different from the view from above:

School teachers imposed standards of discipline, punctuality, and cleanliness that poorer working-class families found hard to meet; school attendance officers denied families their children's earnings . . . . Sanitary inspectors were feared as an inquisitive police, knocking in the night to see how many people were sleeping in how many rooms . . .. Health visitors, eyeing every dark corner of the living-room and every grubby child seemed over-critical of working-class mothers and their homes. Medical Officers of Health sometimes confessed themselves baffled by the resistance of slum dwellers to slum clearance . . . and could not comprehend the attachment of the elderly to their homes and their neighbourhood.

A more recent version of this last particular incomprehension was encountered in the context of local authority planning by Gower Davies (1972) in his study of the Rye Hill area of Newcastle-upon-Tyne. The focus of his investigation was the attempt by the city council's planning department to 'revitalise' a so-called 'twilight area'. In the course of his research the relations between the professional planners and the inhabitants of the area became a central pre-occupation. This led him to make some harsh criticisms of some of the ambitions and practices of the planners and of their impact on the lives of those for whom they were trying to plan.

He was particularly sceptical about the planners' claims to be the guardians and implementers of the public interest and of their self-appropriation of the language of progress, vision, comprehensiveness and human welfare, whereby those who disagreed with them could be dismissed as backward-looking, short-sighted, narrow-minded and selfish. The claim by one Newcastle planner that those in the profession required 'a basic confidence to *know* that you're right when everyone else is saying that you're wrong' (idem, p. 119 emphasis in original) seemed to confirm this over-bearing attitude.

Gower Davies linked this stance with the way in which the public was perceived by the planners. In particular he distinguished between notions of the public as customers and as clients.

> The *customer* is always right: he can choose, criticize, and reject. The *client*, on the other hand, gives up those privileges and accepts the superior judgement of the professional. It is one of the aims of the would-be profession to convert its customers into clients (idem, p. 220; emphasis in original).

Such perceptions of the public as clients have consequences in the way they are treated, as Gower Davies suggests. The Barclay report on *Social Workers: Their Role and Tasks* (1982, p. xii) made a similar observation when it commented that the term 'client' was likely to provoke 'negative reactions . . . as implying an undesirable degree of dependence and perhaps of stigma'. Gower Davies' distinction between 'client' and 'customer' is clearly intended to convey a distinction between the public as object and the public as subject, or between a passive and an active public: in terms of local government service provision it is the difference between a public whose role is simply that of recipient of whatever services the council chooses to provide and a public which has at least some role in determining the nature of that provision.

Council officers are not of course the only elements within local government to come into contact with the public. Councillors, as the elected representatives of the public, may have their own perceptions of those who receive the council's services. Thus Helen Bentwich, a Labour member of the London County Council from 1937 to 1964, constructed her book *Our Councils* (1962) around the notion of 'the grumblers', those 'men and women [who] are grumbling about things which are wrong, and need putting right in the places where they live'. The grumblers constantly complained that 'they really should do something about it' without realising that ultimately 'they' were 'we' (p. 2).

An even bleaker view was expressed in 1949, about that section of the public who lived in council housing, by an Independent councillor from Finchley, Mrs. G. I. Wilson. She feared that council tenants had 'a terrible feeling of irresponsibility' and was concerned that their 'loss of initiative and dependent attitude' were 'attacking the moral fibre of the nation' (quoted in *Labour Councillor*, June 1949). The broader notion that users of council services were in danger of being trapped into dependency was of course to become a staple argument of another Finchley politician in the 1980s.

Some perceptions have been less concerned with moral criticism. One county alderman of the author's acquaintance, having served as a district officer in India under the Raj, saw his local government work as being 'very much like running a native district'; he took a lofty but benign and paternal view of the needs of humble villagers, be they in Essex or in India. He clearly saw them as being under his 'protection or patronage', which the Oxford English Dictionary (1989) describes as the condition of the client.

All three roles we have thus far considered tend to have certain passive qualities associated with them. Apart from the dependency associated with the client role, there is the apathy associated with a low turnout to perform the role of voter or elector, whilst the traditional rendering of the role of ratepayer was always that of the victim, endlessly put upon by others. In recent years however other roles have been identified, in which there is a greater stress on a more active role for members of the local public in their dealings with local government: these active roles are those of the citizen and the consumer.

At the Conservative Party's local government conference in 1989 Margaret Thatcher made no fewer than eleven references to 'the citizen'. In the course of so doing she spoke of the emergence of 'a new kind of council' which 'handed power and responsibility back to the citizen'. In the same year the Labour Party's local government conference devoted one of its sessions to a discussion of *Consumers and the Community*, one of the documents produced as part of the party's policy review for the 1990s. The document advised party members that it had become 'essential that the public sector orients itself more towards the consumer' (Labour Party, 1988, p. 28).

Neither the Conservative Party nor the Labour Party could at this point claim any mutually exclusive identification with notions of citizenship and consumerism respectively. Much of the thrust of the Conservative Government's programme since 1979 had been justified by reference to the need to encourage what has been called 'the sovereign consumer in competitive markets' (Harris and Seldon, 1979, p. 68). As for the Labour Party, the party's final policy review report contained a preface by Neil Kinnock in which he referred to the goal of creating a society in which 'citizens have the means and the self-assurance to take responsibility for their own lives and to fulfil their obligations to others' (Labour Party, 1989a, p. 6). Thus by the end of the 1980s the two major parties had both come to talk the language of citizenship and consumerism, though not necessarily always agreeing on how those two terms might be best interpreted.

The citizen and the consumer could for example be regarded as political and economic creatures respectively. From that perspective the citizen debating public issues in the agora of ancient Greece could be seen as the historical symbol of political democracy. The consumer making judgements on price and quality in the shopping centre would be the contemporary symbol of economic democracy. As such images suggest, debates about public issues amongst the citizens lead to collective political decisions, whereas comparison shopping by consumers leads to individual economic decisions. On that basis one might be inclined to see citizenship issuing in political collectivism, as a left wing concept, with consumerism, issuing in individualism, as a right wing concept. Indeed in their book *Democracy in Crisis* David Blunkett and Keith Jackson (1987, p. 4) suggest a similar contrast, interpreting the local government conflicts of the 1980s as being 'a clash between political democracy and "economic democracy"' and arguing for the defence and extension of the former against the latter.

It is possible to go further than identifying citizens and consumers as the exponents of contrasting forms of democracy. They could be seen as representing wholly contrasting concepts of humanity. Thus Evans and Boyte (1986, p. 5) celebrate the virtue of the citizen as 'one who was able to put aside at times immediate and personal interests and focus on public affairs'. In the same passage they go on to identify the values of citizenship as

> a concern for the common good [and] the welfare of the comm-
> unity as a whole . . . acceptance of the primacy of the
> community's decisions over one's own private inclinations and
> a recognition of one's obligations to defend and serve the public.

This perception of the citizen of civic virtue could then be contrasted with the notion of the consumer as

> the last in a long train of models that depict man as a greedy,
> self-interested, acquisitive survivor . . . a creature of great reason
> devoted to small ends . . . [in] a world of carrots and sticks
> (Barber, 1984, p. 22).

The stark contrast displayed here is similar to that implied by Arendt (1979, pp. 330–1) in which the citizen has opinions whereas the consumer has interests and each, whom she describes respectively as '*le citoyen*' and '*le bourgeois*', represents a different 'model of man'.

However recent discussions about citizenship and consumerism in the context of local government have tended to see the citizen and the consumer as roles which jostle with others for recognition or performance. 'We are consumers and citizens, citizens and electors, electors and tax-payers, tax-payers and contributors, contributors and producers' (Labour Party, 1988, p. 27). If we accept the idea of the citizen and the consumer as roles then we may also acknowledge that these roles may be performed in a variety of ways. The consumer for example may directly and consciously participate in the receipt of some personal services such as housing or social work or residential care, whilst being only indirectly in receipt of regulatory services such as town and country planning and environmental health, or of promotional services such as economic development or tourism. The citizen too, for example, might engage in the 'episodic citizenship of those who enter the public realm only in response to intolerable situations' rather than being committed to any permanent performance of a civic role (Kateb, 1984, p. 42).

Discussing the public in terms of such roles as the citizen and the consumer is not a wholly new development, for it echoes some of the aspirations which were voiced for local government in the past by John Stuart Mill and Sidney Webb. Mill has been described by one of his biographers as being 'everywhere and at all times a good citizen', whilst a more recent commentator referred to him as one of the 'enthusiasts for citizenship . . . [who] would have put us on parish councils and the like in the same way we are enrolled for jury service' (Hamilton, 1933, p. 79; Ryan, 1990). He was certainly an opponent of 'the passive type of character [which] is favoured by the government of one or a few' and he spoke warmly of 'the moral part of the instruction afforded by the participation of the private citizen, if even rarely, in public functions'. As to where such instruction might be obtained he referred specifically to 'the local administrative institutions . . . [as] the chief instrument' of this 'public education of the citizens' (Mill, 1947, pp. 215, 217 and 347). Sidney Webb perhaps took a rather less high-minded view, but even so he saw in local government a potential for the creation of democratic forms of collective self-provision with the local authority functioning as a 'democratic organisation [established] on the basis of the association of consumers for the supply of their own needs' (Webb, 1910, p. 734). The aspirations of Mill and Webb were however to come up against the constraints of representative democracy, bureaucracy and professionalism: it is these very constraints which are now under challenge through the new articulation of the roles of citizen and consumer.

Reappraisals

Since the middle of the 1970s there has developed 'what might be described as a stage of reappraisal in local politics, with the emergence of major debates both between and within the political parties about the role of local government in society' (Gyford, 1985a, p. 80). A crucial element in this period of reappraisal has been a reassessment of local government's relations with its public. This reassessment has embraced the identification of new social groups making their own demands on local authorities and the recognition of the roles of the individual citizen and consumer to supplement, if not to replace, those of the ratepayer, voter and client. This conceptual reappraisal of the nature of the public has been accompanied by a further operational reappraisal, one which examines the ability of local government to function effectively as a means of securing accountability and responsiveness to a more diverse and more active public. This operational reappraisal has taken two forms, both of which may be also seen as part of a broader reappraisal of the workings of the post-war welfare state. There has been first a reassessment of the traditional methods of local government service delivery and second a reassessment of local government's relations with other service-providing sectors, that is the private, the voluntary and the informal sectors. In the first case, established professional and bureaucratic models of service delivery have been called into question for falling short of rising public expectations about accountability, responsiveness and accessibility. In the second case, multi-sector provision has been canvassed as a means of accommodating growing public pressure for the diversity and choice said to be thwarted by municipal monopoly.

Local government thus entered the 1990s engaged in a variety of debates and initiatives arising out of the conceptual and operational reappraisals in which it had become involved. In the next chapter we shall explore the social and political factors which have promoted these reappraisals. We then turn to the operational reappraisals which will be our particular concern in this book. In Chapters 3, 4 and 5 we examine the broad spectrum of recent operational initiatives, ranging from those containing elements of power sharing and participation, through those concerned with forms of consultation, to those focusing on information and accessibility. In chapter 6 we take up the issue of multi-sector service provision and inquire into the prospects for some form of municipal pluralism. Finally, in chapter 7, we place these operational reappraisals and the initiatives which have flowed from them in the context of the conceptual reappraisal of the role of the public and suggest how these reappraisals might also be linked with the recent debate on the nature of the enabling council.

2 Pressures for Change

There have probably been few periods in recent history when change of some sort has not been on the agenda; it is one of the defining characteristics of modern society. Yet the last two or more decades do seem to have been marked by transformations of a very different order and moreover transformations which in different ways and with different timings have affected a wide range of aspects of society.

Cochrane and Anderson, 1989, p. vii.

The social transformations referred to by Cochrane and Anderson have not been without their impact on local government. In the opening chapter we referred to the changing nature of the relations between local authorities and their immediate public, those who use them, finance them and hold them to account. However the whole system of local government itself, as a national institution, and the politics of local government, as a part of the national political life, have both proved liable to change under the impact of social and political transformation. Two particular sets of changes are of importance in this context. One is the gradual move away from a predominantly urban and industrial society towards one characterised by a drift away from the cities and by both de-industrialisation and changing forms of production. The other is the emergence of an increasingly diverse society and of a less deferential, more assertive political culture, both of which have contributed to the appearance of new forms of politics.

After the industrial city

The origins of our present local government system are closely
related to the impact of industrialisation and urbanisation on social
life during the nineteenth century. The problematic nature of this
impact was summarised by Briggs in his account of the Victorian
city:

> The industrial city was bound to be a place of problems.
> Economic individualism and common civic purpose were
> difficult to reconcile. The priority of industrial discipline in
> shaping all human relations was bound to make other aspects of
> life seem secondary. A high rate of industrial investment meant
> not only a low rate of consumption and a paucity of social
> investment but a total indifference to social cost (Briggs, 1968,
> p. 18).

Such indifference to social costs could not however be sustained
indefinitely. For one thing certain social costs, in the form of
epidemic disease, were not always respecters of social class; those
for whom economic individualism was a self-evident truth came to
see a certain self-protective virtue in preventive public health
measures. More broadly it could be, and was, argued that such
measures saved money in the long run: as one writer expressed it in
the 1840s 'it costs more money to create disease than to prevent it'.
Such sentiments created a situation in which '"civic economy" was
a branch of political economy' (idem, p. 21) and in which measures
of sanitary and health reform found a utilitarian justification that
was later to be supplemented by more philanthropic and ideological arguments.

The operation of the various measures of public health reform,
and of other contemporary civic interventions such as paving and
lighting, initially fell to *ad hoc* local bodies and it was not until the
second part of the century that these gave way to a more
integrated, multi-functional form of municipal authority. It was
through the latter form of institution that Joseph Chamberlain as
Mayor of Birmingham was able to boast that the city had been
'parked, paved, assized, marketed, Gas-and-Watered, and
improved' (quoted in Garvin, 1932, p. 202, emphasis in original).
Such a boast conveyed the notion that the city, as a political entity,

provided the opportunity to solve the social problems that it generated as an economic entity. This was a view also expressed by other contemporaries of Chamberlain.

Thus for Sidney Webb (1891, p. 207) it was clear that 'the hope of the future for dense urban communities . . . lies in the wise extension of collectivist action'. For the economist J.A. Hobson the 'raw material of local proximity' needed to be transformed into 'wholesome neighbourhood' by the municipal reformers: he looked to 'civic feeling' to 'safeguard the public welfare against the encroachments of private industrial greed' and to express the 'spiritual dignity of a complex common life' (quoted in Short, 1989, p. 73). The sense of civic purpose which underlay the aspirations of Webb and Hobson and the achievements of Chamberlain found its ultimate organisational expression in the single-tier, multi-purpose county boroughs of the great and middling industrial cities and towns. From the imposing town halls of these authorities were administered the whole range of sanitary, health and utility services which had operated in piecemeal fashion before being taken under their wing. With the town halls securing control of education in 1902 and of Poor Law functions, including hospitals, in 1929 and with the development of new powers in fields such as housing and town planning, there was scarcely any area of the city's 'common life' upon which the county borough council did not touch at one time or another. For some of its inhabitants it provided services, for others it provided jobs, for many it provided both. If 'the period from the late nineteenth century to the Second World War might well be called the heyday of local government' (Stevenson, 1984, p. 307) then the town halls of the county boroughs were the stages on which that heyday was most fully and richly played out.

In an often quoted passage Sidney Webb described the full range of provision which such authorities offered during and for decades after the late Victorian age. He spoke of the town councillor who, despite his professed *laissez-faire* individualism, would nevertheless

walk along the municipal pavement, lit by the municipal gas and cleansed by municipal brooms with municipal water, and seeing by the municipal clock in the municipal market place that he is too early to meet his children coming from the municipal school hard by the county lunatic asylum and municipal hospital, will use the national telegraph system to tell them not to walk through the municipal park, but to come by the municipal tram to meet him in the municipal reading room by the municipal art gallery, museum and library (quoted in Fraser, 1979, p. 171).

The purpose behind Webb's painting of this picture of municipal enterprise was of course to contrast the reality of the councillor's embrace of public provision with his rhetorical claim that 'individual self-help, that's what made our city what it is' (ibid). Yet there is another element implicit in the picture, a sense that all these facilities are 'hard by' one another, or at least readily accessible by a 'walk through the municipal park' or by a short ride on 'the municipal tram'. For Webb was talking of cities with a densely packed population, dependent largely on a widely used public transport system radiating out from the centre. If municipal provision was concentrated organisationally in the hands of the county borough and its town hall staff then much of it was also concentrated spatially in or near the geographic heart of the city where public access was maximised. In these respects the local government of the industrial city during the 'golden age' of its heyday can be seen as one of centralised provision in both organisational and spatial terms.

The same model could not operate outside the cities. In the counties the factors of distance and low population density produced a different pattern of local government. A two tier system of county councils and district and borough councils divided services between them, operating on different geographical scales. The larger counties often found it convenient to adopt various systems of administrative sub-division – area or divisional offices – to cope with the day to day running of services: in some instances both county and district levels became involved in various ways in the joint administration of services, most notably education, through systems of divisional executives. Thus local government in the counties developed in a more dispersed fashion, both spatially and organisationally, than was common in the cities.

One thing however was noticeable and increasingly problematic. Within the counties the one burning ambition of every town of consequence was to escape from the two tier system and to attain the glory of county borough status. The more they were successful in this ambition the weaker the system they left behind them and the greater the incentive for others to follow suit.

The uneasy coexistence of two forms of local government, one for the cities and one for the rural and semi-rural counties, was not seriously challenged in principle however until the investigations carried out in the 1960s by the Redcliffe-Maud Commission (1969). In the debate provoked by these investigations one topic discussed was that of how far a changing social geography required new forms of local government; the question of whether an urban–rural dichotomy provided a secure basis for differing forms of local government was a key issue here. The actual reorganisation of local government which followed the commission's report owed as much to political judgement as it did to any investigatory findings. The most notable casualty of the reorganisation was however the county borough: the cities now found themselves part of a universal two tier system. The metropolitan counties and the shire counties absorbed the old county boroughs, whose proud independence was now judged to be anachronistic in the wake of shifting patterns of population, transportation and labour markets. The conurbation or the freestanding provincial city and its hinterland were now seen as the significant units of social geography around which local government should be reconstructed.

If the reorganisation of the early 1970s was in fact an attempt to come to terms with economic and demographic trends it was perhaps largely an exercise in catching up with developments that had already occurred. Since then however the pace of change has if anything increased and has thereby raised further but rather different questions about the 'fit' between local government and the realities of social change.

One often remarked feature of the 1980s was the de-industrialisation of the British economy, in the sense of the declining share of economic activity or employment held by the manufacturing sector. Manufacturing employment peaked at 8.7 million workers in 1966, falling away to 5 million in 1988; almost half the fall occurred after 1979, partly no doubt a reflection of the severe recession of the early 1980s. Employment in the service sector by contrast grew to the point where by the end of the 1980s it accounted for 14.7 million workers or over 60 per cent of all non-agricultural workers. The experience of de-industrialisation has not been unique to Britain: Britain has however seen 'a greater fall in the relative importance of the manufacturing sectors than most other advanced countries . . . [and] also started to be subject to deindustrialisation in this sense earlier than elsewhere' (McDowell, 1989, pp. 140–1; Ball, 1989, p. 88)

This decline in manufacturing has been accompanied by shifts in the geography of population. After the mid 1970s, according to A. H. Halsey (1987, p. 19) 'a new phase of economic and social transformation occurred'. In the course of transformation

> The shift away from urban industrial manufacturing was accelerated . . . and population movement away from the inner cities towards suburbia, the South East and the new town was discernible. And in the process a pattern has emerged of . . . the newer economy of a 'green and pleasant land' . . . [contrasted with] the old provincial industrial cities and their displaced fragments of peripheral council housing estates (ibid.)

The same process has been described by Hall (1988, pp. 16 and 18) as 'a profound decentralisation of the population, on a very large spatial scale': as part of this process 'the cities – with a few exceptions – have lost their former economic roles' and have yet to acquire new ones.

Such changes clearly bring major problems for local government. Most obviously they impose on city authorities demands for policies to attenuate the impact of decline and to generate new economic activities to compensate for those that have vanished – and all on the basis of a declining local tax base. They also of course bring pressure on the new areas of growth, such as the rural districts and the cathedral and market towns, for high quality services commensurate with the aspirations of the incoming population as well as demands to control the local pace of growth and development.

Taken together the processes of de-industrialisation and counter-urbanisation have thus undermined the social geography upon which rested not only the 'golden age' of local government but also its immediate post-war successor, in which councils had become very much the local arm of a national welfare state. These two processes have left city authorities coping with an ebbing economy and their counterparts in the shires wrestling with the problems of a wave of development. In these terms the key problems have been seen not so much as ones of adapting the structure of local government to fit the new social realities, as of devising policies and seeking resources to meet new local needs. A variety of initiatives in the fields of planning, economic development and public-private sector partnerships for example flourished during the 1980s, as local authorities attempted to grapple with their particular problems of growth or decline. However it may also be argued that the transformations under way in society over the past two decades do ultimately require not only new policies but also new forms of organisation through which to deliver those policies. It has been argued that the form of government appropriate for an industrial era 'becomes over-institutionalized in the post-industrial period. Its large scale bureaucracies become increasingly ill adapted to meet the growing and differentiated needs of the public they serve' (Benjamin, 1977, p. 165). This line of argument has been further developed in the debate about post-Fordism.

The key issue in this debate is whether or not the process of de-industrialisation is being accompanied by significant changes in what remains of the industrial sector, changes which also have an impact beyond that sector. The basic proposition is that we have been witnessing the decline of old style assembly-line mass production methods aimed at satisfying a mass consumer market, of the sort pioneered by Henry Ford: under this system of production work was highly routinised, closely supervised and organised under tight hierarchical control along the lines of 'scientific management' as pioneered by Frederick Taylor. Post-Fordism argues that new technologies are drastically altering production, stocking and retailing methods, leading to a new pattern of small batch production of customised products and employing a more versatile workforce with a greater degree of autonomy on the job. In the latter context post-Fordism also implies a form of post-Taylorism and thereby has a wider significance for systems of management beyond manufacturing industry.

Whether or not the post-Fordist hypothesis is true remains a matter of vigorous debate. Some prefer to acknowledge the development of a degree of 'flexible specialisation', with production of 'specialised goods for particular and changing markets', without asking this concept to bear all the 'end of an era' connotations of post-Fordism (Hirst, 1989, p. 18). Others advise that the arguments of both the post-Fordists and the flexible specialisation theorists should be questioned for lack of adequate empirical evidence (McDowell, 1989; Warde, 1989). One sceptic has suggested that such theorists could be seen merely as diagnosing tendencies, hypothesising about 'the leading edge of the development of those tendencies' (Warde, 1989, p. 13).

However if the post-Fordists or the flexible specialisation theorists have indeed identified a significant trend then certain important consequences might follow for local government. Thus Hirst (1989) draws attention to the importance of the 'public sphere' in regions such as Emilia-Romagna in Italy and Baden-Wurtemberg in West Germany, regions where many industries have followed the model of flexible specialisation. Here the notion of the dense industrial city is replaced by the more loose-knit industrial district of small towns in a rural landscape. Both firms and towns share needs for labour training, higher education, research facilities, public relations, and the harmonisation of production with environmental quality. The outcome which Hirst identifies is the need for local government 'to perform the role of orchestrator of an industrial "public sphere"' bringing together business, labour and the local state to create the necessary institutions and networks.

However the implications of such industrial change do not stop at the need for new roles for local government. They may also entail changes in the organisational structures and procedures of local authorities. This is the case advanced by Stoker (1989) who aligns himself with the concept of post-Fordism as 'a leading edge of change' which has yet to establish its dominance but which carries with it potential consequences of a high order for local government. He sees local government as having been hitherto deeply influenced by Fordist methods of organisation, emphasising largeness of scale, centralisation, hierarchy, corporate management and the provision of a standardised service product. Although it is not made explicit, the precepts and practices of Taylorian management and its advocates were presumably instrumental in the transfer of such methods from private industry to public services. There are however two particular ways in which the Fordist–Taylorian model of local government is alleged to be inadequate in a world moving towards post-Fordism.

One inadequacy relates to 'the scale and scope of modern local government' which makes it 'both a potentially crucial instrument of social change' as well as a 'prime object to be restructured if change is going to take its course'. From this perspective the inherent rigidities of Fordist local government are both inadequate for and antithetical to coping with 'the forces of economic and social change associated with the transition from Fordism' (idem, pp. 148 and 154). This inadequacy is the more urgently problematic, Stoker argues, because the Thatcher government, without specifically embracing a post-Fordist analysis, engaged in a project of reshaping institutions and social relations designed to exploit the transition from Fordism in the interests of creating popular capitalism and an enterprise culture. This is not to suggest that alternative projects compatible with post-Fordism might not be conceivable from other points on the political spectrum (cf. Hoggett, 1987; Stewart and Stoker, 1988; Mathews, 1989). However it does imply that given the reality of the Thatcherite project the government wished to dismantle much of the Fordist form of local government, by fragmenting its structure and opening up public service provision to competition from other sectors.

The second inadequacy of Fordist local government is one which might well have been identified even if the Thatcherite project had never existed, for it relates not to government strategies but to pressure from local service users. Just as Henry Ford originally offered any colour of car so long as it was black, so some local housing departments were reputed to offer any colour of front door so long as it was dark green. This type of attachment to uniform, standardised forms of local service provision no doubt owed some of its origins to bureaucratic convenience and to beliefs in economy of scale and 'rational' use of resources. In some cases it may have reflected professional norms of good or desirable practice: one can imagine the claim that the 'rhythm' of successive dark green doors imposed an aesthetic unity, linking the houses behind their variegated front gardens – though once again some limits may have been set to horticultural variety. Increasingly however the recipients of local services have come to expect them to reflect user rather than provider requirements. In Stoker's words, 'the Fordist approach of providing a standard product for a captive user is no longer viable'. Instead there is taking place a 'trend away from standardised products towards differentiated products aimed at different consumer groups' (Stoker, 1989, pp. 162–4). The need for local authorities to move in that direction does not however need to be accounted for solely in terms of the post-Fordist paradigm. It can also be seen as reflecting the growth of a more diverse and more demanding public whose existence may indeed be compatible with the notion of a consumer led, rather than producer led post-Fordism, but whose origins may lie in a different direction altogether and whose pressure seems likely to move local government ever further away from the centralised, all-embracing county borough model of the golden age of municipal provision.

A more diverse and assertive society

In the previous section we explored the relations between changing patterns of social geography and economic organisation and the policies and institutions of local government. In particular we examined the way in which economic and social changes gradually undermined the model of local government represented by the all-providing county borough, a model that was the pride of those who operated it and the fond aspiration of many who did not. These economic and social changes themselves, though widespread, were not however uniform in their occurrence for 'the uneven social and economic development of place has been a central feature of post-war British society' (Goodwin, 1989, p. 157). One consequence of this uneven development has been the emergence of a greater diversity and disparity between different localities.

> Post-war consensus, constructed around a fairly uniform geography as well as a uniform society, has given way to diversity and disjuncture. Places, as well as people and social groups, have become less alike and there is a greater disparity between various parts of the country (Duncan and Goodwin, 1988, pp. 275–6).

A sense of places, people and social groups becoming 'less alike' and of a growing 'diversity and disjuncture' recurs amongst a number of observers of British society during the 1980s, though the phenomena that they identified often had their origins in earlier years. Thus Allison (1986) saw the 1980s as a period during which many kinds of social division have magnified. The sense of affiliation to a social class declines constantly, but the perceptions of other distinctions intensify: north against south, city and suburbs, rich and poor, employed and unemployed, black and white, right and left, and so on . . . . The picture suggested is of a society literally and slowly falling apart . . . . This is the age of social fragmentation.

A similar if more sharply etched picture was painted by Harrison (1983, pp. 33, 236–7, 434) when he described the inner city as a place of

fragmentation – of communities, families and even individuals . . . that can only be believed if witnessed . . . a mass of conflicts and cleavages: young against old, delinquents against law-abiding . . . the quiet against the noisy . . . rent-payers against squatters; tax-payers against claimants; black against white . . . a score or more possible divisions, and most of them cut criss-cross through each other.

For some the notion of fragmentation had particular significance for its impact on a class-based form of politics. Thus Hobsbawm (1981, p. 14) feared that there was 'a growing division of workers into sections and groups, each with its own interest irrespective of the rest' whilst Samuel (1985) spoke of the rise of 'militant particularism'. For Leadbeater (1988) the fragmentation of class arose from the economic restructuring of the 1980s which particularly divided skilled, full-time workers in prosperous areas from unskilled, part-time and temporary workers elsewhere. Others identified non-class cleavages which cut across those based on class. Dunleavy for example drew attention to a possible public–private sector cleavage between those who worked in and/or obtained goods and services from one or other of the two different sectors and spoke of '*multiple* different public–private cleavages eroding class-based patterns of [political] alignment in different ways' (Dunleavy, 1989, p. 199, emphasis in original). The question of whether or not stratification was being subjected to cross-cleavage, fragmentation or even total disappearance has remained a matter of some debate (cf. Marshall et al., 1989). Yet during the 1980s many of those most deeply concerned over the future of

class-based politics felt the need 'to articulate the needs of the
minorities and the dispossessed . . . as well as the interests of the
organised working class' and to recognise that people aligned
themselves in relation to 'smaller groupings rather than in the sort
of broad class concepts that people saw themselves [in] thirty years
ago' (Livingstone, 1981, p. 18).

Moreover class was not the only social category to be subject to
cross-cleavage or cross-pressure. We saw in the previous chapter
how social groups based on race and gender have formed
significant 'new' publics for local government. Yet there have
been circumstances in which for example the interests of black and
white women have not been identical but have cut across one
another. Thus it has been observed that

> Job-share facilities for example have been an important aspect of
> many [Equal Opportunity] policies and yet the idea of job share
> has been identified as 'institutionally racist' by some black
> women who, locked in low paid work, cannot afford the luxury
> of half a job (Mackintosh and Wainwright, 1987, p. 122).

The notion of a less homogeneous, more variegated society seemed
to draw support from a number of contemporary changes.
Economically, the increasing diversity of society was reflected in
the growth of specialist shops, of 'niche' marketing and of direct
mail targeting. Department stores became converted into assembl-
ages of boutiques and franchise operations; more generally retailers
were warned that in the 1990s they would need to pay more
attention to local and regional consumer differences (*Daily
Telegraph*, 27 September 1989). Large corporations increasingly
reorganised themselves into a series of smaller identifiable cost
centres, whilst small worker co-operatives and self-employment
enjoyed a major expansion throughout the 1980s.

In the media special interest magazines proliferated and self-
publishing became increasingly possible, whilst local and community radio underwent considerable development. By the end of the
decade Sunset Radio in Manchester proposed to offer ethnic music
embracing Indian, Chinese, Greek, soul and reggae, London Greek
Radio was to target the Greek Cypriot community and Bradford
City Radio proposed a mixture of Asian, Afro-Caribbean and
English music. The emergence of such services seemed to confirm

Young's description of Britain as 'a country of distinct publics . . . [with] a great diversity of sub-cultures' (Young, 1985, p. 31).

Some of this diversity reflected the localised presence of ethnic minorities among some of whom a younger generation rejected the integrationist aspirations of their parents and followed instead more separatist strategies entailing own language teaching, religious schools and bans on trans-racial adoption. In 1989 the Inner London Education Authority was funding more than fifty supplementary 'out-of-hours' schools with tuition in Cantonese, Gujerati, Urdu, Bengali and Greek – a mere handful of the 173 languages spoken by the authority's schoolchildren. The issue of multi-cultural education became one of increasing political significance not least for the Labour Party for whom the black vote was of considerable importance: the party that owed more to Methodism than to Marx now operated in a country with more Muslims than Methodists. More generally religion showed an increasing degree of diversity with a rapid growth of differing sects and faiths, both inside and outside the Christian tradition, and with mosques and temples replacing churches and chapels in some areas. Ethnic diversity also expressed itself politically amongst the 'native' peoples of the United Kingdom with the re-emergence of Irish, Scottish and Welsh nationalism which some saw as threatening the continued unity of the state (cf. Nairn, 1981).

Family and household structures came to display an increasing variety, as shown by the growth in cohabitation, single parent families and serial monogamy arising from divorce and remarriage and producing complex extended family networks. The house building industry reflected this variety as its building stock diversified away from the family semi-detached to embrace the studio apartment, the starter home, the executive house with granny annexe and sheltered housing. The cause of the single parent family had been one of the first of a new wave of self-help and mutual aid groups when the National Council for the Unmarried Mother was relaunched as the National Council for the Single Parent Family. An increasing number of such self-help groups emerged to cater for the specific needs of particular sections of the community.

The creation of active organised groups to represent particular interests was seen by Allison (1986) as the more hopeful side of that 'age of social fragmentation' which had so concerned him.

The eighties are also, by reaction, the age of the sponsored anything, of the amenity society and neighbourhood watch, of local sports and artistic and charitable activities which overfill the local papers, of pub quiz leagues and school fund-raising committees.

Within such activities Allison found signs of the 'practices which give meaning to life by relating us to our place, and to each other'. From that perspective the processes of variegation and diversification which could appear to threaten fragmentation and fission might also provide the potential for a healthy and vigorous pluralism of social and political action.

Such a possibility becomes all the more likely if we recall that Britain's growing social diversity before and during the 1980s had been accompanied by the growth of more assertive and more participative attitudes amongst the public. This development was noted for example by Stephen Elkin whose research into the politics of planning in London in the early 1960s had led him to remark on the apparent insulation of the city's local politicians from the views of local people at that time. A decade later however he was struck by the emergence of 'a citizenry growing more knowledgeable of and involved with local government decision making . . . [and] a changing political culture, manifested in an increase in citizen organization' (Elkin, 1974, p. x). A similar perception was shared in retrospect by Arthur Marwick who recorded that during this time

> A new activism was afoot among middle-class residents' groups which broke through the standard apathy of British political culture. Motorway schemes, urban and rural, the siting of new airports, the invasion of suburban streets by heavy goods vehicles, all of these brought militant, and often highly successful, protest groups of (relatively) ordinary citizens into being, giving some real substance to the word 'participation' (Marwick, 1982, p. 176).

A recognition of the emergence of this new activism was experienced in a small way by the present author. Traditionally books on local government had rarely dealt with its politics; and even if they did the publishers had normally adorned the book-jackets (if at all) with dignified pictures of town and county halls. When *Local Politics in Britain* appeared in 1976 the publishers had the front cover two thirds filled with a picture of a demonstration of residents protesting about local traffic conditions, echoing (or foreshadowing) the 'new activism' and those very protests about 'the invasion of suburban streets' on which Marwick was to comment. Assuming that the publishers knew their market they clearly calculated that their prospective readership was ready to acknowledge something of a departure from 'the standard apathy of British political culture' to which Marwick was to refer.

Such a changing culture was confirmed more widely by the Central Statistical Office in 1976 when its annual publication *Social Trends* introduced a new section of statistics on 'Social Participation' and explained this innovation by observing that participation was now 'a significant social characteristic of the present age in British society' (p. 195).

This characteristic was evident in a number of ways, among them a boom in the creation of pressure groups and voluntary organisations of various kinds. Thus of the two thousand organisations listed in the *Voluntary Agencies Directory* of the National Council for Voluntary Organisations (NCVO) in 1989 no fewer than 60 per cent had been founded since 1960, 47 per cent since 1970. Among *Women's Organisations in Great Britain 1987/88* (Women's National Commission, 1989) 46 per cent had been founded since 1960 and 37 per cent since 1970. Amongst environmental groups Lowe and Goyder found a notable rise in the number of national environmental groups and local amenity societies created from the late 1950s onwards. In the case of the local societies their number and their membership 'doubled every six or seven years' between 1955 and 1975: societies grew from 150 to over 1200, with membership rising from 20,000 to 300,000 (Lowe and Goyder, 1983, p. 89).

If amenity groups were sometimes characterised as predominantly middle class in character, particularly preoccupied by the nexus of aesthetics, conservation and property values, they had their working class counterparts in the community action movement whose birth has been recorded as having occurred in 1967 during the Notting Hill Summer Project (Baine, 1975). Community action focused on the need for people in areas of deprivation or under threat of redevelopment to organise in their own defense through combinations of self-help, protest, campaigning and mobilisation. Sometimes making common cause with tenants' associations and public service unions – though sometimes also at odds with the latter – community action groups defended their patches in the inner cities, in rundown council estates and in declining dockyard and shipyard areas. By the early 1980s the movement had become one of the contributory streams to the new urban left which came to dominate a number of Labour councils (Gyford, 1985b, pp. 33–6). This confluence of localised action in working class communities with a wider stream of Labour politics perhaps also had its counterpart on the middle class right: not in the form of the amenity societies – who if any thing foreshadowed the emergence of Green politics – but in the shape of the 'ratepayers' revolt' of the 1970s. The preoccupations of the militant ratepayers groups who formed the National Association of Ratepayers Action Groups in 1974, with their concern over spending levels, the rating system and party politics in local government, clearly pre-figured the stance of the Conservative New Right when it found itself in government after 1979.

The growing assertiveness of the public did not only express itself in the form of the creation and joining of organised groupings. A more diffuse but none the less real consumerism emerged from the 1960s onwards: consumers increasingly asserted their rights against the providers of unsatisfactory goods and services. A growing awareness of the need for consumer rights in the public sector led to the creation of new Commissioners or 'Ombudsmen' to respond to complaints about maladministration in central and local government and in the health service. In due course similar arrangements were made in one or two areas of the private sector such as banking. More generally there were signs that the traditional deference and respect accorded to established authority within British political culture was being displaced by more sceptical and questioning attitudes. In the classic study by Almond and Verba (1963) Britain had once been found to possess a deferential political culture within which the public were willing to trust political leaders with the exercise of power. A re-examination of Britain's political culture in the following decade however encountered much less trust and confidence in government leaders and observed that 'the traditional bonds of social class, party and common nationality are waning, and with them the old restraints of hierarchy and deference' (Kavanagh, 1980, p. 170).

The causes of such developments lie beyond the scope of this book but we may hazard some guesses at some of the contributory factors. The growth of secondary, further and higher education, the development of the mass media and the rise of investigative journalism suggest themselves as sources of a greater consciousness of what government was doing in the public's name. The actual experience of what government was doing, especially perhaps in the case of highly visible and totally irreversible changes to the built and natural environments, must have been a major motivation. The consequences of economic decline should not be overlooked either.

The prism of decline tends to reflect national interest into divided particularistic and sectional interests and to reduce the political electoral utility to which a governing party can put promises of welfare provision (Krieger, 1986, p. 27).

In an era of economic decline the higher aspirations of a more diverse and assertive public thus came into conflict with a governmental system that seemed no longer able to deliver the goods in the way that it had for much of the post-war era. Out of this disjunction between public aspirations and systemic performance there developed

an awareness . . . that new initiatives could not and should not be in the form of large-scale aid administered from on high. They had to come from the roots and move upwards . . . . It is easy to laugh at middle-class worthies campaigning . . . But they did inculcate in the public consciousness an awareness of the limitations of scale, of the exhaustion of resources and of the interdependence of humankind. They made it possible for a new kind of countervailing power to be deployed, appropriate for an age of depletion (Whitehead, 1985, pp. 254–5).

The notion that a changing political culture had its origins in 'the relative deprivation of the times and . . . the perceived responsibility of governments for it' was one of three explanations canvassed by Beer in his attempt to account for 'the broad cultural revolution which swept through Britain during the sixties and the seventies'. One aspect of this revolution was a 'new populism', 'individualist, participatory, majoritarian and egalitarian' in its attitudes to power and worshipping a 'populist trinity' of the quality of life, participation and decentralisation (Beer, 1982, pp. 147, 5, 111, 130). However he notes that another possible explanation rests on the premise not of economic decline but of economic fulfilment. This is the case with the thesis of post-materialism developed by Inglehart (1977), with its suggestion that once basic material needs such as safety and sustenance have been received then individuals will turn towards 'self-actualization needs' with an emphasis on cultural, aesthetic and intellectual satisfactions and with a 'high valuation of participation in economic and political life at all levels' (Beer, 1982, p. 146). At first sight explanations of the emergence of a more participatory political culture on the grounds of both economic deprivation and economic fulfilment seem mutually contradictory. Yet the concept of uneven social and economic development with which we started this section of the chapter suggests that both explanations may be valid but in different places and at different times.

This is the more so when we combine them with Beer's third, political, explanation, namely that the 'new populism' emerged as 'a reaction and an alternative' to 'the centralised bureaucratic state'. His own inclination is to attribute this to a 'value change', an assertion of a new viewpoint about whose emergence 'there was an essential autonomy which escapes structural explanation' and whose ultimate cause 'I do not know' (idem, pp. 146–7). Leaving aside, though not necessarily discounting, the value change hypothesis, Beer's three explanations – two economic and one political – are all compatible given the premise of uneven development. Basically, and rather prosaically, the state may have come to be seen as an obstacle to both materialist and post-materialist aspirations under conditions of deprivation and prosperity respectively, due on the one hand to a lack of resources and on the other to a lack of imagination. It is this obstructiveness of the state which generates political action, aided perhaps by that value change whose origins leave Beer somewhat baffled.

Thus a lack of resources under conditions of economic deprivation would add greater urgency to claims of entitlement to material goods and services, both for established and aspiring client groups, and hence to action by and on behalf of claimants, tenants, welfare rights groups, anti-cuts campaigns, and so forth, anxious to defend or secure their share of the state's limited provision. As for those living under conditions of economic fulfilment their perception of the state's lack of imagination in relation to post-materialist aspirations would produce popular attempts to lead by example, to pre-figure how the state ought to behave, through the promotion of alternative policies, actions and lifestyles: the amenity society 'shaming' the council into action on the environment by carrying out its own 'clean-up' campaign is a common enough example. The do-it-yourself element of the latter strategy is not necessarily confined to post- materialist aspirations: self-help and mutual aid has also been the response of some of those who have found that the state's material resources are inadequate to meet their own particular needs.

Whether we choose to characterise the changing political culture of the last two decades or more as representing the rise of 'social participation', or the 'new activism' or the 'new populism', it has found expression not merely at the level of changing attitudes and values but also at the level of political action. Those changes in form of political action have in turn had major consequences for the politics of local government. They have involved three particular sets of changes. The ways in which the public has sought to participate in local politics have changed; the political parties have had to reformulate their attitudes and their policies to take into account changing public demands; and what might be called the local government establishment, including the local authority associations and various professional and management bodies, has tried to recast old practices and to identify new ones to cope with a more diverse and assertive public.

Politics under pressure

During the course of the research carried out for the Widdicombe Committee (1986b, p. 146) one London council leader referred to 'pressure groups coming out of our ears' when asked about the authority's links with groups in the community. Other councillors interviewed in the same research made it clear that the pressure from more numerous and better organised local interest groups was one of the causes of the increased demands being made on members' time. For some this was a positive development, for they attached much importance to representing the views of particular groups within the wider community. For others the task was not so much one of representing groups as of trying to judge between their competing claims, perhaps a more problematic exercise (idem, pp. 62–3). Although there are no directly comparable research findings the impression from the Widdicombe research is that in the 1980s organisations outside the council loomed larger in the councillor's life than was the case in the 1960s. Although councillors valued voluntary organisations as a means of meeting some social needs in the 1960s they were not disposed to rate them very highly as a means of getting to know the needs and attitudes of members of the public as compared with informal personal contacts (Maud, 1967b, Table 8.8). Yet it is perhaps this latter role of expressing public demands which has seen the most significant development amongst local pressure groups in the subsequent decades. During that period there emerged both an intensification and a diversification of group activity at the local level.

The question of defining the nature of pressure groups has occupied many minds: it has however been claimed that 'hunting this snark saps the enthusiasm' (Jordan and Richardson, 1987, p. 18). Nonetheless it may be helpful to clarify the sort of activity with which we are dealing here. Freeman (1983, pp. 1–2) suggested that we need to recognise a continuum amongst forms of collective group action. At one end there is the interest group with 'a well-developed and stable organization'. At the other end is the crowd, the fad and the trend, 'marked by their contagious spontaneity and lack of structure'. In between are social movements which combine, under some tension, 'noticeable spontaneity and a describable structure' in the form of 'one or more core organizations' along with 'a penumbra of people who engage in spontaneous supportive behaviour'. Stable and well-developed organisations were the kind of groups which local authorities were traditionally well able to cope with, not least because many of them, in the welfare field especially, plugged gaps in council provision as well as making claims on resources. It has been the growth in the other two forms of activity since the late 1960s which has caused local government greater problems of knowing how best to respond.

The 'politics of crowds' has taken various forms at the local level in the recent past. Demonstrations, vigils and pickets have been employed both to publicise the existence of problems and to lobby councillors for their political support. Although such events have required some basic *ad hoc* organisation they have often left no lasting structure once the event or the crisis has passed. The packing of public galleries to cheer or to barrack councillors at key decision making meetings has also required some logistical organisation, but subsequent events in the gallery (and in the council chamber) have sometimes had all the signs of passionate spontaneity. Finally the urban riots of the 1980s, in Brixton and Tottenham in London, in Handsworth in Birmingham, in Toxteth in Liverpool and in St. Pauls in Bristol provided dramatic expressions of the difficulties facing local authorities responsible for inner city areas. At the time and point of occurrence such forms of collective action no doubt very effectively concentrate the minds of local authorities very effectively. Yet in the longer run it may be that the major challenge has been in knowing how to respond not to the crowd in its various manifestations but to the emergence of new social movements.

In addition to characterising social movements in terms of their uneasy combination of spontaneity and structure Freeman also points to their tendency to shy away from traditional forms of organisation based on bureaucracy, centralisation and the division of labour in favour of looser, more participatory models (idem, p. 117). This account parallels that of Dunleavy (1980, p. 157) who distinguishes social movements 'from conventional voluntary organisations and interest groups' by virtue of a number of key characteristics: these include a limited organisational hierarchy, a high level of grass roots activism and participation, a lack of involvement in formal political activity and a bias towards techniques of mobilisation and direct action. In describing this particular organisational style Dunleavy is concerned specifically with the workings of urban social movements, one subsection of the wider whole.

The goals of social movements as a whole have been diverse. Initially they arose largely to promote causes which might broadly have been regarded as associated with the left of politics, focusing on the demands of disadvantaged social groups and excluded minorities and challenging the priorities of a modern industrial economy: the claims and priorities of blacks, women, gays, environmentalists and pacifists were prominent amongst these. Later groups included those perhaps more usually associated with right-wing causes, including opponents of taxation, anti-abortionists and supporters of capital punishment. One particular subsection however composed those groups organised around the local provision of public services, an issue described by Castells (1977) as that of collective consumption: it was the groups who engaged in political conflict in this field that he defined as urban social movements.

Originally Castells confined this category to those movements whose urban struggles could be linked with the party political class struggle as part of the process of transforming society in the direction of socialism. However in his later work he moved away from this preoccupation with links between urban social movements and the politics of class and party (Castells, 1983) thereby allowing a less restricted definition and usage of the term. It is in that light for example that Lowe (1986, p. 4) suggests that we may regard the following as examples of the 'upsurge of urban social movement activity in Britain over the last two decades': the council house tenants' movement, ratepayer organisations, anti-spending cuts campaigns, redevelopment protest groups, the squatters' movement, anti-urban motorway protesters and anti-pollution groups.

The reaction of local authorities to the more active politics of organised interest groups, social movements and crowd behaviour has been varied: but the variety of reaction has not necessarily been random. One account suggests that councils respond to such activities on the basis of three criteria, namely the nature of the group, the nature of its demands and the method by which the demand is communicated (Dearlove, 1973, p. 157). Councils are more likely to respond favourably to groups which they identify as being supportive of the council's goals, making demands in tune with council policy and using established channels of communication. Another interpretation identifies the importance of social networks in allowing the personnel of local government and of the world of group action to meet informally and thereby to enhance mutual understanding and sympathy. Again this is not a wholly random or universal process but one which reflects pre-existing patterns of social relationships. Thus in Conservative Croydon representatives of local commercial interests mingled socially with Conservative councillors so freely and so naturally that exchanges of 'opinions, suggestions and modes of thought pass[ed] almost imperceptibly, like osmosis, from businessmen to politicians and from politicians to businessmen' (Saunders, 1980, p. 324).

In a rather different fashion the old Labour authorities of Bermondsey, Camberwell and Southwark experienced high levels of personal interaction amongst local councillors, council officials, tenants and trade unionists within a locally dominant culture of Labour in which the party was a focus of social as well as of political life. In such a situation pressure group activity was almost non-existent since demands could be accommodated through the networks provided by the Labour party. It was however the eventual inability of these networks to accommodate willingly the demands of new 'outsider' groups, some of them taking the form of social movements representing gays, blacks, squatters and single parent families, which led to increasing internal party turmoil and to a much more vigorous world of pressure group activity within the new London borough of Southwark in the 1970s and 1980s (Goss, 1988).

The willingness or ability of councils to respond favourably to particular types of pressure group is likely to be closely linked to the political character of the council, whether those responses are formal or informal. Stoker (1988, pp. 125–6) has suggested four broad categories of relationship between particular local political regimes and the types of groups to whom they do or do not respond. The four are as follows:

(a) urban areas with left-wing Labour councils: here voluntary sector and community groups, tenants', women's and ethnic groups, single issue cause groups (for example nuclear-free zone campaigns) and trade unions are likely to receive favourable attention, more so than commercial interests;
(b) urban areas with councils under centre-right Labour or (former) Alliance influence: these may be suspicious of organisations seen as motivated by selfish interests (such as middle-class residents' groups) or dominated by extremists (for example tenants' associations) but happy to work with organisations representing the voluntary sector, both sides of industry, professional groups and some environmentalist bodies;

(c) suburban and rural areas where the Conservative and (former) Alliance parties dominate: here the more formal voluntary organisations, amenity groups, residents' associations, farmers and landowners and parish councils are likely to be listened to, unlike campaigners for more controversial causes;

(d) urban and suburban areas under New Right Conservative control may look favourably upon middle class residents' groups, amenity societies and business interests but will be profoundly suspicious of any groups they perceive as 'political' or left wing.

In a system of local government that is increasingly under the domination of party politics the relationship between parties and pressure groups is clearly one of some importance; and as the previous paragraphs imply, certain types of pressure may be more easily exercised through one party rather than another. Yet there is another and perhaps more fundamental aspect of the relationship, for it may be argued that the growth of pressure groups reflects some sort of failure on the part of the parties. Thus it has been argued that in the specific field of urban policy the 'rise of urban protest' reflects 'a failure of political parties to respond to citizens' demands and needs': this failure is ascribed to the habit of the parties of clinging 'tenaciously to ideological positions dating from periods when class and group structures were much simpler' (McKay and Cox, 1979, pp. 274 and 284). If one of the traditional functions of the parties was to aggregate specific demands into broad programmes capable of a wide appeal then it may be that a more diverse and more demanding society has put that role under considerable strain. The decline in individual party membership since the 1950s and the fall in strong party identification amongst the voters since the 1960s suggests that fewer members of the public than previously see a central role for the parties in their political life: similarly the general growth of single-issue politics, of which pressure group activity is the clearest manifestation, would seem to confirm the challenge to the parties.

The parties themselves of course have not been unaware of this challenge and some within their ranks have sought to respond not merely in terms of reactions to individual groups but also by developing broader strategies of how to handle the whole developing phenomenon of the 'new criticism' and of single issue pressure groups. Both the Labour New Left and the Conservative

New Right have produced their own very distinctive approaches, as did the erstwhile Liberal Party, all of which have had some very clear implications for the workings of local government.

The reaction and strategy of the New Right, as they came to dominate the Conservative Party, can best be described as one of downright hostility to the political activities of pressure groups. These criticisms were primarily couched in terms of the perils of organised groups at the national level but the hostility they conveyed also found expression at the local government level. The Conservative *Local Government Brief* (October 1980) rejoiced that under the Thatcher government the days were gone 'when councils are considered as gift-horses to every tin-pot pressure group prepared to shout, harass and blackmail for money' and later on (February 1981) the same source condemned the attempts of 'extreme pressure organisations with little or no public support . . . to launch their weird and way-out policies with local monies'.

Contributing to the making of such attitudes was the notion that ultimately it was the individual rather than the group who was the only legitimate political and economic actor. The proper response to demands for better performance or improved responsiveness by local councils was seen to lie not in facilitating greater political participation but in introducing more market or quasi-market mechanisms into local government along with more stringent financial disciplines. The market mechanism could respond to individual needs more effectively than could the traditional local authority, since:

> independent providers . . . are nearer to public demand than local authorities can even be . . . [since] their perpetual search for profitability . . . stimulates them to discover and produce what the consumer wants (Adam Smith Institute, 1983, p. 3).

For the New Right therefore a more market oriented local democracy was the solution to coping with increasing demands on local government.

This stance was very different from that adopted by the then Liberal Party who celebrated rather than shunned the idea of a wider, more participatory, politics based on group activism. The Liberal Party's annual assembly in 1970 passed a resolution which committed the party to a primary strategic emphasis on community politics; our role as political activists is to help people in communities to organise to take and use power . . . (Liberal Assembly *Final Agenda*, 1970)

This strategy was seen by the party as entailing 'a commitment to participatory democracy' and as embracing more than just locality based communities: 'Much was made of communities of shared interests – gays, blacks, women – as well as local groups waging specific campaigns' (Clay, 1985, p. 4). The outcome was a style of politics which placed stress on doorstep contact with the electorate, on extensive leafleting, on active involvement in local campaigns and on taking up local grievances and issues wherever possible. In office Liberal councillors saw their role as pressing for more open government, for less centralisation of decision making and for increasing communication with, and participation by, local people (Pinkney, 1984).

Within the Labour Party reactions to a more diverse and assertive pressure group type of politics were mixed. The party's local government establishment on the right and centre was wary of developments which it suspected could produce a Trojan horse of middle-class activism directed against Labour's traditional strongholds. For the New Left on the other hand

To be a socialist now is . . . to be where a school or a hospital needs urgent improvement, or where a bus-service, a housing development, a local clinic needs to be fought through against the ordinary commercial and bureaucratic priorities (Hall et al, 1969, pp. 140–1).

Yet the Labour left could not simply embrace a more participatory campaigning politics uncritically, for it wanted answers to questions about how that fluid style of politics related to socialist goals and to the structured, delegate democracy of the Labour movement with its commitment to solidarity based on mandating by majority votes.

For the Trotskyites in the *Militant* tendency during their domination of Liverpool the answer was clear: participation should be channelled through the institutions of the local Labour Party (Gyford, 1985b, pp. 91–2). The party in Liverpool was led by those who claimed 'the immense advantage of a worked-out

Marxist programme, perspective and tactics' and who were sure that 'gay liberation, chairpeople as opposed to chairmen, and token black mayors won't be the things which win us support from workers' (Taaffe and Mulhearn, 1988, p. 17; Hatton, 1988, p. 170). A more open minded approach was taken by the soft left Labour Coordinating Committee, which accepted that 'socialists should be committed to the *principle* of people controlling their own lives, whether or not we like all the immediate results' and even if 'some of the decisions . . . won't always be the ones we would have preferred' (Clarke and Griffiths, 1982, p. 24, emphasis in original; Labour Coordinating Committee, 1984, p. 32). In between these two poles were various elements of the left who declared their genuine commitment to a local politics based on participation, decentralisation and democratisation; yet who also expressed the hope that through such forms of politics a 'Rainbow coalition' could be constructed uniting groups based on class, gender, race, sexual orientation, nuclear disarmament, environmentalism and so on, and mobilising them for the socialist cause.

The politicians were not alone in trying to devise strategies with which local government could meet the accumulated pressures of two decades of social change. There also emerged during the 1980s what Hambleton (1989, p. 8) has referred to as 'managerial critiques' of traditional local government which brought with them their own suggestions as to how councils should respond to more complex and more pressing public demands. One strand of these managerial critiques drew on the experience of the private sector, or rather of those elements of the private sector who were thought to have reaped rewards from their high degree of attention to the needs of their customers. The basic lesson was that which was offered by Peters and Waterman (1982), whose book *In Search of Excellence: Lessons from America's Best-Run Companies* became something of a management bible in some local authorities: excellent companies, they concluded, were distinguished by being 'driven by their direct orientation to their customers' (p. 157). This orientation moreover required the development and maintenance of an appropriate organisational culture to provide the necessary values and commitment amongst members of the organisation. A second, complementary strand of the managerial critique was that developed by Clarke and Stewart (1985) in work carried out for the Local Government Training Board. They developed the concept of a 'public service orientation' which recognised that local authorities existed to provide services for the public, that local authorities would be judged by the quality of those services, that customers demanded high quality and that high quality required closeness to those customers. Councils should therefore concentrate on the quality of their service and on responsiveness to the public as customers.

The initiatives which might follow from embracing either or both of these two notions of customer orientation varied in scope. At one end were ambitious attempts to change the prevailing philosophy of the local authority and to introduce 'core values' emphasising customer orientation, responsiveness and a concern for quality. Much more modest were schemes to redesign and improve access to council offices, making them more welcoming to the public. In the middle range of ambition were plans to monitor customer preferences and service performance and to feed the results into service planning and policy making.

By the start of the 1990s the politicians of right, left and centre and their colleagues in local government management had generated a wide range of initiatives for responding to the pressures generated by the social changes of the previous two decades. These initiatives did not of course find uniform or universal application. Only a small proportion of councils have been controlled directly by the New Right or the New Left or by the Liberal Democrats and their predecessors, though of course the presence of a central government dominated by the New Right after 1979 allowed some of their initiatives to be imposed from the top down rather than being generated from the bottom up. As for local government officers, not all of them found the time, or had the desire, to read *In Search of Excellence* and for some chief executives documents on new styles of management were not the most pressing pieces of paper to cross their desks.

The implementation, wholly or in part, of these initiatives was thus patchy, depending upon the vagaries of local politics, the pressures of central government and of bodies such as the Audit Commission, the initiative of individual council leaders or chief executives and the urgency of local problems amenable to new solutions. Nonetheless between them they amounted to a comprehensive repertoire of policies and practices which were available for local authorities to employ as appropriate, or sometimes as legislation demanded. This variety is apparent merely from listing some of them: public participation, user involvement, consultation and co-option arrangements, decentralisation, privatisation, opting out, use of the voluntary sector, encouraging self-help and mutual aid, market research and opinion polling, changing the organisational culture, improving reception facilities, developing customer relations and marketing, and devising mobile and one-stop service systems. Some of these flow from clearly political strategies, others from more managerial concerns; one or two originated in purely pragmatic responses to a particular problem. Together however they form part of a wide-ranging new repertoire of modes of local authority service delivery. In the chapters that follow we shall explore in more detail the individual components of this new repertoire and discuss some of the questions provoked by their implementation.

3 Participation: Taking Part

The need for responsive local government and for people to participate was a constant theme of many of the official reports of the 1960s.

Community Development Project, 1977, p. 56.

In this chapter and in the two which follow we shall examine some of the initiatives which local authorities have launched in their attempt to make their services more participatory, more responsive and more accessible to members of the public. The range of ventures which can be directed to these ends is considerable, ranging from those which entail ceding some degree of power to the public to those in which the emphasis is placed more on presentation or on what Hague (1990, p. 33) has described as 'largely cosmetic changes'. One much quoted attempt to classify such a range of initiatives was that of Arnstein whose 'ladder of citizen participation' contained eight rungs, although she warned that in the 'real world of people and programmes, there might be 150 rungs with less sharp and "pure" distinctions among them' (Arnstein, 1971, p. 177). Arnstein's ladder was constructed with specific reference to her analysis of federal social programmes in the United States in the 1960s with their aspirations for 'maximum feasible involvement of the poor' and it reflected her deep suspicion of the practical 'chicanery' which she felt underlay some of the official verbal allegiance to ideas of participation (idem, p. 178). The principle behind the typology which was the product of that suspicion is not however dependent on it, for it serves to crystallise

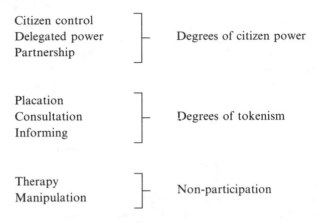

Citizen control
Delegated power　　　　Degrees of citizen power
Partnership

Placation
Consultation　　　　　　Degrees of tokenism
Informing

Therapy
Manipulation　　　　　　Non-participation

Arnstein's 'ladder'

the more general point that relations between public authorities and the public can vary all the way from 'keeping them happy' (but in the dark?) to allowing them an active share in decision making. In the context of British local government one simple three-fold typology is that described by Hampton (1987, pp. 127–8):

> Participation in service provision can be seen as a means by which individuals may protect their rights as consumers of public goods and services; it can be described as the right to consultation; or it can involve the full . . . concept of people sharing in the processes of policy-making and service provision.

Here we shall adopt a variant of just such a typology, grouping the initiatives examined into three broad categories. First, in this chapter, we shall look at those in which there is some measure of 'sharing in the processes of policy-making and service provision', in which there is some measure of participation, defined as 'people . . . taking part, with others, in their local government' (Boaden et al., 1982, p. 12). Then, in chapter 4, we look at initiatives lying broadly in the field of consultation, acknowledging that the public at least has the right to be heard even if it does not take a direct part in decision making. In chapter 5 we concern ourselves with experiments focusing on the provision of information about, and access to, the council and its services.

The forms taken by these various initiatives may thus be broadly characterised as *participative, consultative* and *informative*, though those categories each cover a variety of initiatives and are not always mutually exclusive. The various services themselves also present different contexts for such initiatives. In some cases, such as the personal services of housing, education and social services, there can be an enduring relationship over a period of years between those who use and those who provide the service. In the protective or regulatory services such as environmental health, licensing, town planning and consumer protection, the relationship may focus more episodically on the application of policies: the same may be said of such promotional or developmental activities such as tourism, heritage promotion and economic development. Moreover in the case of the personal services it is largely, though not exclusively, private individuals and their families who are the prime recipients of the service. In the case of protective and promotional services the recipients are more likely to include a mixture of both individuals and commercial and other organisations. Given this variety of services and recipients in addition to the varied aims behind our three categories of initiative it is not surprising that the outcome is one of a considerable diversity in the types of activities now under way. We now turn to our first category of initiative, that which embraces some degree of public participation in decision making.

There has been a common theme to the search for mechanisms to secure more responsive local authorities and to allow a greater degree of public participation. That theme is one of taking account of external interests when decisions are being made in committee rooms and council chambers. There is an underlying recognition that neither the professional wisdom of the officers nor the electoral credentials of the councillors can necessarily provide all the raw material needed for decision making. Some sources of knowledge, of expertise or of opinion may not be tapped through the formal channels of professional bureaucracy and representative democracy. Other devices may therefore be needed to supplement those channels.

The search for such devices has certainly been pursued with some degree of energy since the 1960s but it would be wrong to assume that the search only began in that decade. Such an assumption would in particular overlook a very long standing procedure, namely that of the co-option of non-councillors into membership of local authority committees.

Co-option

The practice of co-opting individuals into membership of local bodies is one which in fact pre-dates the reforms of the Municipal Corporations Act of 1835. Before that date such bodies as the improvement commissioners and the un-reformed municipal corporations would routinely perpetuate their existence by co-opting new members whenever a vacancy arose. In such circumstances of course co-option was not so much a supplement to the electoral process as a substitute for it. Traces of this practice still exist in the power of parish councils to fill casual vacancies by co-option if no electors call for the holding of a by-election.

The parliamentary debates over the Municipal Corporations Act addressed the issue of the relations between co-option and election. The House of Lords took the view that there was a clear need for 'a permanent and unelected element' in local government, the absence of which 'would destroy the checks which had hitherto existed on the democratic principle' (Redlich and Hirst, 1970, p. 132): or as Hasluck (1936, p. 176) put it, 'a non-elective element was necessary to steady the wild incapacities of the representatives of the ignorant multitude'. The price which the Lords exacted for allowing passage of the 1835 Act was the introduction of the aldermanic system whereby the elected councillors added to their number by choosing non-elected aldermen to form one quarter of the total membership of the council. This reformulation of the co-optive principle, designed to temper electoral pressure through the presence of the local equivalents of elder statesmen, persisted until the abolition of aldermen in the 1970s.

Outside the council chamber other institutions of nineteenth century local government also employed the co-optive system. School boards for example would 'co-opt docile female relatives to form a ladies committee, to organise womanly work' such as visiting children's families, investigating diet and health and promoting the cause of education for girls. Some boards co-opted women to fill casual vacancies on the board itself: such women often held their seats at subsequent elections so that co-option thus became a useful mode of entry for women into local electoral politics (Hollis, 1987, p. 192).

The power of councils to co-opt non-elected voting members onto their own committees was first established by the Local Government Act 1894 and extended in subsequent legislation. In the 'golden age' of local government before the second World War, it became a widespread practice in particular embracing committees dealing with education, pensions, maternity and child welfare, public assistance and allotments. Whether or not the practice was a good one became a matter of some dispute. Finer (1933, p. 220) saw co-option as 'another remarkable addition to the technique of democracy . . . [which] may one day prove to be its salvation'; in sharp contrast, Laski (1935, p. 86) feared that 'the worst failure in the committee system has been its use of the power to co-opt'.

Defenders of co-option cited a number of justifications for the practice. Simon (1926, p. 86) for example saw co-opted members as people who 'keep the committee in constant and direct touch with important organisations whose friendly co-operation is essential'; moreover they were 'people who are keen on their work, expert in certain aspects of it'. Finer (1933, p. 220) also cited the opportunity to add expert knowledge to a committee's deliberations as a major advantage which provided 'rich resources of scholarship, mind and energy'. Co-option of representatives of voluntary agencies in the welfare field was seen as useful 'for the purpose of liaison and co-ordination' (Warren, 1948, p. 86); virtue was also seen in 'the representation of interests directly affected by the work of the committee' (Hadfield and MacColl, 1949, p. 66). Examples of the latter included provision for the co-option of allotment holders on to allotment committees, of teachers on to education committees and of women as members of maternity and child welfare committees (unless there were at least two women councillors in membership). The acquisition of expertise, the promotion of good inter-organisational relations and the representation of specific affected interests were thus claimed as the important benefits of co-option.

The sceptics, such as Laski, mounted their criticism on two basic grounds, those of practice and of principle. All too often, they argued, co-optees were in fact being chosen for their party loyalty; indeed even Finer (1933, p. 221) deplored the tendency to use co-option as a 'compensation prize' for party candidates defeated at the local elections. Laski however argued that, in a paradoxical fashion, party based co-option, whilst a travesty of the true purpose of the practice, reflected the realities of an increasingly party based local government, for 'if the co-opted member is not connected with a party group he tends to have less influence than his special experience would warrant' (1935, p. 87). Questions of practical politics apart, the other major objection was the more fundamental one of principle, namely the undesirability of giving power to individuals who lacked any direct responsibility to the voters, especially any direct responsibility for financial decisions.

The arguments between supporters and opponents of co-option rumbled on inconclusively for several decades until the 1980s when 'the system of co-option of non-elected members' was listed amongst the terms of reference of the Widdicombe Committee of Inquiry. In announcing these terms of reference in the House of Commons on 6 February 1985, the then Secretary of State for the Environment, Patrick Jenkin, expressed his concern that co-option was being used in some cases as a device for appointing majority party sympathisers, an echo of Laski's complaint fifty years earlier.

The extent of co-option discovered by the investigations of the Widdicombe Committee (1986a, p. 90) revealed that the practice appeared to have declined since the inquiry by the Maud Committee twenty years earlier. By 1985 there were about 6000 co-opted members compared with 16000 in 1965. In the meantime of course there had been a substantial reduction in the number of local authorities as a result of the reorganisation of the 1970s, from over 1800 to 520, but the fall in co-opted members was disproportionately greater than that reduction itself. Co-option was least common amongst shire districts and most common in the London boroughs. Apart from those committees where co-option was a statutory requirement – education committees and police committees (Scotland excepted) – it was mainly to be found in the fields of social services, leisure, personnel and housing. Additionally it was characteristic of committees set up to deal with race relations and women's issues, especially in London and the metropolitan districts. In these cases, as in the case of housing, co-option was often seen as a means of expanding the representation of those groups who were left under-represented by electoral democracy – ethnic minorities, women and council tenants.

The Widdicombe Committee (1986a, p. 91) commended the latter aim but concluded that such co-opted representation should take an advisory form rather than include the right to vote: 'it is wrong in principle that non-councillors should be voting members of committees with powers to take decisions'. The conclusion of the committee was thus that only councillors should have the right to vote on decision taking committees, that non-voting advisers should be able to attend meetings of such committees and that the established arrangements for co-opting teachers and church representatives on to education committees and magistrates on to English and Welsh police committees should be subject to review. The proposed move away from co-opted members with voting rights was regretted by those who saw it as a means of broadening the basis of representation on committees. It is perhaps a sign of how far preoccupations have changed since 1835 that co-option, originally advocated as a means of diluting democracy and curbing public influence ended up being defended as a means of extending democracy to a wider public.

Government reaction to the Widdicombe recommendations was somewhat ambivalent. It accepted the principle that only councillors should be voting members of decision making committees and sub-committees; however it held back from applying this principle to education or police committees and it allowed departures from it in respect of certain very localised committee functions. The provisions of the Local Government and Housing Act 1989 included the ruling that no-one other than an elected councillor might be a voting member of a decision making committee as distinct from a purely advisory committee. Exceptions to this rule however embraced not only police and education committees but also committees and sub-committees concerned (a) with the management of a whole or part of a single housing estate, provided it did not contain more than one sixth of the authority's stock and, (b) with the management of council-owned land or buildings on a single site within a budget laid down by the local authority.

These last two exceptions made it possible for co-opted voting members to sit on local committees or sub-committees dealing with housing estate management and with the management of other facilities such as community centres and sports halls. In that respect the co-option provisions of the 1989 Act were judged to leave 'room for experiment with new ways of extending local democracy' (Hambleton, 1989, p. 19) through an element of user participation.

User participation

The concept of the 'user' of council services is one which poses some problems, as indeed does the concept of 'use' itself. Someone who borrows a book from a library or who plays a game of squash or goes for a swim at a sports centre is using a council service in a different way from a council house tenant or a resident in an old person's home. For the tenant or the resident, as also for the school pupil or the college student, their use of the service may well be a key element in the structure of their life, directly affecting its basic quality both now and perhaps in the future. For them the use of the service entails some form of continuing relationship. For the book borrower or the sports enthusiast however their use of the council's facilities is essentially made up of a series of specific transactions across the issue desk or the reception counter; it is not built into the fabric of their lives – though bibliophiles and sports fanatics might contest this perhaps?

Definitions of the 'user' may also differ from service to service. A sports centre may cater both for individual swimmers, squash players and so on, and also for organised clubs: the requirements of the two types of user may not always coincide. Users of local authority housing are clearly the tenants and their families; do they include prospective tenants of new housing, who may have views on design and layout? Users of the education service presumably include pupils and students; but some regard parents and prospective employers as the effective if not the physical users of the service. In the case of the social services there may sometimes be doubt as to whether the term 'user' means for example the disabled person or the elderly person or whether it also embraces the family members who contribute to their care or are concerned about their welfare; in some instances the notion of being 'referred' to a social worker may actually be taken to imply the absence of any quality of autonomy as a user.

Given the fact that the natures of both use and user differ from service to service and sometimes within services, there has been no uniformity in the experiments in user participation which have taken place in recent years. Some of the experiments moreover have been generated at the local level; others have represented responses to encouragement from, or the requirements of, central government. Here we will look specifically at developments in the fields of housing, education and social services, where not only is there some form of continuing relationship between user and provider but also some degree of mutual commitment, whether through the landlord–tenant contract or less formally through relations such as those of teacher and pupil (or parent) and social worker and client.

The landlord–tenant relationship between the local authority and the council house tenant is perhaps the most formalised relationship between provider and user in local government. Yet it derived basically from the type of such relationship which traditionally existed in the private sector; it did not aim to address any new issues which might arise in the different circumstances of large scale public sector housing management. Indeed it was not until the late 1960s that pressure emerged for a new approach to local authority housing management which would embrace elements of tenant participation.

Hague (1988) has identified four stages in the development of tenant participation. Until 1968 it was simply not on anyone's agenda: house building and rent levels were the key issues for tenants, housing managers and councillors alike rather than forms of housing management. Then from 1968 to 1974 there grew pressure from tenants themselves for more say in housing decisions, especially in reaction to contemporary concerns over standards of repair and new methods of rent assessment. In the years from 1974 to 1979 the Labour government of the day began to promote the idea of tenant participation, especially in the form of housing co-operatives; this development, Hague suggests, had corporatist overtones in that it reflected a desire to incorporate tenants into the difficult business of managing housing with reduced resources. Finally the period after 1979 saw both the New Right and the New Left embracing the tenants' cause but offering very different solutions to their problems, from the right to buy and opting out at one end of the spectrum to decentralisation and democratisation at the other. The end result of these stages has been the accumulation of a variety of forms of tenant participation: in legal terms housing authorities have been required by the Housing Acts of 1980 and 1985 'to enable those of its secure tenants who are likely to be substantially affected by a matter of housing management . . . (a) to be informed of the authority's proposals in respect of the matter and, (b) to make their views known to the authority' (1985 Act, Section 105). Councils must consider any views expressed by tenants before coming to a decision.

Local authority responses to such requirements have been varied. One survey showed that out of ninety-six respondents thirty-eight were content merely to notify tenants by letter of council proposals and to await their response; a further thirty-five used varying combinations of letters, leaflets, press notices, public meetings and direct contact with tenants' organisations; and twenty-three had introduced either area consultation committees or tenant co-option onto the main housing committee (Community Rights Project, 1986a). Another review observed that ideally procedures should entail involvement '*both* with representative tenants' associations *and* with individual tenants'; it also commended the use of meetings rather than relying solely on written representations since 'tenants are generally more inclined to articulate their feelings orally rather than in writing' (Bartram, 1988, p. 11).

Bartram describes one particular exercise, developed by Tameside Borough Council, which combines individual participation by tenants with the involvement of tenants' associations. It concerns the procedure for discussing house modernisation schemes and has the following elements:

1. Firstly, tenants' associations are invited to preliminary meetings to discuss design options.
2. Secondly, show houses are opened to demonstrate these options, and officers take note of tenants' comments. These are open both in the evenings and at weekends and *all* Housing Renewal Officers are present to explain and to listen.
3. A further meeting involving tenants' associations is then held to discuss the plans drawn up so far, and to make changes where necessary.
4. Approximately four weeks before the start of each scheme another public meeting/exhibition is held to demonstrate choices once again. Drawings of each house type and option are displayed, along with samples of gas fires, kitchen units,

bathroom units, etc. Officers are present to answer questions
and to offer advice.
5.   The choice is given to tenants as to whether they move into
temporary or permanent alternative accommodation. Several visits are made to the tenants in order to establish their
preferences.

Tenants are visited individually to obtain their choice of design at
least six weeks before modernisation is due. They are visited again
two weeks before modernisation is due to find out their preferences
for decoration. Officers have sometimes had to visit tenants in the
evenings and at weekends to complete the surveys on tenants'
choice (idem; emphasis in original).

A venture such as this clearly involves more than hoping that
tenants will turn up at whatever event the council decides to
arrange. It requires the council to go out to visit the tenants as well
as having the latter attend a meeting or an exhibition. Council
officers and tenants meet on the latter's home ground as well as the
former's: the net result has been not only greater tenant satisfaction
but also the avoidance of council expenditure on proposals that
would have proved unacceptable to the households involved.

Whatever arrangements are made for responding to the views of
individual tenants they operate within the framework of what has
been described as 'the power relationship between councillors and
housing managers on the one hand and tenants on the other'
(Clapham, 1990, p. 68). Active tenants' associations can be one way
of attempting to redress the potential one-sidedness of this
relationship; but such bodies tend to have a fitful existence,
emerging and disappearing in response to the waxing and waning
of local problems or of the enthusiasms of a handful of individuals.
Some authorities have recognised the desirability of their tenants
having a more stable collective voice and have therefore devised
ways of providing the necessary support.

Sheffield for example has tackled the question of financing
tenant groups through the raising of a two pence per week levy
on house rents for each tenant. Tenants can opt out of the scheme,
but over four-fifths have elected to contribute to the levy whose
proceeds go to tenants' associations recognised by the council and
having a properly constituted and elected set of officers and
committee. Greenwich has approached the problem of funding

tenants' groups through its voluntary sector grants scheme but has also provided a broader form of assistance through the employment of five tenant support workers. Their functions include providing administrative back-up, assisting with accounts and other financial procedures, encouraging participation in meetings through the arrangement of transport and crèches, and developing links between tenants' associations and other community groups: in addition tenants' representatives have been encouraged to visit other local authorities to learn from relevant initiatives elsewhere.

Tenants' associations are perhaps the most basic expression of collectively organised user participation in housing. More ambitious in their scope are the various forms of housing co-operative which now exist. A survey carried out for the Department of the Environment (DOE) in 1986–7 found a total of 605 housing co-ops in England and Wales (McCafferty and Riley, 1989). Nearly two-thirds of these were owned by their members, who had either a collective or an individual share in the equity. Just over a fifth took the form of tenant management co-ops where the property was owned by another body, usually a housing association or a local authority. It is with the latter variety that we are concerned here.

Tenant management co-ops have been defined as 'voluntary associations of tenants who enter into an agency agreement with their landlord . . . to carry out housing management and sometimes rehabilitation on their estates' (Birchall, 1988, p. 113). Amongst the merits claimed for them is that of 'consumer control over the design and refurbishment of housing and over its management and maintenance': a DOE review concluded that such co-ops offered some economic benefits, few if any disadvantages and that 'where there is full tenant commitment . . . and where tenants receive adequate support and training' then they could 'strengthen communities, encourage self-reliance, and provide local consumer control of housing management' (Department of the Environment, 1989, pp. 8–9).

As the above references to 'commitment' and to 'adequate support and training' indicate, tenant management co-ops are not an easy option: nonetheless recent research suggests that they can provide tenants with a satisfactory system of maintenance and repair and also offer 'an effective way of involving tenants directly in the management of their own housing' (McCafferty and Riley, 1989, p. vi). Such success is however achieved only after some effort and co-ops such as these have so far been largely confined to London and Scotland, where local authorities have committed themselves to their promotion.

In Islington, some thirteen tenant management co-ops had managed by 1988 to produce better performances in respect of repair costs, void rates, re-let times and rent arrears than amongst the rest of the council's house stock. They had also overcome initial fears of control falling into the hands of a small clique, of early enthusiasm fading away under the pressures of demands on time and energy and of possibly discriminatory decisions on housing allocation (Power, 1988; Morton, 1989). Another London authority, Wandsworth, has also promoted management co-ops, though in a different political climate from Islington, that of the Conservative right rather than the Labour left: co-operatives may have their roots in early socialism but they can also be embraced by the right in the name of 'promoting active citizenship, increasing choice and reducing individuals' dependence on state agencies' (Department of the Environment, 1989, p. 3).

Wandsworth's Co-operative Development Team was involved in the gestation of some eleven possible management co-ops in the 1980s, of which four were fully established by 1990 with a further seven in various preparatory stages. For people interested in such ventures the team has made available an information pack clarifying such issues as model rules, co-op decision making, support and training, the management agreement between the council and the co-op, arrangements for repairs and maintenance, finance, allocation of dwellings, rent collection and equal opportunities. The council urges co-ops to 'make a special effort to ensure that their committees represent a cross section of the membership': in addition co-ops are reminded that the times and places of meetings should be arranged so that 'as many people as possible can attend' and that provision should be made for people with children and for old people needing escorts (Wandsworth, 1988).

The degree of commitment required amongst co-op members may be daunting for some people. One possible half-way house between the pro-active role of a management co-op and the more reactive or responsive role of a conventional tenants' association is that represented by the estate management board (EMB) promoted by the Priority Estates Project set up in 1979 as a joint DOE and local authority exercise in tackling the problems of unpopular (and often poorly managed) estates. The setting up of an EMB takes place under the provision of Section 10 of the Housing and Planning Act 1986 which allows a local authority to delegate management and maintenance to a third party, in this case the EMB. The EMB for any individual estate will consist of a majority of elected tenant representatives plus councillors representing the local authority and a small number of co-opted individuals. The EMB, once constituted, negotiates a management agreement with the council, specifying their respective powers and duties: this agreement requires approval by a majority of the tenants in a consultation exercise and by the Secretary of State before it can come into effect.

Under such an agreement the EMB becomes responsible for the control and management of an estate budget, the running of an estate office, including housing maintenance and repairs, rent collection and arrears, allocation and lettings, open space maintenance, cleaning and caretaking, and the necessary training of staff and tenants. The merits of such a scheme have been identified by the Priority Estates Project as follows:

- It establishes a *formal partnership* between the tenants and the local authority, one stage removed from Council political and bureaucratic structures.
- Through the management agreement, a degree of *local autonomy* over estate management is ensured.
- It *empowers the tenants* without loading sole responsibility onto them.
- It provides for good estate-based management from a team of *well-trained staff* who themselves have greater freedom to manage within the terms of the agreement.
- Although the EMB must be supported by a clear majority of tenants *it does not depend on high levels of direct participation* for its success.
- The tenants retain their *status as Council tenants.*
- It ensures that *decisions are made locally.* (Zipfel, 1989, p. 7, emphasis in original)

Similar advantages were identified by West Lancashire District Council (1989) when it produced an information sheet about a proposed EMB for residents of its Digmoor estate in Skelmersdale:

The main point of the proposal is to give Digmoor people more say in how their estate is run. A local committee (or Board as it will be known) will be set up consisting of resident representatives elected from the various areas of Digmoor plus a number of Councillors nominated by the Council. The Council will give this Board the responsibility for ensuring a high standard of management of Council housing on the estate by overseeing the work of the Neighbourhood Housing Office and the budget for managing and repairing the housing.

The Council will still own the housing and fix rents. The security of Council tenants will not be affected but there will be more say for local people. (Emphasis in original)

Digmoor residents were also assured that 'you will be given every encouragement and training if you choose to get more involved' in the work of the EMB. In 1990 the Digmoor scheme was awaiting the approval of the Secretary of State along with other EMB proposals from Birmingham, Blackburn, Bristol, Burnley, Rochdale, Rossendale and Stoke-on-Trent. The Bloomsbury estate in Birmingham became the first to receive ministerial approval for an EMB in August of that year.

The EMB schemes bring together user representatives, council representatives and co-optees to undertake the management of locally based staff and resources within an overall framework of policy and finance set down by the local authority. In those terms they bear at least a passing resemblance to a much larger compulsory initiative, not in housing but in education, namely the local management of schools (LMS) introduced into England and Wales by the Education Reform Act 1988. Indeed two years before the passage of that act, one commentator had made a similar connection between the two services by suggesting that 'if the tenants of council estates are to be offered responsibility for their management, with a local office to serve them, then the legally constituted school governing body is clearly worth considering as an organisational model' (Burgess, 1986, p. 24).

Burgess's remarks were made in the context of his account of Cambridgeshire's financial management initiative for schools which began in 1981. As this date suggests, the notion of devolving some elements of management down to school level was one which pre-dated the 1988 Act: related questions about accountability in education and about responsiveness to users' needs were being asked throughout the 1970s and 1980s. In the early 1970s localised experiments in new and more participatory forms of school government that involved parents, staff, pupils and the local community were launched in Bristol, Humberside and Sheffield. Partly in response to the interest provoked by these initiatives the Taylor Committee was set up by the government in 1975 to conduct an inquiry into the management and governments of schools in England and Wales. The committee's report *A New Partnership for our Schools* appeared in 1977 and commended the idea that every school should have its own governing body, rather than being governed as part of a group of schools, and that each such body should contain equal numbers of local authority representatives, school staff, parents and representatives of the local community; a step in this direction was taken in the Education Act 1980 which required all schools to have representation of parents and teachers on governing bodies.

One commentator has seen the concern for greater local control of schools in the 1970s as being a 'primarily middle-class and professionally orientated movement' reflecting the gradual disappearance of the traditional grammar and direct grant schools, as a result of which 'one powerful and articulate section of upper middle-class society has largely lost control over its children's education'; on that reading the demand for parent involvement in school government was an attempt to re-assert that lost middle class control within the comprehensive system (Bacon, 1978, p. 190). There was however another element in the 1970s debate, in which parents were not seen as being the sole users of the education service. Against a background of national economic difficulties increasing attention was being paid to 'the vocational preparation of young people for their future economic roles on the grounds that . . . the service had neglected employers and society as legitimate users of education' (Ranson, 1990, pp. 186–7). A third factor was that of the attitudes of teachers as a profession, who some felt were clinging to out-dated notions of accountability. Margaret Maden, then herself a head teacher, expressed regret that during the 1970s teachers had shown;

> no sense in their training . . . of an accountability beyond a fairly small and tight professional group . . . . They failed to consider

how important it was to talk with and to listen to people beyond
the boundaries of schools, the parents, the local community,
employers, and all those other stakeholders of whom we are all
too conscious now (quoted in Whitehead, 1985, p. 204).

It was a combination of these concerns about parental rights,
vocational preparation and the accountability of the professionals
which fed the educational policies of the post-1979 Conservative
government. The Education Acts of 1986 and 1988 in particular
addressed the issues of the form and the function of school
governing bodies in the light of these concerns.

The Education (No. 2) Act 1986 provided for the election of
parent governors in equal numbers to those appointed by the
education authority, for the election of teacher governors in
addition to the headteacher, and for the co-option of other
governors, amongst whom members of the local business community were to be included if they were not already found amongst the
other governors. It also required governors to make a report to an
annual parents' meeting. The Education Reform Act 1988 gave all
primary and secondary schools with more than 200 pupils control
over their own spending. The intention, according to circular 7/88
from the Department of Education and Science, was 'to secure the
maximum delegation of financial and managerial responsibilities to
governing bodies that is consistent with the discharge by the
Secretary of State and by the local education authority of their
continuing statutory responsibilities'; the outcome would be that
'the governing body will control the running of a qualifying school
with its delegated budget'. This arrangement for LMS, the circular
warned, was 'concerned with far more than budgeting and
accounting procedures': indeed once LMS came into operation in
1990 governing bodies began establishing sub-committees to deal
with staffing, the curriculum, premises and pupil-related matters as
well as finance.

The first round of elections of nearly 100000 parent governors
under the 1986 Act, held in 1988, produced wide variations of
competition and turnout. A survey published in the *Times
Educational Supplement* (21 October 1988) found that in 40 per
cent of schools no elections were held because not enough parents
came forward: 10 per cent of the schools reported unfilled
vacancies. Where there were elections turnout averaged 43 per

cent for primary schools and 35 per cent for secondary schools. Some unease was provoked by the finding that one parent governor in eight was a teacher and, subsequently, by allegations that political party activists had also secured election in their parental roles. The shortage of candidates in some schools and the unfamiliarity of the LMS work load for both new and experienced governors highlights the problem of giving people the confidence and the skills necessary to do the job adequately. The 1986 Act required local education authorities to arrange, free of charge, the training necessary for governors. Many had already provided this in a modest fashion but the coming of LMS in particular made it all the more imperative to do so. Essex, for example, expanded its training for governors into a Governors' Support Project whose activities included the preparation of governors' training manuals, the organisation of a regular programme of courses, liaising with and supporting locally based self-help groups of governors and developing resource and information banks for both governors and trainers.

Introducing elements of user participation both into education and into housing is facilitated by the existence of a clear focal point around which to build structures and procedures, namely the school and the housing estate. The same can not be said of 'the disparate activities covered by the personal social services which lack any clear focus or identity' (Bamford, 1990, p. 3) ranging as they do across a spectrum of domiciliary, residential and community based services available to the elderly, to children, to disabled people, to the mentally ill or handicapped and to others in need or at risk. Nonetheless a concern for greater responsiveness to the users of social services has been evident at least since the report of the Seebohm Committee in 1968, which called for the creation of advisory forums attached to the area offices of social service departments with consumers of the services amongst their member-ship. A similar proposal, for local Welfare Advisory Committees with clients' representation, was made in the Barclay Report in 1982. Neither of these specific proposals was widely taken up: a survey of 116 authorities in 1985 elicited replies from 20, of which only seven had set up any sort of advisory committee (*Community Care*, 28 March 1985). On the other hand, as we saw earlier, the social services have been one of the chief fields in which the machinery of co-option has been used within the formal local authority committee structure. Some 48% of social services committees for example had co-opted members in 1985 (Widdi-combe, 1986b, Table 7.1). Often however these arrangements did not involve clients directly but embraced representatives of voluntary groups who acted as surrogates for the actual service users themselves.

A quite different approach from that of creating committees or other forums is that of setting out principles, guidelines or charters identifying the rights of users. As a result of its examination of five social services departments in 1987 for example, the Social Services Inspectorate commended a number of initiatives as examples of good practice. In the context of encouraging user participation they applauded;

- clear statements of agency expectation about user participation;
- opening case conferences to, for instance, children, to other users and their carers;
- using a 'contract' approach to provision and receipt of service;
- encouraging the formation of user committees in day and residential centres.

Similarly they approved of arrangements to allow users 'maximum feasible choice' over such matters as deciding between staying at home or residential care, keeping open the option of returning home after a period of residential care, and determining the daily regime of getting up, going to bed and what to eat within residential care (Barnes, 1988, pp. 30–1).

In line with this approach Croydon produced a *Users' Rights Charter* for social services clients in 1988 giving the following undertakings.

Users of our Services have the right to:
Personal independence, personal choice and personal respons-ibility for their own actions.

Have their cultural, religious, sexual and emotional needs accepted and respected.

Have their personal dignity respected by others, and be treated as individuals, whatever their disabilities.

Be consulted about decisions affecting their daily lives, especially those involving risk.

Look after their own personal needs as far as they are mentally and physically able.

Privacy for themselves, their belongings and their affairs, including the right to receive visitors in private.

Freedom to enjoy their sexuality and to have it recognised by others.

The same access to facilities and services in the community as any other citizen, including registration with the medical practitioner and dentist of their choice.

Education and information relevant to their individual needs.

Choose whether or not to mix with other people in the community, either by going out or by inviting people into homes, hostels or sheltered flats.

Decide whether or not they receive official or personal visitors.

Be addressed by staff in the way in which they choose.

See records which are held by the department containing information about them, in line with departmental policy on access to records.

Have their complaints considered according to agreed and publicised principles.

Such charters are a useful expression of intent but they may well need to be supplemented by quite specific instances of what users' rights mean in practice. Buckinghamshire's *Guidelines for Work with the Elderly*, issued in 1981, specifies for example that the principle of residents' choice embraces such matters as 'the degree of clutter or order in their rooms', 'locking their rooms and cupboards', 'choosing to take the risks of normal living' and the right to 'choose bath days and bath times and who, if anyone, helps them'. Another means of specifying rights, which can also spell out the mutual obligations of social worker and user, is the contract approach to service provision, which was among the initiatives commended by the Social Services Inspectorate and referred to above.

Some social workers now draw up, write down and sign contracts with their clients, with the acknowledged intention of specifying what the agency will and will not provide and what the client for his or her part will have to contribute to the bargain.... Such contracts of course also define the obligations of the worker and the organisation providing the service and more particularly the limits to their rights which they accept in return for guarantees from the client (Smith, 1987, p. 80).

The notion that social worker–client relations should move away from the subordination of the latter to the former found clear expression in a working party report by the British Association of Social Workers, *Clients are Fellow Citizens* in 1980, which explored the mechanics of making clients' rights effective. It argued that clients were entitled to such citizenship rights as information, access, complaints, redress and participation. The report has been described as having evoked a 'ready response' from within the social work profession. 'It is now common place to find young people in care contributing to their services, to see day centre attenders involved in planning and evaluating their own programmes and to find in homes for the elderly a range of devices from residents' committees to advocacy schemes designed to strengthen participation and involvement' (Bamford, 1990, pp. 59–60). The willingness of some social workers to respond positively to pressures for participation and involvement may reflect in part the emergence within their ranks of a radical analysis of the traditional claims of professionalism during the 1970s. This analysis with its recognition that 'the client is now assumed to be able to make some judgement of his own needs' (Leonard, 1973, pp. 113–14) was similar to one that developed at the same time within the ranks of the town planning profession: they too took up the question of public participation.

Public participation and popular planning

It has been observed by Hampton (1990, p. 17) that during the 1970s 'the phrases "public participation" and "planning" went together as easily as "fish and chips"'. The Town and Country Planning Act 1968 had given local authorities the duty of affording members of the public the opportunity to comment on structure and local plan proposals before their formal adoption. The Skeffington Report on *People and Planning* published in 1969, had provided advice and recommendations on how this duty could best be performed. During the following decade there was a wealth of experimentation with various forms of public participation in planning as the first of the new generation of structure and local plans were launched. This was a period in which the planning profession seemed to be in the vanguard of attempts to create a more participatory style of local government: its efforts provoked considerable debate about the true nature of such a style and about whether planners were truly concerned with the interests of the public or merely with creating their own constituency among that public (see Hain, 1980).

During the 1980s however, circumstances changed in a number of ways. In 1981 the government's circular 23/81 from the Department of the Environment announced 'a change of policy based upon experience' which aimed to discourage planning authorities from doing any more than the statutory minimum in respect of public participation. If councils were disposed to be more ambitious than that then they would need to be 'satisfied that the further work and delay that it entails is clearly justified'. Such guidance derived from the Thatcher government's concern that the planning process had become excessively time consuming and expensive, especially from the point of view of developers. It was also accompanied during the succeeding decade by various measures designed to whittle away the scope of local authority planning, through the creation of urban development corporations, enterprise zones and simplified planning zones and through the promotion of a more market-led form of planning. One observer has concluded that the net result was that the 1980s saw 'a retrenchment and abandonment of the participatory movement' in planning (Thornley, 1989, p. 2).

Certainly participatory planning lost something of its 1970s' high profile in the 1980s. This however reflected more than mere abandonment in the face of government discouragement. For one thing participation in planning had become no longer the main stream but rather a tributary to a much wider flow of initiatives of a broadly participatory nature in a number other local authority services. The 1980s also saw a measure of taking stock as authorities learned from the experience of the 1970s and tried to refine both the goals and the techniques of the participatory process in planning.

One review of the experience of the 1970s concluded as follows:

The problems of participation were assumed to be technical – what media to use – rather than strategic. Objectives were rarely discussed, the audience was assumed and the outcome was scarcely evaluated . . . . Participation in planning to date has tended to be planner orientated . . . . The planners compose the publicity to announce their proposals and disseminate it through channels over which they have control, and at times which are convenient to their programme (Boaden et al., 1982, pp. 65 and 67).

The search for better approaches to participation preoccupied a number of authorities during the 1980s and the sorts of conclusion to which they came were similar to those arrived at by Manchester in a review of its own experience. Manchester City Council (1986) identified a number of key requirements for successful public participation in planning. They may be summarised as follows:

1.   Both the council and the public need to be clear about the purpose of the exercise from the outset; are the public being informed, consulted or more actively involved in decision making?
2.   It is necessary to identify in advance exactly who is to be involved from amongst the public: are there specific target groups and do they have particular problems with attending meetings or understanding procedures?
3.   A variety of methods need to be used to reach the public from large meetings to informal groups to opinion polls.
4.   Where groups are being regarded as spokespeople for a wider constituency, agreement should be reached at the start on a 'test of representativeness': what counts as representation and who is authorised to act in that fashion?
5.   Both the council and the public must accept that public involvement will add to the time taken, not only for policy making but also for implementation.
6.   Advance agreement should be secured on mechanisms for reporting back to those taking part.
7.   The role of council employees must be clarified to all concerned, especially when they are involved in helping groups to formulate their views and to present their case.

During the 1980s a number of authorities attempted to devise approaches to public participation which addressed some of the issues identified by Manchester. One example was the work carried out for its Central Area District Plan by Sheffield City Council in 1986 and described by Alty and Darke (1987) on whose account we now draw. The city centre had relatively few residents but a large number of users: the Council decided to pay particular attention to those users whose needs might otherwise have been overlooked – women, senior citizens, ethnic minorities and disabled people. Accordingly, in addition to using a range of conventional publicity techniques (media coverage, exhibitions, films, letters to organisations, public meetings) the council also identified nine target groups whose opinions should be sought: women, parents with young children, the elderly, disabled people, the unemployed, the low paid, young people, Asian communities and Afro-Caribbean communities. Relevant organisations were invited to send representatives to form advisory groups for each of the target groups: the council then hosted and serviced a set of meetings at which each group could prepare its response to the draft plan.

Despite some pitfalls, including the early break up of the unemployed group and a low degree of involvement of Asian women, the various groups each held several meetings, timetabled and conducted as conveniently and informally as possible, during which participants grew in confidence and gradually developed their own collective views. These were then conveyed directly by each group to two or three members of the council's planning committee at a series of individual 'hearings' followed by one final plenary meeting for all the groups with the councillors. The councillors responded to the group both orally at hearings and the plenary meeting and later in writing.

At the practical level the outcome included a number of specific proposals for the central area of the city relating to parking, subways, child-care, personal safety, signposting, toilet facilities, city centre housing and community group premises. Over and above that, most of the advisory group members felt that the exercise had been enjoyable, educative and genuinely influential, whilst the councillors felt that they had heard some genuine views from 'ordinary people'. A key element in the apparent success of the venture was the work of the planning officers who were provided to support the work of the advisory groups. The nature of that support varied from chairing meetings, taking notes and arranging room bookings and child care to explaining the implications of policy proposals and drafting initial versions of group submissions. This clearly cast the planners concerned in a challenging role, where their task was neither to defend their department nor to pre-empt what the advisory groups might want to say but rather to act as enablers who facilitated the emergence and expression of the groups' own ideas.

Sheffield has not been alone in devising participation schemes which embrace both targeting and enabling strategies. A similar exercise was carried out in the production of the Central Newham Local Plan prepared by the London Borough of Newham (1989). As part of the process of plan preparation, the opportunity was taken to conduct a social audit of local needs, not all of them directly related to land use planning, in an area of predominantly high density residential development: the centrality of Central Newham is geographical rather than commercial or administrative. The social audit was structured around the work of ten working parties made up of people from voluntary and community groups, public bodies and schools. Each was concerned with one of ten sets of needs, namely those of the following: under-fives, young people, women, ethnic minorities, people out of work, people with disabilities, the elderly, the mentally handicapped, the mentally ill and alcohol and substance misusers. The choice of target groups or issues rested on certain pragmatic judgements: problems of the under-fives were seen as 'politically current' whereas those of gays and lesbians were not; single-parent families were seen as having problems which were practical issues and politically current but whose study was beyond the scope of available resources (Best and Bowser, 1986).

In addition to public meetings, exhibitions and a major involvement of local school-children as part of the Local Plan publicity, in which around 2000 people were involved, the social audit working parties determined their own agendas, modes of consultation and final output. Consultative mechanisms included questionnaires, discussion meetings, a video and brain storming sessions. Each working party was provided with assistance from planning officers who gave administrative and clerical help but tried not to intrude into its deliberations: as in Sheffield their role was one of enabling and facilitating. The final outcome was that 'the working parties identified a range of needs for their different client groups. As many as possible have been addressed in the Local Plan'. The published plan itself identifies fifty two individual policies addressing the particular needs of one or more of the target groups: other policy proposals which had no land-use implications were referred to the relevant service committees (Newham 1989, pp. 8–9; Best and Bowser, 1986).

Both the Sheffield and the Newham exercises were forms of public participation designed to secure inputs into a plan being produced by the local authority: they were not designed to secure the production of the plan itself by the local public. This latter however was the aspiration of the 'popular planning' initiative promoted under the aegis of the GLC in the early 1980s. With the abolition of the GLC itself in 1986 the initiative has now receded into history: yet its experience does throw light on some aspects of participation which are of wider and still contemporary significance.

The concept of popular planning originated in the field of economic and industrial strategy rather than of land use and development. It grew out of the experience of the 'alternative plans' produced by workers at Lucas Aerospace and Vickers in the late 1970s and was crystallised in a declaration *Popular Planning and Social Needs* produced by Coventry Trades Council in 1981. The core element was the idea of 'planning from below – planning that is based on people coming together in their workplace and community organisations to formulate their own demands and wishes for the future' (GLC, *Jobs for a Change* bulletin, June 1984). The particular case to concern us here is the experiment in producing the *People's Plan for the Royal Docks* in 1983.

The stimulus for this exercise was the announcement of a public inquiry into the proposal for a short take off and landing airport on land between the Albert and King George V Docks. Campaigners against the airport had already won the backing of the GLC, which now agreed that its Popular Planning Unit should assist the Newham Docklands Forum in drawing up an alternative 'people's plan' to present at the public inquiry. The plan was duly prepared and its proposals presented at the inquiry: they emphasised local needs for training and jobs, rented housing, better public transport and improved facilities for children. The plan was scorned by the leading barrister for the London Docklands

Development Corporation – 'a people's plan . . . ridiculous. I have never heard of such a thing!' (Newham Docklands Forum, 1983, p. 3). However 'local people felt that at the very least their views had been presented in a positive way' (Mackintosh and Wainwright, 1987, p. 315) even though the eventual outcome was the granting of planning permission for the airport.

The final version of the plan had been prepared by an officer of the GLC's Popular Planning Unit but was based upon drafts prepared by locally based working groups dealing with such issues as dockside industry, housing, community needs, recreation and new technology. These drafts in turn tried to reflect the views of local organisations and of individuals for whom 'surgeries' were held on the housing estates. The whole process however, despite affording local views the chance of being presented 'in a positive way', revealed some fundamental problems which have been chronicled by Brownill (1987 and 1988).

Some of these problems are those identified by Manchester City Council (1986) and referred to earlier: the problem of the respective obligations of GLC funded staff to their employer and to the local docklands community is a case in point. Four particular problems perhaps merit special mention. First, the need to comply with a pre-determined timetable for the public inquiry meant that the emphasis came to rest on producing a plan rather than on developing popular skills which would have required a longer time-scale. Second, the role of women tended to be confined to work on domestically related issues: dockside issues were 'macho stuff', the prerogative of male trades unionists in particular. Third, 'the idea that once people were consulted then a spontaneous flood of ideas would flow was not to be' (Brownill, 1988, pp. 16–17): local people's history of being the objects rather than the subjects of decision making produced problems of how far they should be prompted or stimulated into discussion by those more experienced than themselves. Fourth, the People's Plan had to fulfil two simultaneous roles, articulating local views but also respecting broader GLC policies.

Ultimately perhaps all four of these problems are related to one overall issue at the heart of both popular planning and public participation: which is more important, the production of a plan or the development of an effective participatory process? Is the process designed to generate a good plan, or is the plan the occasion for developing a more open process? Those are the sorts of questions to which old professionals (and politicians) and new activists may have different answers. It is however the former rather than the latter who have statutory authority on their side: in that sense the problems encountered by the People's Plan spell out some of the limits still in operation in respect of promoting participation as a valued end in itself rather than simply as a means to other ends.

4 Consultation: The Right to be Heard

> Deciding to consult is a commitment from the Council to consider the views of local people when final decisions are made.
>
> Harlow, 1990, p. 5.

The right to take part and the right to be heard are not of course wholly divorced from one another, not least because the former surely implies the latter. Yet people may also be given the opportunity to express their views, for example at public meetings, without this entailing the opportunity of playing an active part in service provision or policy making. Indeed for many people the right to air a grievance or to ask a question or to make a suggestion may be the limit of their desire for involvement in local affairs. Similarly some councils may well be willing to sound out local opinion without going so far as to devise arrangements for more active local participation. In this chapter we examine some of the initiatives directed to permit or to encourage the expression of local public opinion.

Forums for consultation

Co-option has been one device by means of which councils have been able to respond to advice and opinion from those outside the ranks of council members and officers. It is not of course the only such device; moreover it is a device which depends upon a pre-existing structure of committees and sub-committees on to which co-option can take place. Such committees have for the most part been chiefly concerned with service provision. However it is also possible for councils to establish committees and other forums that are designed not to oversee service provision but to provide specifically for consultation with particular sections of the local community.

The decision about what should be the format and the procedure to be adopted for consultative purposes is one which requires some thought, since there is no uniformly appropriate mechanism. Harlow District Council (1990, p. 22) has provided a useful checklist of the questions which need to be answered before any consultation process is set in train:

- What sort of issues do you think it is worth consulting the public about?
- Why do you want to consult?
- At what stage in the planning/policy process do you want to seek people's views?
- Whose views are you seeking?
- Will some people's views count more than others?
- What should be an acceptable level of consultation?
- Do you want the views you receive to be as representative as possible?
- How will you encourage people to put forward their views?
- How can you best attract the people whose views you are seeking?
- How will you consult people?
- Once you have drawn people into the consultation exercise, how can you encourage them to put forward their views?
- How much information will you give your consultees, and how can it be best presented?
- How much weight do you plan to give the views and arguments expressed?
- What will you do if the views expressed contradict your plan?
- How will you inform people about the decisions taken?

The answers to such questions will of course differ from place to place and from time to time but at least by addressing them a local authority may hope to adopt an appropriate consultative procedure for whatever ends it has in view.

Since the 1960s a number of local authority services have experimented with a variety of consultative mechanisms. Some councils have established consultative and liaison committees with social service user groups and voluntary organisations in line with the recommendation of the Seebohm Report in 1968. Housing departments have set up consultative committees and councillor-tenant meetings. Leisure and recreation departments have devised ways of consulting users of their facilities in the sporting and artistic fields. Planning departments have employed a variety of means to consult public opinion on planning proposals since the publication of the Skeffington Report in 1969. These mechanisms are directed variously at user groups or in the case of planning at a wider public. There are however, some consultative mechanisms which are designed to cater neither for user groups, nor for the generality of the public. They aim to respond to specific publics defined by such criteria as gender, ethnicity, economics and geography: they embrace committees and other forums dealing with women's issues, race relations, the interests of commerce and the concerns of localised areas or neighbourhoods within the authority. It is these to which we now turn.

By 1989 some forty-three local authorities in Britain had set up some form of committee to address womens' issues, following a precedent set by the GLC in 1982. The exact form and status of these bodies differed from council to council. A survey in 1987 found that amongst thirty respondents, ten were full standing committees of the council, seven were sub-committees of a policy and resources committee, six were advisory groups to standing committees or sub-committees and seven were subsumed within wider equal opportunities committees and sub-committees. Five of the committees confined membership to women only and twenty-one provided for the co-option on to the committee of non-councillors, often with specific provision for black women, lesbians, the elderly and disabled people (Edwards 1988). Very often the committees themselves have set up a variety of working groups dealing with such issues as child care, women's rights, health, employment, prostitution, transport and housing. Attempts have been made to discuss these issues at open meetings with participation facilitated by provision of crèches, by special facilities for people with disabilities, by translation for Asian women and by encouraging contributions from those unused to speaking at meetings.

The aims of women's committees are broadly similar throughout the country. The terms of reference of one in particular give some idea of what the aspirations are: they are those of Brighton's Women's Committee set up as a full standing committee in May 1986 'to work with and on behalf of women in Brighton'. The committee's terms of reference are as follows:

1. To facilitate an examination of the structure of the council and its procedures in order to ensure that a women's perspective is incorporated in its work, by working with other council committees, developing guidelines, and advising on their implementation.

2. To advise other council committees on proposals for reviews of the activities of the council both as provider of services and contractor of goods and services, to examine the council's work in terms of women's needs and views, and to advise on recommendations arising from such reviews.

3. To work with the Personnel and Equal Opportunities Committee, within the context of the council's Equal Opportunities Policy, to achieve equal opportunities for women in the council's employment and to advocate the adoption of similar policies to other employees in the area.

4. To assist other committees to monitor the activities of the council and committee reports on these activities to ensure that women's views and needs are fully considered.

5. To work with other committees on specific projects for women in Brighton.

6. To work with women's groups, other voluntary and community organisations, tenants' associations and trade unions to encourage improvements in services and facilities for women in Brighton, to campaign for such improvements, for positive policies and legislation on women's rights and to defend existing rights.

7. To provide assistance to encourage the foundation of new women's groups and to support projects for women provided by women's groups and other non-statutory organisations.

8. To liaise with and make recommendations to Her Majesty's Government, East Sussex County Council, other statutory organisations, and companies about matters affecting the welfare and interests of women in Brighton.
9. To seek, in all areas of the committee's work, to ensure that the welfare and interests of women who also suffer discrimination on grounds of race, disability, sexuality, age or class are given full consideration (Wilkinson, 1988, pp. 9–10).

Making due allowance for their different focus, the terms of reference of race relations committees possess to some degree a similar tenor to those of women's committees. In the case of Islington for example the council's standing orders ascribed the following terms of reference to the race relations committee.

1. To initiate and develop policies in respect of all aspects of race relations in and affecting the Borough and its inhabitants and to establish the present and future needs of minority communities.
2. To ensure that the council's policies and activities are non-discriminatory and to monitor their implementation by the council's committees.
3. Where appropriate to take maximum advantage of grants, etc, available from central Government and other sources.
4. To provide advice and support to organisations on race relations matters.
5. To engender co-operation and liaison with and between public authorities throughout the Borough on matters of race relations.

Both of these terms of reference articulate the desire to respond to the needs of a particular section of the public whose interests are seen as having been previously down-played or totally ignored. Moreover just as women's committees have made provision for representation of particular sub-groups of the female public, so too race relations committees have identified particular ethnic constituencies requiring representation: in Camden for example these have included the Irish, the Cypriots, the Afro-Caribbeans, the Chinese and the Bengalis. A further similarity has lain in the common creation of (usually rather small) women's units and race relations units within local authorities to provide administrative and research support for the respective committees.

There is however one problem with which race relations committees have had to cope that has not been encountered by the women's committees. Before the emergence of race relations committees dialogue between local authorities and the black communities was often conducted through previously established local community relations councils (CRC), reborn in 1990 as racial equality councils. The representativeness of CRCs varied from place to place; some were predominantly black peoples' organisations; some had good links with all or most ethnic groups, others with few or even none; some were predominantly white with only token black representation. Such questions of representativeness have sometimes posed a problem and ethnic minority groups might then demand direct access to local authorities rather than rely on intermediary bodies such as the CRCs. Race relations committees were able in some cases to provide more direct access but the co-existence of the two forms of representation produced a varied pattern of consultative mechanisms.

Gay and Young (1988, pp. 30–1) recognised four basic positions in respect of consultation on race equality issues. Some authorities were 'generally resistant' to any positive relationship with CRCs which they viewed as representing 'sectional interests'; some were 'comfortable enough' with their local CRC and were prepared to grant it 'a monopolistic position in the consultative process', some developed their own race relations mechanisms and preferred to set up 'new consultative structures in which the CRC played no significant role', and some were willing to incorporate the local CRC within consultative mechanisms devised by the authority but to regard it as one among several bodies 'within the constellation of ethnic minority organisations'.

Whatever the consultative structure, and whatever the relative roles of race relations committees and CRCs, the general question of 'representativeness' has remained capable of generating controversy. Prashar and Nicholas (1986, pp. 13–18) have recounted some of the problems encountered in this field, including disagreements over such issues as the accountability of co-optees on to council race relations committees; the rights of black organisations as against black individuals as the constituency of representation; and the merits or otherwise of election by public meetings. Part of the problem of course is that 'the ethnic minority population is not a static demographic fixture' and that because of this ethnic representativeness is rarely 'so tangible a thing as to be captured at one point in time and maintained thereafter by constitutional formulas' (Gay and Young, 1988, p. 33). However in practice some such formulas are frequently used to organise representation, whether on CRCs or on council race relations committees. In some cases this may produce structures which 'emphasise inequalities between consultors and consulted' (Ben-Tovim et al., 1986, p. 101). Equally though a lack of formulae or structures can pose problems. This difficulty has also complicated the workings of some women's committees and their sub-groups. A desire to maximise the openness of meetings and to minimise hierarchical procedures could sometimes mean that notions of representation and accountability became confused: 'both the attendance and the decisions of these meetings could shift from week to week . . . they can be and have been taken over by groups that are organised enough to hold caucus meetings in advance' (Goss, 1984, p. 127).

The problem of how far consultative procedures on race relations and on women's issues can be truly representative of the constituencies they serve may well be capable of only partial solution. In that respect of course such procedures share the same difficulty as the wider system of representative democracy within which they are located. Whatever their problems however, they do clearly constitute an attempt to respond to the interests of those who have always been under-represented by conventional electoral politics. The same has not however been true of consultation machinery directed at the world of commerce and industry.

The local government franchise at one time gave businessmen a 'business vote' as commercial ratepayers in addition to their vote as ratepaying householders. Moreover, in the days when much local business was indeed truly local in terms of ownership and management, businessmen and shopkeepers played a prominent part in council affairs. Indeed the pre-1939 golden age of local government has also been called the 'golden age of the shopocracy' on that account (Stevenson, 1984, p. 314). In those days, it seemed, 'businessmen were entrenched in the lives of their localities and had both the time and the inclination to devote to local government service' (Dearlove, 1979, p. 185). Since then, although employees and managers continue to be disproportionally well represented amongst councillors (Widdicombe 1986c, Table 4.5), they have become less clearly identified with the immediate interests of local business. The changing nature of labour markets may well mean that their place of business and their place of political residence are divorced, linked only by commuting: the financial control of once-local firms has increasingly passed into outside hands through mergers and takeovers. The result is that 'ownership and control are no longer fused in the hands of a locally resident and politically active bourgeoisie' (Dearlove, 1979, p. 240). One consequence of this disjunction between local politics and the ownership and control of local business was the feeling amongst businessmen that the private sector was no longer adequately represented locally and that it was suffering especially from 'taxation without representation' in respect of the levying of the non-domestic rate (Sherman, 1970, p. 4).

Bridging the gap between industry and local government required machinery which was not always ready to hand. One instance where industry itself facilitated the liaison is that of Sussex, where the Federation of Sussex Industries, founded in 1945 and now embracing nearly 200 firms, has developed a clear role in representing the private sector to the public sector. The Federation is now routinely consulted on highway and planning matters by both county and district authorities; it has been a major channel for recruiting school governors from member firms; it has provided volunteers to take part in school curriculum development work; it has collaborated with the two county councils in staging industrial and business exhibitions; and it has represented its own members and other groups at discussions with county and district councils on rate levels. Its director general has claimed that 'there is hardly an aspect of local government in Sussex concerning which the Federation is not interested and on which its views are not sought' (Miller, G., 1987, p. 89).

The Federation of Sussex Industries may be a body peculiar to that county but in other places local chambers of commerce have sometimes performed a similar role as the voice of local economic interests. This has been particularly the case in relation to discussion of the government's inner area programmes where the ministerial guidelines made it clear that before giving the necessary approvals to local authorities it would 'expect . . . to be satisfied that the voice of the private sector has been heard' (Department of

the Environment, 1981, p. 2). A similar requirement for consultation with local industry and commerce has been built into the
provisions for producing local economic development plans under
the Local Government and Housing Act 1989. Chambers of
commerce or of trade have often provided the means for enabling
consultations such as these to take place. In Leeds for example the
local chamber (usually in the person of its assistant director) was
'granted observer status at all meetings of the inner-city sub-
committee, sitting with the local authority's officers at the table,
and being asked to contribute to the discussions' (King, 1985, p.
215). It became particularly involved in such issues as financial aid
to small firms, the urban aid programme and the Youth Training
Scheme. Grant (1983) found evidence of rather similar close
relations between local councils and chambers of commerce in
Birmingham and Norwich though a wider study by Stewart (1984)
found that many chambers lacked the resources to engage in
sustained dialogue with their local authorities. However the
introduction in 1984 of procedures for the compulsory consultation by local authorities of non-domestic ratepayers saw many
chambers thrust into a consultative role for want of any other
obvious spokesman for local industry and commerce.

Now that the level of non-domestic rates is determined
nationally some of the significance of such local consultations
has clearly been lost although they are still required by the Local
Government Finance Act 1988. The initial years of rates consultation however produced a number of problems for the participants.
Relations between councils and commerce were not always good
and meetings were sometimes overshadowed by assumptions of
incompetence and inefficiency held by business representatives
about their local authority opposite numbers. Businessmen tended
to assume that economy and cost cutting were the key issues rather
than quality and cost-effectiveness in service provision. Finally,
despite their commercial expertise, business representatives were
often completely lost in the intricacies of local government finance,
especially given the constantly changing rules of the game in the
years concerned. Whether such consultation exercises could have
been, or in a different context may yet be, a learning exercise
remains to be seen.

Having considered consultative machinery aimed at publics
defined by gender, race and economic interest we now turn to

those aimed at specifically localised publics, those who live in the various geographic sub-areas which make up a local authority. Some of the most ambitious recent ventures in this field have been bound up with wider schemes of service decentralisation and we shall consider them later on in that context. At this stage however we will examine three particular consultative mechanisms whose origins lie outside any such decentralisation schemes.

The first of these mechanisms may perhaps be best described as an example of consultation by correspondence; it relates to the rights of English parish councils to be notified of applications for planning permission and to express their views upon them; in practice this usually entails the submission in writing of the views of the parish council rather than any regular meetings between parish and district. For some parish councils in rural or semi-rural areas under development pressure, this particular form of consultation can be of considerable importance since planning applications can raise issues affecting the basic physical character of the village or hamlets which constitute the parish. Whatever the significance of any such planning issue however, the views expressed by a parish council may be only one amongst several. The district council as planning authority may also receive representations from the local amenity or conservation society if there is one, from owners of property adjoining any proposed development site, from other interested individuals and from the district councillor or councillors whose ward embraces the parish. If all these views are consistent then together they may make some impression on the councillors who form the district planning committee; if they are not consistent however, then there is no necessary reason why the views of the parish council will be accorded greater weight than those of other interested parties.

In taking part in this particular form of consultation, parish councils, especially in small communities, may sometimes find local planning issues becoming rather personalised despite the advice that 'personalities should . . . normally be disregarded'. The giver of such advice regretfully noted however that 'this is a fact with which many parish councillors often find it difficult to come to terms' (Storey, 1986). Parish councils do not of course enjoy the advice of professional officers versed in planning policy or planning law, though they may have elected members in their ranks who possess some relevant expertise. In the absence of such advice parish councils may well express views which seem to express a local 'common-sense' but which fall outside the scope of the district council's planning powers as determined or interpreted by planning legislation, the county structure plan, statutory local plans, government circulars and various forms of supplementary planning guidance. This can sometimes lead to the parish feeling that the district wilfully ignores or over-rides the views it has expressed. Thus what is one of the most common forms of consultation of local opinion by district councils can on occasion produce a degree of mutual incomprehension: further intervention by the district's councillors and planning officers may then be needed in order to clarify matters and to restore good working relations.

The consultation of parish councils by district councils is of course a procedure involving two elected bodies. Our two other examples of sub-area consultation are ones which have entailed a widening out of consultation beyond the ranks of elected members, in Rochdale and in Richmond-upon-Thames. In the case of Rochdale our concern is with the area committees first set up in 1983 in the neediest areas of the borough in connection with the council's Community Based Action Area Programme, which embraced the creation of Housing Improvement Areas and General Improvement Areas and related schemes of environmental improvement. This venture preceded the council's current commitment to a more ambitious scheme of neighbourhood decentralisation. The common purpose of the eight area committees was to ensure that local residents were involved in the management of the various improvement programmes; the format of the committees however varied from area to area. Some were made up of ward councillors plus representatives of residents' organisations and community groups operating within the area; others coupled this arrangement with the holding of open forums before the committee meetings at which residents could raise any local issue which concerned them. Residents' representatives on the various committees also met amongst themselves on several occasions in order to discuss their role and to suggest ways of improving the effectiveness of the committees.

The recommendations of the area committees were referred to the Community Based Action Area Sub-Committee of the Housing Committee for final decision and more often than not were accepted. From 1986 the area committees were also enabled to give their views to the planning sub-committee dealing with planning applications on any important development proposals in their areas: other service committees also began to consult the area committees on their own proposals before taking any final decision. All the area committee meetings were open public meetings and attracted attendances varying from less than ten to over a hundred. They were originally seen as a means of giving 'an additional formal status to consultations'(Rochdale Metropolitan Borough Council, 1987 para. 1.1) in specific action areas, building upon but not necessarily replacing more informal street level meetings. In retrospect they proved to be one of the building blocks from which a more ambitious and wider-ranging scheme of decentralisation eventually grew.

The Rochdale consultative machinery employed a committee structure which enabled the views of local representatives to be transmitted into the formal procedures of the council via service sub-committees and main committees. This contrasts with the arrangements in Richmond-upon-Thames where twice-yearly area consultation meetings are essentially designed as occasions on which local residents can question their councillors without however being part of any committee structure. The Richmond meetings, begun in 1984, occur in May–June and October–November each year in ten locations, each covering from one to three wards. The ward councillors are usually all in attendance together, sometimes with the chair of the relevant committee if any major policy item is due to be discussed. The agendas for the consultation meetings are partly derived from the council itself, partly from amenity societies and residents' groups who are invited to submit items and partly from individuals who may make their own suggestions. The range of issues which can thus be covered is wide; the agendas for the autumn cycle of meetings in 1989 give some indication of the scope. The council itself had placed items on all the agendas dealing with poop-scoops and animal wardens, the unitary development plan for the borough, the community charge, a proposed environmental charter, and a highway defect reporting scheme. Issues raised by local groups or individuals were very localised but tended to be concentrated in the fields of traffic, parking, development proposals and environmental nuisances.

The format of the meetings is essentially that of a two hour question and answer session, with the councillors having been briefed beforehand by officers on known agenda items. There is also space for other items to be raised from the floor, without notice, to which councillors respond as best as they can. The mood of the meetings varies; some residents are on first name terms with their councillors and clearly inhabit the same world of political and pressure group activity: others have come there to protest over some burning issue and are more concerned to give the councillors a grilling, and on occasion to challenge or even abuse them, rather than to continue politely the latest stage in some on-going discussion. At one of the autumn meetings in 1989 a councillor who suggested that 'we ought to pass on' to the next item was assured by one angry protester that 'you can all pass on as far as I'm concerned'. Generally however the meetings are low key; perhaps they are livelier in the outer reaches of the borough with less easy access to the council offices, and in those instances where opposition politicians can use them as a platform to criticise the ruling group. An attendance of three or four dozen would be a respectable figure, though some will drift away after their issue has been dealt with, whether in satisfaction, in sorrow or in anger. At the end of the meetings complaints will have been aired, policies explained, undertakings given, progress chased and a number of problems marked down to be 'taken up' with the relevant council department.

The agendas of the Richmond area meetings do tend, perhaps inevitably, to focus on geographically based problems rather than on those that might arise from experience of specific council services. They are concerned largely with the role of the council as regulator of the local environment rather than as the provider of specific services such as housing, education or social services. This does not mean that the borough is blind to the need to consult particular service users as well as local communities. Indeed Richmond operates, for example a system of seven area housing committees containing both tenant-representatives and councillors and intended to allow consultation on housing management issues. Ventures such as those of Richmond are thus clearly cast in the shape of area or service based structures. Members of the public may however also wish to express their views on particular issues as and when they arise regardless of how they fit into council structures. This requires rather different procedures.

Petitions, questions and complaints

One historian has observed that the British public have sometimes supplemented the institutions of representative democracy 'by petition, by agitation or by riot' (Perkin, 1973, p. 6). In the recent past the truth of this observation has been confirmed by the inner city riots of the 1980s and by the widespread demonstrations against the introduction of the poll tax in 1989 and 1990. Less widely noted was the emergence, or re-emergence, of the petition as a way of making public demands on those in authority, at least at the local level.

'Getting up a petition' is in fact a fairly common response amongst those concerned by some actual or possible decision by a local authority. An unpopular planning application for example may well provoke local residents into signing a petition against the granting of planning permission: such a petition would then normally be referred to the members of the planning committee at the appropriate meeting. Similar arrangements may well be made to handle other sorts of petitions as and when they are submitted. In some cases however the procedure has now become more formalised and even incorporated into council standing orders. A survey by the Community Rights Project (1986) found that of 262 responding authorities some 59 had provision for the presentation of petitions and/or the receipt of deputations at council meetings: three of those authorities – Afan, Haringey and Walsall – also extended this provision to committee and sub-committee level. The nature of such provisions varied in respect of such matters as whether or not, or for how long, petitioners might address the councillors and whether petitioners could be questioned by councillors.

The kinds of issues raised by petitions and the numbers of people putting their names to petitions are naturally very varied. An analysis of the experience at Sheffield enables us to illustrate the variety both of issues and of the extent of support. During 1988 a total of 43 petitions were presented at nine council meetings, bearing a total of 43689 signatures. Seventeen petitions had fewer than one hundred signatures, ten had more than a thousand. The largest, with 19401, protesting at proposed branch library closures was organised by the National and Local Government Officers

Association (NALGO) Libraries Shop Stewards Committee: it secured a reprieve, or at least a stay of execution, for the threatened branches. The range of issues covered can be seen from the meeting on 8 June 1988 when eight petitions were presented. They referred to cars parked in a school access way, inadequate cutting and maintenance of some grass verges, a request for double yellow lines in a particular street, support for the council's opposition to clause 28 of the Local Government Bill, the reduction of a local library's opening hours and three proposed closures   of a child nurture unit, of a young people's narrow boat project and of a swimming bath.

As this list suggests, the petitions fall broadly into two categories, those drawing the council's attention to a local problem requiring remedial action and those reacting to the council's own policies or proposals. In the former case the outcome usually has been a referral to the appropriate committee to see if and when the necessary work can be done within policy and within budget. Petitions relating to the council's own proposals inevitably get a mixed reaction. The closure of the narrow boat project referred to above was re-affirmed, despite the petition, at the subsequent meeting of the Family and Community Services Programme Committee. On the other hand, at another council meeting petitioners secured the withdrawal, 'for the present time', of charges which had been levied by the Education Programme Committee for the use of school premises. Petitioners asking that the City Hall ballroom be reserved only for ballroom dancing and not made available for heavy metal discos found that they had opened a Pandora's box. The Leisure Services Programme Committee was told that on investigation the council's safety officer had now reported that the ballroom floor was unsafe for any form of dancing: further discussions would therefore have to take place as to the future use of the ballroom.

The reception of petitions at council meetings can allow for a brief face-to-face exchange between councillors and petitioners, though the procedures are normally designed to prevent the development of debate between the two parties. A similar facility is afforded by those councils who have introduced a public question time into their meeting agendas. This idea was pioneered by Bracknell in 1974 but had spread to at least eighteen others by the time of the Community Rights Project survey of 1986. The detailed arrangements vary from authority to authority: some require advance written notice of questions, others do not; most specify a maximum length of question time, usually 15 or 30 minutes, others leave it open-ended; and some lay down rules limiting how many questions one person may ask and rejecting questions that have been asked at a preceding meeting. As with petitions the subject matter of questions can be quite varied. Chelmsford Borough Council, for example, received in 1989 questions about the town's ice rink, the cost of planning appeals, a street parking scheme, the indoor retail market and the closure of a doctor's surgery. In most cases the questions at Chelmsford are oral rather than written, with the replies following suit: one consequence of this is that neither questions nor answers are fully recorded in the council's minutes though the topics raised are referred to therein. One topic, that of the future of the indoor market, produced numerous questions from a crowded public gallery: the answers were so far from satisfying the questioners that eventually the council meeting had to be adjourned to allow passions to cool.

Asking a question at a council meeting, or at a committee meeting as some councils also allow, usually involves attendance at the town or county hall, which may in itself be inconvenient or even daunting for some people. This difficulty is mitigated in the case of Basildon, whose committees are mainly area-based and meet at venues within their local areas. Four of the seven area committees permit a formal public question time; at their January 1990 meetings they generated seventeen, seven, four and three public questions respectively. The other three area committees provide for periods of adjournment during which members of the public may express their views, though these are not part of the formal business. Both formats however are facilitated by the easier physical access arising from the use of local venues at which to conduct the meetings.

There is one particular local authority committee which is perhaps especially likely to arouse in members of the public the feeling that they would like to ask a question or even make a statement, that is the committee or sub-committee dealing with applications for planning permission to develop or to change the use of land or buildings. The possible impact of proposed developments upon particular localities or individual households may be such that those affected may feel frustrated if they are uncertain whether or not the planning officers or the councillors have grasped the full implications. A few councils, including Clydebank, Rhymney Valley and Calderdale, have adopted procedures designed to deal with this problem. Clydebank's chief planning officer has outlined his council's procedure as follows:

> I describe the proposal and answer any questions from members. Then applicant and objectors are each allowed a maximum of 10 minutes (although five minutes is usually more than enough) to present their case. Each is then asked questions by members before withdrawing to the public gallery. Members then debate the issues, with applicant and objectors still present, and decide.
>
> In practice, requests to be heard are relatively few. It is reckoned by all involved that the little extra time involved is well worthwhile in achieving fair and good decisions (Gregor, 1990).

Questioning need not of course be confined to the arena of formal council or committee meetings. We have already encountered the area-based consultative meetings in Richmond-upon-Thames, which allow residents to question their own ward councillors. A variation on this scheme is provided by the regular series of Civic Conferences held by Havering. Started in 1974, these are held every two months with participation being based on a membership of about 100 local organisations, each of whom is entitled to be represented at the conference meetings. Any of these organisations is entitled to put one question to each meeting of the conference, giving three weeks notice in doing so. Replies are given at the conference by the appropriate committee chairs, with supplementary questions being allowed: the presiding Mayor may occasionally open up a wider debate beyond the level of question and answer if it seems appropriate so to do. On average something like twenty questions are handled at each conference, ranging from small, highly localised problems to major issues of council policy: the attendance averages out at around fifty people per meeting, most of them from the organisations which have tabled the questions of the day. Copies of both questions and replies are available in the public library for reference after the conference has taken place.

The subject matter of both questions and petitions under the procedures we have just considered is almost invariably one of public policy and its implementation, rather than of personal or domestic concern. Sometimes of course the distinction between public policy and personal concern is not a watertight one. Planning issues for example can give rise to disagreements not only about what constitutes the best general policy but also about the consequences of policy for individual households or properties: the same can also be true in other fields such as housing. Even so it is likely to be the public policy aspects which are most readily aired by means of petitioning and questioning in an open forum. Few people are likely to wish to air their own private circumstances and problems before a formal audience of councillors, officers, press and public. They may prefer the privacy offered by a councillor's surgery, a telephone call, a private meeting or correspondence. However if they are at some stage dissatisfied with their treatment then they may wish to make some sort of formal complaint. They may choose to do this with the assistance of their own local councillor; but if they do not, or if they are dissatisfied with their councillor's efforts, then they are dependent upon whatever arrangements the council has for dealing with complaints.

There are some complaints procedures which are made available by law. The right of public inspection of local authority accounts, for example, carries with it the opportunity to question the auditor and to make objections on matters related to the accounts. Local authorities may be taken to court and their decisions may be made the subject of judicial review, though the law on his last topic has been described as 'complex to the point of being almost unpredictable' (Birkinshaw, 1985, p. 58). In the field of education, local authorities are obliged by the Education Act 1980 to provide an appeal procedure for parents dissatisfied with their child's secondary school allocation: in addition, the Education Reform Act 1988 requires authorities to provide arrangements for dealing with complaints on curriculum matters.

The whole range of local authority services are of course within the remit of the local government ombudsman, the Commission for Local Administration; the Commission's powers are confined to questions of maladministration, which entails a council having done something it should not have done, not doing something it should have done, or doing something the wrong way. On that basis maladministration can cover neglect and unjustified delay, malice, bias or unfair discrimination, failure to tell people of their rights, failure to provide advice when requested or providing inaccurate or misleading advice, failure to have proper procedures and failure to follow the council's own agreed policies, rules or procedures. Complainants approaching the ombudsman are normally required to have given the council concerned a chance to deal with the matter.

This latter requirement has provoked some authorities into establishing their own complaints procedure, if only to safeguard their position in respect of possible ombudsman investigations. The ombudsman produced a recommended code of practice for the handling of complaints in 1978, updating it in 1982, although its adoption remained voluntary. In recent years however, the issue of complaints procedure has taken on a new salience. Reviewing its existing procedures, for example, Buckinghamshire County Council (1989, p. 1) observed that 'a clear, positive and well publicised complaints procedure should be an important part of Customer Care'; it also judged that the council would need 'to embrace the systematic monitoring and evaluation of complaints as an important aid to assure the effectiveness of service provision, and as part of its developing performance management process'.

Buckinghamshire's comments reflect the two faces of council complaints handling, namely its function for the complainant and its function for the management of the authority. A survey of 152 local authorities in England carried out by the University of Sheffield concluded that of the 63 which claimed to have authority-wide complaints procedures some 45 had procedures designed mainly to serve 'managerial functions' and 'internal bureaucratic needs' rather than being geared to public needs (Seneviratne and Cracknell, 1988, p. 183). In the case of social services departments for example, complaints procedures seemed to be used 'as protection for social workers who seemed all too aware of the necessity of making their decisions accountable in an increasingly critical environment' (ibid). More specifically Birkinshaw (1985, p. 79) has ascribed the social service practice of maintaining a central register of complaints as 'a response to widely publicised tragedies of child death'.

However, the concept of complaints handling as being not only a management tool for monitoring performance but also an important means of relating to complaining service users has significant implications for the sorts of procedures that ought to be adopted. At the most basic level of course any such procedure is only of use to service users if they are aware of its existence: in the Sheffield study only eighteen authorities had publicised the procedures outside the organisation. In its own review however, Buckinghamshire (1989, p. 11) stressed the importance of informing the public about complaints procedures not only in terms of 'good consumer relations' but also because a widely publicised and consistent procedure 'would remove the suspicion that those with the ability to make "high level" contacts obtain the best treatment'. Apart from giving the procedure wide publicity, further recommended practices have included the following:

1. allowing a variety of formats of complaints, oral as well as written, rather than using standard forms;
2. the appointment of an officer with specific responsibility for dealing with complaints;
3. a deadline for processing complaints;
4. a system of registering and monitoring the handling of complaints;
5. provision for higher level review if the complainant is still not satisfied;
6. written reasons for all responses and conclusions;
7. evaluation of any lessons to be learnt from complaints. (Birkinshaw, 1987; Seneviratne and Cracknell, 1988; Local Government Training Board, 1988)

One authority whose procedures have attempted to address such requirements is Braintree District Council, whose complaints procedure is publicised in leaflets available from council offices, libraries and Citizens Advice Bureaux. The council's version of the recommended practices outlined above is as follows:

1. complaints are accepted in any form, other than that of an anonymous letter;
2. a Quality Standards Officer is appointed in each service department to register and handle complaints; in addition a Quality Manager in the chief executive's department offers a

'helpline' telephone number for complainants who are uncertain how to proceed;

3. all complaints are acknowledged and there is a target response time of seven working days, failing the achievement of which complainants must be given an explanation of the delay;

4. in addition to registering complaints, the Quality Standards Officers each prepare a departmental monthly return of complaints and their outcome to the Quality Manager who reports to the council's management team with a summary of all complaints; the management team consider each one individually to see what lessons may be learned;

5. complainants who are not satisfied with the handling of their complaint have the right to have it reviewed by the chief executive and, if that fails to satisfy, by the chair or vice-chair of the council;

6. all complainants receive written responses to their complaints; visits to or from complainants may also occur if they are agreeable to this;

7. the council's Policy Committee receives a quarterly report on complaints and members then consider whether they reveal the need for action; for example, a concentration of housing repair complaints in one locality in 1988–89 led to a change in the way repair jobs were placed with sub-contractors in that part of the district.

Defining and categorising complaints under such a procedure can never be wholly watertight. Braintree's complaint categories for reporting to the management team and to members seem fairly straightforward:

(a) Dissatisfaction with the council's decision: the council's decision has been properly made but the customer is unhappy with it.

(b) Employee's attitude: the customer is aggrieved at the attitude of the employee e.g. rude, insolent, surly etc.

(c) Delay in responding: the length of time taken to respond or to do something has prompted the customer to complain.

(d) Dissatisfaction with the action taken: action by the council in pursuing a solution to a problem or the way the matter has been generally handled is not to the customer's satisfaction.

(e) Dissatisfaction with the standard of service: the standard of service laid down by the council is achieved but the customer feels more should be done.

(f) Miscellaneous: any complaint not falling within any of the other categories.

(g) Housing repair delays: delays in completion of housing repairs.

Both the categorisation and the handling of complaints at Braintree aim to ensure that both the council and the complainant draw some benefit from what might otherwise be a counter-productive experience. The chief uncertainty about the procedures lies in the grey area of when exactly a problem becomes a complaint, an issue on which some members have claimed to be unclear. Nevertheless Braintree's procedures are an attempt to strike a balance between the needs of management, members and the public when complaints are being made. They also form part of the council's broader concern with its relations with its service users, with its image in the local community and with its reputation in the world of local government.

Opinion polling

The organising of petitions, the asking of questions and the making of complaints are all mechanisms which require members of the public to take some form of initiative in order to ensure that their voices are heard. However a local authority might have its own reasons for wishing to sound out public opinion and might thus launch its own ventures in this respect without waiting for local people to express their views spontaneously. In some cases such an exercise might be part of a broader strategy of public relations and marketing, designed to inform as well as to consult the public about the merits of local services. However this need not necessarily be the case and we shall consider opinion polling here, whilst dealing with public relations and marketing in the following chapter.

The carrying out of research and surveys into public opinion on local authorities and their services does not in itself imply the conscious adoption of a public relations or marketing strategy. Indeed some councils undertook such ventures well before the latter concepts began to appear on the local government agenda, usually because there was some pressing issue on which councillors sought local public reaction. Islington for example commissioned an opinion survey by MORI on attitudes to rates and spending in 1982; Sheffield commissioned one on attitudes to rate-capping and services in 1984; and in the latter year both Test Valley and Christchurch sought the public's views on proposed boundary re-organisations. These moreover were merely a few of the more than eighty surveys carried out for local authorities by MORI in the 1980s: other authorities have commissioned similar work from other firms or conducted their own research.

Although such surveys have become increasingly popular over the past decade or so they are not without their problems. Rushing into such exercises without a clear perception of their purpose for example is a recipe for disaster. Thus the Local Government Training Board (1988, p. 84) has advised councils of the basic need to distinguish between obtaining '"hard" facts for a performance review exercise . . . [and] "softer" information about attitudes and perceptions'. An opinion survey may uncover the facts but group discussions or unstructured interviews are more useful for exploring attitudes and perceptions. Clarity about purpose and methodology is not the only problem however; nor do problems end when decisions have been made about who is to do the work and at what cost. There are important issues that arise once the work has been done and the results are to hand.

A key issue is that of how the findings of any survey are to be interpreted and what weight is to placed upon them, as the following observations indicate.

The subjective perceptions of a service . . . bear no *necessary* connection to that service's or authority's objective performance, efficiency or success. A good service, by any objective standard, might forever be unfavourably perceived because expectations are inappropriate. Measurements of dissatisfaction might tell us more about people's aspirations for what 'should be' than their opinion of 'what is' . . . . Whether these opinions are subsequently judged to be appropriate by some other yardstick is a separate issue (Newcastle-upon-Tyne City Council, 1985, p. 1; emphasis in original).

The matter of relating the public's subjective perceptions to the demands of 'some other yardstick' is closely linked with the question of how far the priorities of elected members (the 'other yardstick'?) should be waived in favour of public opinion. However that conundrum is solved, councillors may still feel that opinion polling in some way undermines their role as public representatives, leaving the pollsters claiming to be the true voices of the people. On this issue councillors can be sometimes rather on the defensive: 'I don't need opinion polls – I walk through my ward every day of the week' as one councillor put it. Councillors may of course conduct their own assessments of public opinion quite apart from surveys carried out by professional pollsters. Liberal Democrat councillors in Richmond-upon-Thames in 1990 for example invited local residents to complete a tear-off slip from a door-to-door news-letter giving their views on the best balance between improving or maintaining services or cutting them to meet the government's community charge estimate of £341 a head for the borough. The results of this exercise however were not quite the same as those obtained from differently worded questions on the same topic included in the council's annual survey of residents' attitudes, which showed a greater concern for defending services than did responses to the councillors' own poll. Faced with such conflicting evidence of public opinion councillors no doubt felt free to make their own judgements when it came to setting the level of the charge.

Officers and their departments can of course also be on the defensive if the results of a survey seem to cast them and their services in a bad light. They may too have genuine reason to feel that they alone are not to blame. As one report expressed it: 'The expression of some public dissatisfaction with a service should not be seen as a criticism of the employees who deliver the services. It can be a result of policy, resources available or, as with dog fouling, more the actions of the public' (Norwich City Council, 1987, para. 11). Given the sensibilities of councillors and officers there is always the temptation to receive the results of any research or polling rather gingerly, to highlight the good responses, to excuse the bad ones, to issue a Pollyanna-ish press release and then to hope that the findings can be quietly allowed to lay on the shelf and gather dust. The more robust alternative is to try and utilise them as 'a useful addition to policy making on services' as the Norwich report suggested (idem, para. 10).

One authority where a reasonably systematic attempt was made to follow that course is Braintree, for whom MORI conducted a residents' attitude survey in 1989 involving both group discussions and face-to-face interviewing. The results of the MORI survey were considered by all the council's committees and a series of action targets agreed in the light of public attitudes (Braintree District Council, 1989). Amongst them were the following:

-   Additional expenditure on litter bins together with a scheme for commercial sponsorship of bins.
-   An increased level of daily cleaning for public conveniences.
-   The production of a 'green charter' on the environment.
-   Additional car parking provision on the council's housing estates.
-   Further installation of entry phone systems in council flats.
-   Greater publicity for the council's housing advisory service.
-   The expression of concern to the two local MPs over the council's limited ability to provide new housing to rent as a result of government legislation.
-   Better marketing of local youth facilities.
-   More activities for children during school holidays at the council's sports centres.
-   Pressure on British Rail to improve commuter car parking provision.
-   Production on a trial basis of a quarterly civic newspaper in order to improve public awareness of the council's services and activities.

Opinion polling need not be confined to assessing attitudes about existing services: it may also be used to guide local authorities who are uncertain about whether or how to proceed with new initiatives. Reading for instance took this course in respect of implementing a Labour manifesto commitment to decentralisation of services. Before committing itself to any particular scheme the council commissioned research from the Safe Neighbourhoods Unit (1987) which carried out detailed consultations with a quarter of all households in four areas of the borough. This revealed particulary strong support for decentralisation amongst council tenants, elderly people, women and households with children. Overall, residents favoured the idea of one-stop local offices providing access to, or information on, the services of the council and other agencies, which could deal with problems without reference back to the council's Civic Offices and which were sited within fifteen minutes walk of where they lived. On the basis of such findings the council felt encouraged to begin a gradual programme of decentralisation focusing initially on two specific areas where the demand for such a move seemed to be especially strong.

The Reading survey also found that over two thirds of residents were not aware of the full range of council services and required better information. This finding is similar to that made in the case of Braintree, where two thirds of the residents polled agreed that they 'don't really know much about what Braintree District Council does'. Their main concern was for more information on the services available to them and on whom to contact at the council in respect of different problems (MORI, 1989, pp. 66 and 70). It is such questions of information and access that we examine next.

5　Information and Access

> The hallmark of any good service assumes an ability to make available to the public a quality service not otherwise provided. It must recognise that people wish different things and provide its customers with information on what is available . . . . It is considered that this authority should . . . raise standards, improve services and improve the delivery of them. This is the challenge of the 1990s.
>
> Roxburgh District Council, 1989.

The overwhelming majority of people are likely to prefer local government services that match their needs and circumstances; not everyone however necessarily wishes to secure this through sustained involvement in participative or consultative procedures. Indeed they may take the view that it is the council's job, not the public's, to ensure that the demands of the latter are anticipated and accommodated. As the above comments from Roxburgh suggest it can be seen as the council's responsibility to 'provide its customers with information' and to 'improve the delivery' of services. The attention paid by local authorities to these aspects of its relations with the public are our concern in this chapter.

Even if there were no pressures at all for measures of participation or consultation, councils would still need to pay attention to their treatment of the public for the reasons set out by Walsh (1990, p. 25):

> Relations with providers are particularly important for services, especially where we are offering advice, help or counselling. The service may be, in large part, the relationship.

In similar vein Clarke and Stewart (1990, pp. 9–10) refer to the dependency of much public service delivery upon an 'interaction between provider and user' which has its own 'moment of truth' whenever such interaction takes place, be it a housing officer meeting a tenant, a social worker assessing a client or a receptionist dealing with an inquirer. It is in the light of the importance of such interactions and relationships that attention needs to be paid to such considerations as availability of information and ease of access to services, and also to the surroundings and the manner in which they are provided, all of which can make or mar the 'moment of truth'.

Improving access

For some members of the public a very basic need may be that of access to information about the workings and policies of the council, about the availability of services and also perhaps about council files relating specifically to themselves. The first and last of these are now covered by legislation enacted during the 1980s.

The Local Government (Access to Information) Act 1985 drew on the particular experience of Bradford, where an all party agreement on open government had been enshrined as clause 46 of the council's standing orders. The clause provided the basis for the draft bill which eventually became law as the 1985 Act. The Act gave to the public the statutory right to attend meetings of all committees and sub-committees and to inspect and to copy not only committee reports but also the background documents on which the latter have drawn. Some councils have gone further than the minimum requirements of the Act or did indeed anticipate them. Calderdale for example agreed in 1983 that members of the public could record the proceedings of council committee and sub-committee meetings if they gave prior notice of their intention so to do.

In 1987 the Access to Personal Files Act provided for the right of access to personal files other than those held on computer and thus covered by the Data Protection Act 1984. Regulations under the 1987 Act were introduced in 1989 in respect of social services and housing and in 1990 in respect of education. They allow social work clients, council house tenants and applicants and parents and pupils aged sixteen or more to see and copy their own files, to correct mistakes and to place their own statements in the files. These rights however only apply to information recorded after 1 April 1989 in the case of social services and housing and after 1 September 1990 in the case of education.

Neither the 1985 nor the 1987 Act dealt with access to services themselves. A traditional complaint about local authorities was that members of the public sometimes had great difficulty in finding the right person to deal with their problems; they were passed around from office to office or from one telephone extension to another rather like a puzzling and unwanted parcel. No doubt such confusion could have arisen because of uncertainty about the nature of the problem, or because it involved more than one department; but whatever the reason it hardly made life easier for those who experienced it.

One attempt to avoid such difficulties has been the development of the one stop service shop, such as that introduced by Westminster City Council in January 1986. Prior to that date people visiting City Hall were confronted with a situation in which there were:

1. Fifteen main departmental contact points.
2. Contact points on twelve different floors in City Hall and in other buildings throughout Westminster.
3. Over 250 callers a day needing to visit more than two floors and two departments.
4. Glass screens separating the staff from the public, producing an unfriendly atmosphere.
5. No facilities for confidential interviews or discussions.
6. No provision of public toilets, facilities for disabled people, public telephones or photocopying machines.

The one stop shop overcame these problems by providing:

1. An access point for all council services and information on one floor.
2. Links to other council buildings by phone or by facsimile machines.
3. A computerised database of council information.
4. An open counter service with staff who have had training in public awareness skills (and self-defence).

5. Private interview rooms
6. Toilets, photocopiers, telephones, seats and a special counter
    for disabled people.

Since it first opened, the City Hall one stop shop has been dealing
with between 300 and 600 callers a day with certain cyclical peaks
such as electoral registration queries in the autumn and rates/poll
tax queries in the spring. The counter staff, who are drawn from
the individual council departments, basically fulfil a reception or
'clearing house' function rather than one of providing detailed
professional advice: but they do of course know where such advice
can be found. For those who use the shop, questionnaires are
available to enable them to give their views on the service they have
received: the results are scrutinised by the council's Press and
Public Relations Section to identify any action needed. The overall
ambience of the shop is certainly unlike the more austere
surroundings of some town hall reception areas: the carpets, the
background music, the indoor landscaping, the open counters and
the furnishings are perhaps more reminiscent of a travel agent's
office. Such a commercial comparison is not accidental: it reflects
the approach of the council leader Lady Porter, who was described
by her chief executive as believing that the council should 'try to
provide precisely the same service as retail establishments give to
their customers . . . she equated local residents with customers'
(*Municipal Journal*, 9 December 1988).

A small number of authorities have followed Westminster's
example and set up their own versions of one stop shops, some
of them with particular features of their own. Bradford for example
opened a one stop Information Centre in 1989 at the City Hall,
with others at Keighley and Shipley. The City Hall centre provides
a contact point for all council services, together with information
on local organisations and their activities, free 'hot-lines' to all
council departments, space for displays and promotions by both
the council and outside bodies and a tourist information centre. In
1990 a Job Spot was added to advertise council job vacancies,
along with a campaign aimed at women 'returners' seeking to get
back into employment and needing help with re-training and job
searching: a further development was the provision of information
on recreation, youth services and more generally 'what to do in the
summer'. As in Westminster, the staff at the three Bradford centres

were all trained in customer care, whilst staff with Asian language abilities were also employed where appropriate. The atmosphere at the centres was intended to be clear, bright, friendly and welcoming. Oddly enough such a move 'up-market' from old style council offices brought its problems: the council launched a 'Need it fixing?' campaign in 1990 to reassure people that over-flowing dustbins and broken pavements could still be reported in the new surroundings.

A further variant of the one stop idea is that of the Norwich Advice Arcade opened in 1987. The city council's own advice service, which covers housing, consumer affairs and welfare rights, is located there and also administers a larger advice arcade which provides accommodation for more than twenty other, mainly voluntary, organisations. These include the Citizens' Advice Bureau and Age Concern, along with other bodies who rent space on either an annual or a sessional (half-day) basis. Such bodies have included Physically Handicapped and Able Bodied (PHAB), Men-cap, Norfolk Bus Information Centre, Norwich Community Health Council and the Norwich Crossroads Care Attendant Scheme. Something like 300 callers a day use the advice arcade, either in person or over the telephone and the council itself regards the facility as 'a unique example of co-operation between the City Council and the voluntary sector' and observes that 'the ease with which the public can move between the services has proved popular' (Norwich City Council, 1988, p. 3).

In some authorities local libraries have begun to assume functions rather akin to those of council information centres. In Dorset for example county council departments increasingly use libraries as the location for exhibitions and sometimes for meetings: the highways and planning departments, and some district council planning departments have been particulary active in this respect. Voluntary sector organisations too have looked to the county's libraries as a resource centre able to provide help and guidance. Bradford too has used its libraries as a preliminary contact point for providing council information. Not only do the libraries attract a wide cross-section of the public and have extended opening hours, they are also 'considered by their users as "neutral" places in contrast to the "hostile" environment' of council offices (Clipsom, 1987, p. 123). The library service in many counties does of course also have a long tradition of taking its own services to the people through the development of the mobile library service. Essex for example had its first library van with a capacity of 2500 books in 1930: sixty years later eighteen mobile libraries were catering for over 500 stops within the county.

The principle of taking services to the people need not be confined to libraries. Newport for example has experimented with the use of adapted single decker buses, on hire from the bus company, for use as polling stations in locations without appropriate voting places: 'the buses were driven in in the morning and driven out again in the evening'. The possibility of 'taking the votes to the people' by using the buses on a circulating basis within a given polling area has also been canvassed, though this would presumably need a change in electoral law (Dyer, 1988, p. vi). No such problem however confronts the introduction of a mobile office service providing a small scale version of a one stop shop.

Richmond-upon-Thames introduced a mobile office system in 1985 with a caravan located initially at ten sites, later reduced to six, on specific days of the week. The caravan provides a range of information leaflets together with computer and telephone links with council departments and staff from finance and housing. Although the scheme was launched with a good deal of publicity the impetus was not maintained and the scheme was slow to build up a regular public. Siting changes may have contributed to this: so too may the problems of dealing with queries outside the realms of housing and finance. For these the staff may have to act as a referral agency rather than provide an answer on the spot, though they try to do the latter whenever possible. In some ways perhaps the scheme may be seen as a halfway house between a full one stop shop and a system of area based decentralisation. By 1990 the council was taking cautious steps towards the latter with the opening of local offices for housing and social services in three areas of the borough.

The decentralisation of services has been a major field of innovation in local government since the early 1980s with Walsall and its thirty-one neighbourhood offices usually being seen as the pioneers. Certainly Walsall became something of a model for other, mainly Labour, authorities, not least perhaps because it couched its hopes for decentralisation in an explicitly political language. As well as dealing with housing problems the neighbourhood offices also provided welfare benefits advice and dealt with some aspects of social services such as meals on wheels and home help: but they were also seen as a focus for rebuilding a sense of political community amongst local people by bringing residents, council officers and services into more direct contact. As one of the council's neighbourhood officers expressed it: 'People need a little less faith in the experts and a bit more in themselves. You need a system of political education; which, in an indirect way, the Neighbourhood Offices provide' (Seabrook, 1984, p. 142).

Although Walsall's initiative was perhaps the first of a new wave of politically conceived decentralisations, other authorities had made similar moves in the previous decade. Cunninghame for example decentralised its housing service into four area offices on the initial recommendation of its new Director of Housing in 1974: his colleagues in environmental health and recreation agreed to decentralise some of their functions and personnel at the same time (Lindsay, 1986). At roughly the same period there was 'a small but growing trend' in the social services towards social workers operating on a patch or neighbourhood basis (Hadley and Hatch, 1981, p. 154). The decentralisation of services in the 1970s and 1980s thus reflected both professional and political motives: the provision of more geographically accessible service offices and a more responsive service has been accompanied in some authorities by aspirations towards using decentralisation as an agency for a more democratised form of decision-making about service provision, a strategy which we will examine in our concluding chapter.

By 1990 over fifty authorities had embanked on schemes of service decentralisation, usually starting with housing but also sometimes embracing environmental health, planning and social services. The geographical pattern of decentralisation has varied widely. Islington has provided twenty-four neighbourhood offices giving an average coverage of one office for every 7000 inhabitants. In Tower Hamlets, Norwich and Basildon seven neighbourhood offices have been established, in each case serving an average population of 20000, 17000 and 23000 respectively. The decentralisation of services has on the whole been a more common objective than that of decentralising political influence or power. A survey of thirty local authorities conducted by Arnold and Cole (1987) for example found that the improvement of effectiveness, accessibility and public relations outranked greater democratisation as objectives of decentralised housing services. Even so, despite the relative modesty of ambition of decentralising service delivery rather than decision-making, such efforts have not been without problems of their own. The construction or conversion of premises for neighbourhood offices is clearly a major item of expenditure; so too may be new computer technology to link neighbourhoods with remaining town hall offices; staff may also need training for new ways of working in environments designed to be user-friendly and to break down traditional inter-departmental boundaries. New working conditions, close public contact and fears about future career patterns may prove problematic to some staff, whilst councillors may prove uneasy about their role in relation to new neighbourhood institutions.

Despite the difficulties, the introduction of decentralised services does seem to have proved a worthwhile innovation, though much of the evidence so far is piecemeal or anecdotal and the question of whether the benefits outweigh the costs may sometimes be a matter for political judgement. Thus a review of the evidence on the impact of decentralised housing services found it hard to tell whether more accessible services, changed attitudes and better communication between staff and tenants adequately counter-balanced problems with staff morale, costs and rising demand (Cole, 1987). Such uncertainties underline the need for more monitoring and evaluation of these initiatives called for by Hambleton, Hoggett and Tolan (1989).

Decentralised offices, the use of mobile service vans and the provision of one stop shops, despite their virtues, may nonetheless fail to solve access problems in large rural authorities with a thinly scattered population. Here the use of information technology may provide part of the solution. Montgomeryshire for example has introduced an experiment involving the siting of computer terminals in sub-post offices, allowing local people access to information on some aspects of housing and finance and also providing a means of arranging appointments with council staff.

Whatever forms of access to the council are provided they may lose much of their utility to the public if the experience they provide is not in itself helpful and pleasant. That is why, for example, the opening of one stop shops has involved much consideration of details of design, lighting, furnishing, signposting and reception. Thus in launching its own experiment with a system of 'local shops' across the district Wrekin District Council (1987, paras 2.1 and 2.2) stressed the need for such facilities to be 'friendly, attractive' places, providing a 'friendly and efficient' service with opening times that would 'relate to local requirements'. This stress reflected not only the new local authority interest in the service shop concept but also a wider concern over the nature of reception facilities and of across-the-counter relations between staff and public.

Arun District Council (1987c), for example, in their action plan *Working for the Public*, referred to alterations to the Civic Centre reception area, which had been re-designed 'to give a more welcoming first impression' to those arriving with problems and queries. The action plan also included proposals for staff to attend seminars and discussion groups exploring the concept of customer care, for training in telephone use, plain English writing and reception behaviour and for better briefing of reception staff by individual service departments as new issues or problems emerge which may produce enquiries from the public. The context of good customer care at the reception desk can be gauged by the *Customer Care Code* produced by the housing department of Leicester City Council (n.d). The Code, distributed to every household in Leicester, included the following reminders to staff:

> Be polite, courteous . . . and sincere. Don't pass customers round – there's nothing worse than being transferred numerous times before finding the right person – try and put yourself in their shoes.
> Give full attention to the customer's enquiry. Make the customer feel welcome and important. Don't assume the customer knows what you mean – CHECK.
> Don't use office jargon when talking or writing to a customer. Be simple and concise.
> If you have to say no to a customer's request explain why and offer an alternative if you can.

The reception function is not of course a one-way process. People coming in with problems or queries are in fact bringing in information about the council's performance or lack thereof. Some chief officers have thus concluded that they may have something to learn by sitting at the reception desk themselves from time to time. The former chief executive of Wrekin who spent

45 minutes at the reception desk every Monday morning claimed that 'It was a good way to keep my feet on the ground' and that it helped him 'to learn how customers are treated' (Grice, 1989) as well as being a good exercise in improving the quality of the 'moment of truth' in provider-user relations.

Public relations

Relations which are based on the provider-user interaction are not the only relations with which councils may need to concern themselves. They may also wish to place particular service relationships into the wider context of a council's overall philosophy and objectives, to inform members of the public of their nature and to persuade them of their virtue. For this purpose they may enter into the field of public relations, whose purpose in local government has been described by a past president of the Institute of Public Relations in the following terms:

> to ensure that the local authority enjoys the reputation it deserves and to help it deserve the reputation it wants (quoted in Richardson, 1988, p. 5).

Public relations was certainly a growth area in local government during the 1980s, testified to by the establishment of a Local Government Group within the Institute of Public Relations and by the organisation by that institute of the Local Government Public Relations Awards sponsored by the *Local Government Chronicle*. However local government interest in public relations in fact predates the 1980s even if it did not fully flower until that decade.

In 1946 NALGO produced its own *Report on Relations between Local Government and the Community* which argued that a greater public knowledge of local government was a pre-requisite of any greater public involvement. Reaction to the report was mixed but in 1947, after discussions with the local authority associations, the government set up a Consultative Committee on Publicity for Local Government, chaired by the Parliamentary Secretary to the Ministry of Health, John Edwards. The committee favoured a wider use of publicity by local authorities and in response to this view the Local Government Act 1948 made it lawful for local authorities to incur expenditure in connection with providing information on individual services and on local government matters generally, including the arranging of lectures, the making of films and the mounting of exhibitions and displays. Edwards made it clear however, in winding up the House of Commons second reading debate on 19 November 1947, that 'there is certainly no intention of empowering local authorities to run newspapers'. In retrospect the emphasis at this stage seems to have been very much on publicity as the handmaiden of extra-mural education in 'civics'.

A rather different approach however can be seen in the wake of local government reorganisation in Greater London in the early 1960s and elsewhere in the early 1970s. Many of the new authorities addressed themselves to questions of identity and recognition. In the London Borough of Camden for example, although 'the question . . . of presenting an image of the new Borough was very secondary' to the business of making the new organisation operational the council nevertheless broke new ground by deciding to seek a symbol, or a logo, rather than the traditional coat of arms. It also sought a clear house style for design and printing and a uniform colour for its vehicle fleet (Wistrich, 1972, pp. 54 and 248–9). A few years later it was rewarded with congratulations from the *Times* (4 September 1970) which judged that Camden 'with its clasped hands symbol and orange dustcarts . . . [had] probably established its identity in the public mind better than most of the 1964 vintage London boroughs', many of which were to follow its example.

Creating a clear identity may not only be a matter of addressing the public outside the authority: there may be a desire to do something similar for those actually working for the authority. For example a communications audit carried out for Norfolk County Council by Profile Public Relations (1988, p. 2) stressed the desirability of developing 'a unified county council identity', not only amongst the public but also amongst employees working in a range of localities scattered across a large and diverse county. This view was one which the council itself subsequently endorsed: a central public relations unit was created, including a press officer and a publications officer under the head of the unit; the style of the council's annual report was re-designed; a 'mission statement' was adopted setting out the purpose behind the council's work; and proposals were drawn up for clarifying the overall corporate image of the authority both for its employees and for the public.

Concern for identity, image and recognition has however spread beyond the matter of establishing a clear perception of authorities in the minds of the public and employees. As local government came to realise that it needed to woo the public rather than treat it as a captive market so too did it become anxious to present an image that was not only clear but also positive and friendly. In some cases local authorities also came to see themselves as being under attack by some of the central government legislation of the 1980s and addressed themselves to questions of image as part of their defensive strategy. This involved varied combinations of logos, house styles and slogans, sometimes forming part of a concerted publicity campaign. Edinburgh for example produced T-shirts, balloons and advertisements with the council's slogan 'Improving Services, Creating Jobs': that particular slogan was eventually to be ruled unacceptable by the Scottish Court of Session on the ground that it contained no information and its deployment was therefore an improper use of the council's money. A similar fate befell the GLC's slogan 'Keep the GLC working for London', though 'Working for London' was allowable. In this case the political implications of the former slogan were at the heart of the issue: this in turn was an instance of a wider debate about the point at which local government public relations might become unduly politicised.

The conjunction of a more demanding public and a more politicised environment in the 1980s was certainly paralleled by a noticeable increase in public relations activity within local government. A survey conducted in 1986 by Franklin (1988a) found that of the 416 responding local authorities there was a public relations department, or at least a public relations specialist, in 91.4 per cent of counties, 92.9 per cent of metropolitan districts, 86.4 per cent of London boroughs, 87.5 per cent of Scottish regions, 35.4 per cent of English and Welsh shire districts and 28.2 per cent of Scottish islands and districts: some 62 per cent of the respondents reported increased budgets for public relations over the preceding three years. The scale of public relations activity varied from council to council. One third of councils undertaking public relations work had only one full time specialist; at the other end of the scale 10 per cent had ten or more public relations staff. Seventeen of the largest eighteen departments were in local authorities controlled by Labour.

The scope of public relations activity naturally differs between authorities; it embraces varying combinations of press and media relations, publicity and information, campaigns and promotions, customer relations and internal communications within the authority. One activity which has gained considerable attention during recent years, despite John Edwards' assurance to MPs in 1947, has been the production of local authority newspapers. The nature of these publications varies, though a tabloid format is common: as for size, the *Brighton Line*, the *York Citizen* and the *Stirling Tribune* for example produced eight page issues in the winter of 1989–90; the *Ipswich Angle* ran to twelve pages; and the *Stoke on Trent City News* topped them with sixteen pages.

Apart from size there are a number of other variables arising from different editorial policies. Stirling's newspaper for example contains no commercial advertising, whereas that of Ipswich devotes the equivalent of two of its sixteen pages to display advertisements from local retailers and service sector firms. Some newspapers concentrate on council business, others extend their coverage to the local implications of the work of other agencies such as the police, the health authority or central government. Some contain detailed listings of available and forthcoming facilities, events and meetings; others are more in the nature of reports back on activities carried out or decisions made by the council.

Publications such as these can have a very wide circulation since they are invariably free to the reader and are often delivered through the same distribution networks which circulate the commercial free newspapers. They are thus a useful device for informing the public of the council's past, present and future activities and for providing such basic details as the names, addresses and telephone numbers of council departments and of local councillors. The exact number of authorities producing such newspapers is unknown, though Franklin (1988b) discovered 97, with the highest incidence in metropolitan districts and London boroughs, where 30.6 per cent and 24.2 per cent of councils respectively issued them. Labour authorities were nearly three times as likely as Conservative authorities to produce a newspaper and their papers' content addressed issues such as social policy, welfare rights, equal opportunities, unemployment and education, topics which were largely absent from their Conservative counterparts which gave greater emphasis to leisure, entertainment, transport and road safety and which contained a greater proportion of commercial advertising.

Labour's greater enthusiasm for council newspapers, its use of them to discuss politically controversial issues, its track record in establishing well staffed public relations units in some authorities and its linking of public relations work with campaigning, as in the cases of Edinburgh and the GLC, led some of its opponents to raise charges of 'propaganda on the rates'. Expressing his concern at the possibility of councils engaging in 'overt political campaigning at public expense', the Secretary of State for the Environment, Patrick Jenkin, asked the Widdicombe Committee to prepare an early interim report on local authority publicity (Widdicombe, 1986a, p. 18). In the event the committee members were not unanimous in their findings: the majority view however was that local government publicity should not be used to promote the interests of a political party but that councils should nevertheless be able to use their powers to support or to oppose legislative changes and to inform the public about local government generally as well as about specific services (Widdicombe, 1985).

The government's legislative response, in the form of the Local Government Acts of 1986 and 1988, went further than the Widdicombe majority had suggested. It restricted councils' scope for publicity to material relating to the specific functions and services of local government rather than to the generality of matters relating to local government. However the primary test was to be that set down in section 27 of the 1988 Act, amending section 2 of the 1986 Act; this prohibited the publication of any material 'which, in whole or in part, appears to be designed to affect public support for a political party'. The appearance was to be construed in terms of the content, style, timing and likely effect of such material. How such considerations might be interpreted by the courts remains yet to be seen. In any event the legislation in this particular respect is not a wholly new departure. 'Party political publicity has always been unlawful for a local authority . . . [the legislation] seeks to reduce this common law principle to statutory form' (Allen, 1988, para. 8.1)

The debate about the proper purpose of local authority publicity is not confined to the question of its use for partisan purposes by local politicians. Professional practitioners themselves may have views which conflict with those of colleagues. Thus for example Franklin (1988a) found that although public relations specialists and chief executives agreed in giving top priority to media relations, chief executives then went on to give customer relations second priority, whereas for public relations staff customers came fourth after publicity and campaigns and promotions. However it should not be assumed that all public relations specialists take such a view. Guttridge (1987) for example has argued that customer relations should be the top-most priority, more important even than relations with the media. This moreover would require recruiting staff with a rather different background, with fewer from journalism and more with experience in advertising, campaigning, fund raising, exhibition organising and marketing.

Marketing

The notion that marketing could have something to contribute to local government might well seem to be rather bizarre, a 'contradiction in terms' as Vielba (1986) puts it. However Vielba goes on to suggest that although marketing had its origins in the market based private sector rather than in the public services, local government interest in 'marketing as the vehicle for increasing responsiveness and effectiveness reflects an openness on the part of many public sector authorities to private sector management ideas' (idem, p. 14). Most of the traditional definitions of marketing certainly reveal its private sector origins, as in the Institute of Marketing's definition of it as 'the management technique which identifies, anticipates and satisfies customer requirements profitably' (quoted in Crouch, 1986, p. 75).

Yet it is arguable that some authorities were pursuing just such a course of action twenty or more years ago, without recognising it as marketing, when they entered into the business of attracting industry to their localities. Attracting employers away from the south to the north or from the conurbations to small towns was often pursued under the title of industrial development or employment promotion by the councils concerned: it was an exercise which sometimes had losers as well as winners, as different local economies underwent radical restructuring; but it was in many ways an exercise in marketing, albeit it one of marketing a place or a locality rather than a local authority itself.

There is another variant on the local authority marketing of place which has become increasingly common, namely that of encouraging tourism and attendance at all manner of conference centres, historic buildings, museums and other recreational facilities. Hampshire for instance set up its own central marketing unit in 1987 following a study into 'the marketing of the tourist attractions owned by the county council . . . historic sites, country parks, museums and similar properties'. The aim was to 'generate increased revenue and at the same time improve the product on offer to the public . . . [and] add to the overall attractiveness of the county as a place to visit and in which to reside' (Webster, 1988, p. 110). Clearly such activities are a variant or development of the sort of promotional activities which many resort towns have indulged in over the years. Even so, the promotion or marketing of place has never been wholly free of controversy, whether it has been directed at tourism or industrial development: some people have feared the changes in character which local communities might undergo in the wake of successful promotion of resort facilities or industrial estates.

Controversial or not, the marketing of place in the sense described above, is a readily recognisable local government activity with two or more decades of experience behind it. What is much newer is the notion of applying the idea of marketing to the local authority itself and to its services. Such a notion is still incomprehensible in some quarters, where marketing is an unknown entity.

Some officers think of it as virtually identical with public relations . . . . Some think of it primarily as a research function. Some think it is all about modern graphic design . . . [or] that the marketeers will help to sell things like sponsorship packages, membership of the fitness suite or a training programme. But selling is not marketing . . . .

The marketeer must be allowed to play a substantial role in helping to determine what, in view of customer preferences, changing market conditions, and the actual and potential competition, the council should or should not be providing (Tam, 1989).

The perspective presented us by Tam is thus one from which marketing is seen as a key ingredient in the process of deciding what services should be provided, to whom and on what financial basis. This view is similar to that expressed by Stewart (1986, pp. 4–6) who sees the marketing approach as one which forces the local authority to ask some key questions about its services and their users.

- Who are the users of the service?
- Who are the potential users of the service?
- How is the service related to demand? . . .
- What do users want from a service?
- What do they in fact receive from the service?
- What difficulties are encountered by those using or trying to use the services? What causes those difficulties?
- What suggestions have customers for service improvements? . . .
- How will demand be affected by the price and in which segments of the market will that be most felt?
- Are these likely effects in accordance with the policies of the authority?

The asking of questions such as these implies that traditional patterns of service provision can no longer be taken for granted, for if they could such questions would be superfluous. Echoing the debate about post-Fordism, Walsh (1989, p. 3) relates the emergence of marketing in local government to the necessity to 'move from the era of the mass production of standard services to the flexible production of non-standard services'. Councils making such a move towards 'more sophisticated and varied services in a more complex environment . . . will need to develop the skills of marketing' in order to understand more clearly 'the concerns and needs of the public' and to make services more widely accessible.

Walsh goes on to argue that hitherto the middle class have gained more from public services than have more disadvantaged groups, not least because they have understood and manipulated the system more effectively. He suggests that 'marketing techniques of analysis may help to determine more clearly who needs to benefit from services, and how to distribute them effectively' (idem, p. 17). Such techniques of analysis he divides into strategic marketing and consumer marketing. The two cannot be divorced however, for the first is concerned with questions about what services to produce, for which markets or groups and through which distribution system, whilst the second is concerned with the consumers' experience of and reaction to the services they are offered. Answers to such questions do in turn require the sort of knowledge available through the use of market research.

As to why local authorities should address themselves to the sorts of issues identified by Tam, by Stewart and by Walsh, one answer is that provided by the Institute of Public Relations (1986, para. 5.3(e)). The institute suggests that particular council services may need to be marketed for one or more of three reasons

- to be viable they need a minimum number of consumers;
- the council wishes to attract income;
- the council believes it is socially desirable to increase take-up.

One set of services which seems particularly likely to have some cause for concern on these three points is that of leisure and recreation provision. Local authority leisure facilities have always been in a competitive situation to some degree, having to compete with the attractions offered by the private sector, by clubs and indeed by neighbouring authorities since patterns of usage need be no respecter of local government boundaries. The prospect of possible privatisation of leisure facilities adds a further urgency to the necessity to deal effectively with questions of securing the best use of resources. Moreover there can also be problems of untapped or latent demand to which an effective response can be beneficial socially as well as financially. Thus one review of leisure facility marketing recounted that

[there are] groups in the local community who consistently show very little or no desire to use leisure centres. A classic example of such a group are women from certain ethnic groups whose religious and/or cultural norms preclude physical/sporting activities. More surprising is the fact that women generally have displayed a marked lack of demand . . . it is possible that the lack of demand is due to misconceptions of the 'product' on offer and a communication task is identified. A composite resolution to such a problem may well be to consider the introduction of a new product which will satisfy the leisure needs of this segment [of the market] and, then, communicating it effectively. This has been done to great effect with popmobility sessions aimed at women and also with Asian dance lessons aimed at this minority segment (Smith, 1988, pp. 42–3).

Exercises in marketing need not be confined to services remaining in the council's charge: they may also be regarded as desirable in order to secure the retention of services which are open to the possibility of users opting out.

Proposals for allowing schools or council housing estates to opt out of local authority control must first be tested by a poll – though one at the ballot box rather than one conducted through market research. Such events may well test the public relations and marketing skills of councils if they are concerned to minimise the extent of opting out, or conversely if they are keen to encourage it. In either case however, they reflect the need of local authorities to adjust not only to the demands of public opinion and public relations but also to the possibility of local service provision being organised from outside the traditional structures of local government. For there is a body of thought which has argued that the way to secure better services is not to adopt participative, consultative or informative strategies within the public sector but to open up that sector to competition from other quarters to secure a more pluralist pattern of provision.

6 Diversity, Pluralism and Choice

Local authorities are no longer regarded as necessarily the only, or best, providers of their traditional services.

Audit Commission, 1988, p. 1.

In chapter 2 we saw how the post-war consensus was challenged by the emergence of what Duncan and Goodwin (1988, p. 276) called 'diversity and disjuncture'. Part of this challenge has involved a reappraisal of the functioning of the welfare state, within whose operations local government has long played a key role. The basic drift of that reappraisal has been described as 'a very general movement away from centralism and towards a belief in ordinary people' (Barclay, 1982, p. 204). Within that general movement there has been a variety of ideas as to what should replace or at least complement centralised bureaucracies, whether at national or local level. One view has been that identified by Willmott (1987, pp. 30–1):

Two fundamental aims are increasingly recognised as worthwhile objectives of policy. The first is to help people to come together in meeting their needs and tackling common problems. The second is for public services to strengthen voluntary and informal structures and to work with rather than against them.

A rather different view is that which has been described as 'market orientation'.

This has sought in various ways to return to the individual the power to choose between alternative ends and means in social policy. Such a choice is exercised, by and large, through market decisions made by the individual as a consumer (Bulmer, 1989, p. 191).

Both these views in turn have been embraced by the advocates of a 'mixed economy' of welfare, often termed 'welfare pluralism'. In the words of two of its proponents:

> welfare pluralism can be used to convey the fact that social and health care may be obtained from four different sectors – the statutory, the voluntary, the commercial and the informal. More prescriptively, welfare pluralism implies a less dominant role for the state, seeing it as not the only possible instrument for the collective provision of welfare services (Hatch and Mocroft, 1983, p. 2).

Welfare pluralism has been able to appeal to a wide range of political opinion. For the right it can provide 'a politically convenient formula for . . . reducing the role of the state' whilst those on the left may welcome its 'anti-bureaucratic, anti-centralist, anti-professional implications' (Johnson, 1987, pp. 60–1). Advocacy of welfare pluralism has had its parallel in the field of local government. The notion of the local authority as the self-sufficient direct provider of services, characterised by a uniformity of standard of provision, has been called into question. Public provision is seen as having limited the choice available to different individuals or groups or localities: a more varied range of providers is thus canvassed in order to secure greater choice for a more diverse set of publics.

> The use of private contractors, management buy-outs, the development of co-operatives, the creation of a local authority company, grants to voluntary bodies, the stimulus to self-help, partnership with the private sector, the use of public contractors and joint action with other authorities, all have to be considered for the provision of services . . . there is a requirement to recognise diversity where needs, opportunities and problems vary (Clarke and Stewart, 1989, pp. 5 and 7).

The argument for this type of approach was summarised very clearly in the White Paper *Caring for People*.

> Stimulating the development of non-statutory service providers will result in a range of benefits for the consumer, in particular: a wider range of choice of services; services which meet individual needs in a more flexible and innovative way; competition between providers, resulting in better value for money and a more cost-effective service (Department of Health, 1989, para. 3.4.3).

The specific reference being made here was to community care, but the case being made was one which had far wider implications. It implied that throughout local government 'authorities will need to operate in a more pluralist way than in the past, alongside a wide variety of public, private and voluntary agencies' (Ridley, 1988, p. 25).

It would of course be quite incorrect to assume that until recently local authorities were never associated with other agencies in carrying out their functions. Cousins (1982, pp. 155 and 152) for example has referred to 'the misty ground between the public and voluntary sectors' at local level and to the 'galaxy of bodies which exist to link local authorities to the voluntary sector and to the wider community'. Indeed when the virtues of welfare pluralism were initially canvassed by the Wolfenden Committee in *The Future of Voluntary Organisations* (Wolfenden, 1978) they were related to what was seen as an already existing situation in which statutory and non-statutory sectors worked side by side and in which the expansion of the latter need not be at the expense of the former. However some have argued more recently that the role of the non-statutory sector should not be merely ancillary or additional to that of the local authority: it should also in some cases displace, rather than assist, councils in the direct provision of services.

Any discussion of such a development requires us to make some attempt at distinguishing between the various elements of the non-statutory sector. The debate about welfare pluralism has generally distinguished the statutory sector from the private, the voluntary and the informal sectors: this was the approach of the Wolfenden Committee and it is echoed in the remarks of Hatch and Mocroft (1983, p. 2) quoted above. The boundaries between the sectors are not wholly watertight: Hadley and Hatch (1981, p. 93) for example observe that the voluntary sector ranges 'from organisations no less formal than those found in the statutory sector to some that are so informal that they hardly merit the term organisation'. Nonetheless, allowing for such difficulties, this three fold division of the non-statutory sector will be used to order our discussion in this chapter.

The informal sector

Informality implies a lack of structure, and that in turn may suggest some problems in identifying the content of the informal sector. However the work of Abrams and his colleagues provides us with a useful starting point. They distinguish between two informal systems. One is a 'traditional' system based on 'relatively tightly defined, stable relationships, above all those of kinship . . . particularly female centred ones'. This 'world of mutually supportive kin, neighbours, friends and co-workers' was very much the informal sector as perceived by the Wolfenden Committee. It does however co-exist with, and may be in course of displacement by, 'a distinctively modern informal system', one based not on the 'normative bonding' of stable relationships but on 'choice, mutual interest and reciprocity': it is a system of self-help and mutual aid and provides 'the means whereby people sharing a need or a problem can come together to give help and support to each other' (Abrams et al., 1989, pp. 7 and 11).

   The traditional informal sector was well described in some of the community studies carried out in the two decades after the second World War, notably for example the work done in Bethnal Green by Young and Willmott (1957). The patterns of family and neighbourhood life which such studies portrayed have since altered under the impact of economic change and urban redevelopment: yet the more recent work of Willmott (1986, 1987) suggests that informal care still remains a reality, even if it now operates in a less tightly knit form within a more mobile and more dispersed society. In times of difficulty

   the bulk of care comes from close relatives. This is especially true of personal and domestic care and especially so when the need for it is continuous . . . . But this does not mean that other relationships are negligible as sources . . . there is substitution by more genealogically distant relatives when closer ones are absent and by friends, even neighbours, when no relatives at all are available (Willmott, 1986, p. 108).

The links of local authorities with this evolving system of informal care are in some cases minimal or non-existent: relatives, friends and neighbours carry out the tasks of housekeeping, cooking, shopping, gardening and personal care with little or no involvement by their local council. Yet increasingly local government is being drawn into a closer association with the informal sector beyond existing provisions such as home help and 'aids and adaptions' to permit domestic life to continue. 'In social policy in particular the key phrases are "community care" and "supporting informal carers"' (idem, p. 104): as we shall see, the two phrases are not unrelated.

Community care was placed firmly on the public agenda by the government's response to Sir Roy Griffith's report *Community Care: Agenda for Action*, published in 1988. The 1989 White Paper *Caring for People* and the National Health Service and Community Care Act 1990 embraced the idea that local authorities should take the leading role in organising and monitoring community care. The government defined community care in its White Paper as 'providing the right level of intervention and support to enable people to achieve maximum independence and control over their own lives': its objective was one which it claimed to share with previous governments, namely 'to promote community based services which encourage and prolong independent living' (paras. 2.2 and 2.12). This approach is one which responded to 'the declining popularity of institutional care' which was crystallised by 'research in the late 1950s and the 1960s demonstrating the harmful consequences of living in total institutions . . . the submission to rigid regimes, the loss of the ability to determine one's own routines' (Johnson, 1987, p. 67).

The nature of the role to be performed by local authorities under the government's proposals would revolve around the creation of a 'mixed economy of care' as the White Paper described it. Authorities would act as 'arrangers and purchasers of care services, rather than as monopolistic providers . . . by developing their

purchasing and contracting role to become "enabling authorities"'
(paras. 3.4.7 and 3.1.3). They would be expected to make use
'whenever possible of services from voluntary "not for profit" and
private providers in so far as this represents a cost effective care
choice': where the authority itself was the main or sole service
provider it would 'be expected to take all reasonable steps to secure
diversity of provision'. However large or small its own direct
provision of services the authority 'will continue to play an
important role in backing up, developing and monitoring private
and voluntary care facilities' (paras. 3.4.1 and 3.4.3).

The government's concept of community care seems mainly to
entail the transfer of provision of care by statutory personnel to
provision by personnel from the voluntary and private sectors with
the local authorities in a monitoring and back up role. However
there was also a recognition in the White Paper that 'the great bulk
of community care is provided by friends, family and neighbours'
and that local authorities should 'do all they can to assist and
support carers' of this sort by providing 'advice and support as well
as practical services such as day, domiciliary and respite care'
(paras. 1.9 and 2.3). This of course brings us to the second of
Willmott's 'key phrases' – 'supporting informal carers'.

The reality of the informal element of community care is that the
bulk of it comes from relatives and that 'the relatives are more
often women than men and are often daughters and daughters-in-
law' (Willmott, 1989, p. 60). This reality was expressed by Finch
and Groves (1980, p. 494) in the form of a double equation:
community care equals family care equals care by women. It has
led some to argue that an expansion of community care which
relies on the traditional informal system based on relationships,
especially those of kinship, should be resisted since it undermines
women's search for equality (see Dalley 1988). However, so long as
informal care persists in some degree so too will the need for
support for those who undertake the caring role.

Defining the nature of the appropriate support for carers is
clearly an exercise which ought to take account of the views of the
carers themselves. Yet given the pressures under which some of
them live they may well be unable to spare the time or the energy to
orchestrate their views themselves: this in turn implies that local
authorities may need to take the initiative in the matter. One
council which has done so has been that of Birmingham, where it

has been estimated that over 100000 people are involved in informal care, with nearly a quarter of them devoting at least 20 hours a week to the task. Between 1987 and 1990 the city council engaged, with the cooperation of the health authorities, in a Community Care Special Action Project, one element of which was a programme of carers' consultations, based upon the recognition that carers have a claim on the local authority's attention just as much as do those for whom they care (Jones, 1988).

Birmingham's carers' consultation involved a series of open meetings in different parts of the city, out of which there grew a number of networks and groups addressing specific issues raised at the meetings. Given the size of the potential audience of carers, the total attendance was small – 330 in the first two years of the project: those carers most able to come to discuss lack of support were understandably likely to be those who were already comparatively well supported, a perhaps inevitable example of the Catch 22 paradox. Jones (idem, p. 58) also records that 'Non-English speaking carers have been noticeably absent from our Special Action Project's meetings for carers, despite our distribution of translated posters and advertising of the availability of translation at each meeting': in response to these particular problems the project obtained resources from the King's Fund Informal Caring Support Unit to carry out a short-term inquiry into the needs of carers from ethnic minority groups.

From its consultation meetings the council obtained a clearer view of the problems experienced by those who provide the traditional form of informal care. These problems included the absence of help or advice outside office hours; the havoc caused by changes of personnel or timetable or routine, for example in the home help service; the difficulties with transport facilities; the sense of isolation; the adequacy or otherwise of day care provision; the need for respite for carers and for holidays for both the carer and the cared for; the problems of obtaining and coping with equipment and adaptation; and the search for information and advice (Prior, Jowell and Lawrence, 1989). Identifying such problems was in itself a first step to searching for a solution and the end result was an Action Plan designed to address the issues raised by the carers (Lawrence 1990). Hearing of carers' difficulties direct from those concerned may have given added impetus to the search for solutions. As one senior officer involved expressed it: 'I heard about our services from these carers in terms that never survive transmission up the hierarchy' (Jones, 1988, p. 59).

For some people, coping with the problems of caring can be too urgent to wait for the attention of local government. Instead they resort to the organisation of self-help and mutual aid, the 'distinctively modern' model of informal care which we saw defined earlier on by Abrams et al. (1989). Self-help and mutual aid is not however confined to questions of caring and in that respect it can be seen as a more variegated element of the informal sector than the more specifically care-focused traditional informal system. It also goes beyond the Victorian and individualist connotations of self-help associated with the writings of Samuel Smiles, for it expresses itself in collective action and mutual support organised by those who share a specific problem or circumstance.

The range of concerns covered by self-help groups was well illustrated in a series of articles under the title 'Initiative' published in *New Society* in 1986 and 1987: reports on some 68 of the groups were later gathered together in book form (*New Society*, 1988). The groups covered the fields of women's issues, health promotion, handicap, ethnic minorities, housing, education, the arts, young people, employment and crime. They were all locally based groups, dealing with the problems of local people. As such they were only one example of the self-help phenomenon, for others exist at a regional or national level: but it is perhaps at the local level that the growth of such groups has been most marked in the recent past and it is of course groups operating at that level which are most likely to have dealings with local government. Such dealings may not always be easy. The self-help movement often represents a rejection of, or an absence of, formalised professional structures: as such its component groups can be assertive and demanding, insisting on defining their own needs and solutions. Yet at the same time they may be looking to local authorities for moral, material and financial support in many cases.

Some local authorities may largely restrict their involvement with local self-help groups to the provision of grants. This in itself is not an unproblematic relationship; questions about the size of the grant and about how far it is effective in fulfilling the council's aims – if these have been specified – can always be raised in respect of any individual group. Such questions are of course all the more searching in times of limits on local authority expenditure.

Sometimes there will also be arguments about the virtues of grants to particular categories of groups: the legitimacy of council grants to any group other than those promoting the interests and values of White Anglo-Saxon Protestant heterosexual males has been vigorously contested by some local politicians and by some sections of the public and the press. Such debates have perhaps encouraged the notion that self-help and mutual aid is very much a sectional business, with sharply defined and perhaps antagonistic groups clamouring for resources in what may be a zero-sum game.

However the practice of self-help need not be confined to particular sections of the community seen as defined and separated by some specific characteristic or condition. It may also be taken up on a more collective basis by local communities themselves as suggested by Abrams et al. (1989, p. 12).

> When extended to the level of the local community as a whole . . . the principles of mutual self-help come to constitute community development, which emphasises community organisation that promotes self-determination, local control and participatory democracy.

Stirling District Council provides an example of this sort of conjunction between self-help and community development, an example which goes beyond a mere funding relationship between the council and local groups. As part of a wider 'Going Local' programme, which has involved the setting up of decentralised housing offices, the creation of consultative area committees drawing in representatives of local groups, and 'customer care' surveys of service users' experiences, the council has also encouraged what one officer described as 'hands-on self-help initiatives'. Initiatives have mainly been in fields such as job creation, environmental improvement, community facilities and the development of tourism. Amongst these schemes have been the carrying out of planting by residents in Aberfoyle and Callender; the creation of a steering committee to form a housing co-operative in St Ninians; the establishment of Cowie Community Enterprise to set up a wood-cutting business and a community cafe; and the formation of a Bannockburn Heritage group to generate interest and income from visitors and tourists.

In some cases the council has provided small scale capital for 'pump priming' purposes: but it has also pursued a strong marketing strategy to attract funds from sources such as the Scottish Education Department (SED) the Scottish Development Agency, the European Social Fund, British Coal, British Petroleum and other private sector sources. In the case of one community hall, in the village of Throsk, the council provided funds but the construction work was done entirely by the literally hands-on labour of local people. In Cowie and Plean, where SED money was forthcoming for constructing community halls, local opinion was consulted about their location, design and facilities and their management entrusted to locally elected management committees.

As well as supporting particular local projects, Stirling has also concerned itself with helping local groups to set up and to survive. The council's Resource Centre offers a wide range of advice and assistance to local community organisations on matters such as fund-raising, local government procedures, publicity, exhibitions, and printing. Meeting space and training facilities are offered and an Economic Development Unit provides advice to potential community business projects. For those uncertain of how to go about organising themselves, the centre produces a range of leaflets on such thorny subjects as 'Starting a Group', 'Organising Petitions', 'Community Group Constitutions', 'Being a Secretary/ Treasurer', 'Writing Minutes', and 'Public Meetings'. In all these ventures there are clear affinities with notions of community development transcending self-help, in which 'Neighbours helping each other was but a part of a process of making the area a better place to live in and of winning or generating resources, skills and participation' (Abrams et al., 1989, p. 128).

Such initiatives by the council have reflected a mixture of political commitment and financial realism. The political commitment was expressed in a strategy document for the period 1988–92 *Partnership with the People* (Stirling District Council, 1988) which stressed the importance of community based participation. The council's leader said that the authority aspired to create 'a whole new consultative process where a community's needs are identified by the community itself' (*Stirling Tribune*, November 1988). The financial realism was reflected in one officer's judgement that 'one of the reasons why the council adopted initiatives involving the public sector, the private sector and the voluntary sector was the realisation that the public sector would not be able to finance developments on its own in future'.

Any close involvement with self-help groups by a local authority clearly raises delicate issues of how far the former can maintain their character if they become reliant, even if only in part, on council support of some kind. One local authority for example claimed that an expansion of council funding over a ten year period had 'transformed what was an unpaid "self-help" sector into a professional, paid non-statutory sector' (Bradford City Council, 1988, para. 2.1). Such problems however are not confined to the self-help sector. More formally organised voluntary bodies are often in receipt of financial assistance from local authorities, who are themselves now under increasing pressure to ensure that they receive value for money in respect of any such grants. Relations between local government and the more formally organised voluntary sectors are thus undergoing particular pressures of their own.

The voluntary sector

The National Council for Voluntary Organisation (NCVO) has described the voluntary sector as 'diverse and dynamic and therefore difficult to define'. Its own definition of a voluntary agency is that of 'a self-governing body of people who have joined together voluntarily to take action for the betterment of the community, established otherwise than for financial gain': on that basis the NCVO has estimated that there are over half a million such voluntary organisations in England (NCVO, 1988, p. 1). The number and diversity of such organisations embraces a great range of agencies from highly organised national bodies such as the British Red Cross Society and Help the Aged to small local self-help groups such as the Black Carers Support Group in Lozells, Birmingham. On that basis it would clearly be possible to regard many of the self-help and mutual aid groups, referred to in the previous section as being part of the voluntary sector rather than the informal sector. However, we regarded the informal sector as being underpinned by relationships of kinship, neighbourliness, friendship, mutuality and reciprocity: we can also identify a more formal voluntary sector wherein there are 'consciously organised roles and tasks . . . [within] a more bureaucratically structured form' (Abrams et al., 1989, p. 6).

This distinction between an informal sector and a more formal voluntary sector is similar to the classic distinction made by Beveridge (1948) between mutual aid and organised philanthropy as the major forms of voluntary action. It also resembles a more recent distinction made by an NCVO working party between self-help and mutual aid on the one hand and service provision on the other: in the case of service provision 'volunteers typically raise funds to pay for services provided by a combination of professionals and volunteers', in some cases supplementing or complementing statutory provision with the aid of public funds combined with voluntary activity and funding (Nathan, 1990, p. 17). It is this service provision role of the formal voluntary sector which concerns us here.

Relations between the voluntary sector and local government have a long history, with local authorities recognising that voluntary organisations have a useful role to play in some form of service provision. In 1951 for example the Conservative local government conference was reminded of four specific virtues of voluntary sector service provision. It could conduct experiments with new services – 'the first duty of the voluntary organisation is to act as herald and forerunner'; it could concentrate on special needs, or work 'too limited and specialised for the local authority itself to carry out'; it could work jointly with local authorities, with the latter's resources being used 'to amplify voluntary funds and services'; and it could be employed and funded as the local authority's direct service agent where the law allowed (Kingsmill Jones, 1951, pp. 6–7). Nearly forty years later the 1990 Labour local government conference was also reminded of the merits of the voluntary sector. The sector could be innovative, experimental, unbureaucratic, cost-effective, closely linked to the views of the local community and able to pursue high risk political strategies, and to campaign for change (Dubs, 1990). Both these perspectives from different dates and different points on the political spectrum stress the innovative and practical utility of the voluntary sector.

The more recent Labour view goes on to highlight the sector's political and campaigning potential, though perhaps the Conservative reference in 1951 to the voluntary organisation as 'herald' conveys a similar message. The implicit notion here of a dual role –

providing services but also campaigning on the issues to which they relate – identifies an aspect of the relations between councils and voluntary organisations to which we shall return later.

As far as service provision is concerned the variety of tasks undertaken by the voluntary sector with local authority support includes play schemes, youth clubs, community transport, conservation projects, unemployed people's centres, advice centres, day centres, village halls, and women's centres (NCVO, n.d). In making grants to voluntary bodies for the provision of such services local authorities may be guided by their own particular criteria. Richmond-upon-Thames for example requires to be satisfied on four key points before making a grant. How cost effective will the provision be, compared with alternative arrangements? How many people in the borough are likely to benefit? During what hours will the service be available? Is the service accepted by the council as being necessary but not possible to provide directly in the current financial climate? (Enterazi, 1988.) In Hackney (1988) attention is paid to the need for groups to undertake annual self-assessments of performance and also for them to be run according to stipulated procedures, to adopt an equal opportunities policy and to combat positively racism and sexism.

One particular service with a long tradition of voluntary sector co-operation with local councils is meals on wheels. This service originated as a voluntary sector initiative in the second World War, with local authorities being allowed to make grants in 1948, and to provide cooking and transport facilities in 1962. The outcome has been very much a 'mixed economy' of meal provision. This is clearly illustrated by a survey of meals on wheels provision carried out by Essex County Council (1989). The county council's own involvement as social services authority is limited to a grant to each of the fourteen district councils within the county. The meals themselves are cooked variously in the kitchens of schools, hospitals, town hall canteens, the Womens' Royal Voluntary Service (WRVS), a private caterer and a factory canteen. The organisation and carrying out of the delivery of the meals is again in varying hands – district councils, the WRVS, Age Concern and the Salvation Army.

The meals on wheels service is not a particularly controversial one and it seems a well established and much appreciated instance of multi-agency provision. Two aspects of it however may be of some wider significance. The service depends, in its current form, on a supply of volunteers adequate to match the demands for meal delivery. Demographic trends suggest a substantial growth in the number of elderly people and thereby a likely increase in service demand: this could be further accentuated by moves towards care in the community instead of in institutions. Voluntary service provision depends upon an adequate ratio of helpers to helped: a combination of demographic trends and community care policy could create problems in maintaining such hitherto workable ratios. That in turn might lead to pressures for payment of helpers to ease the recruitment problem, thereby following a similar pattern to that taken by other elements of the voluntary sector, namely the employment of paid staff in addition to volunteers.

The other aspect worthy of note concerns the relationship between pluralism and choice: as we have seen the virtues of diversity and choice have been much mentioned in the context of welfare pluralism. The meals on wheels service is certainly diverse in the sense of its being a multi-agency operation. Yet at the point of consumption choice of agency is non-existent. In the case of Essex, if you live in the Maldon district your food will be cooked, organised and delivered by the WRVS: if you wanted, for any reason, to be provided for by the district council or the Salvation Army, you would need to move to Thurrock or to the Hockley area of Rayleigh. In this situation pluralism in the sense of multi-agency provision does not automatically imply diversity and choice for the service consumer, except perhaps at the cost of moving house. The latter option in turn of course does not require multi-agency pluralism, as witnessed by the practice of parents house-buying into the catchment areas of favoured local authority schools.

The mixed economy of meals on wheels provision did not of course arise as a deliberate response to arguments in favour of pluralism in service delivery. It is indeed a classic case of innovation from within the voluntary sector followed by an increasing though limited involvement on the part of local government. In recent years however, there have been more deliberate attempts to develop the role of the voluntary sector in local service provision. Four main considerations underlie these attempts. Firstly the central government is keen to reduce the scope of public sector services as a matter of political ideology. Second, and as a consequence of the first consideration, compulsory competitive tendering has been introduced for some council services, which in turn has led some councils to consider what social services they might also contract out even if not obliged so to do. Third, financial pressures on local authorities encourage them to seek possible savings even without a formal tendering process. Fourth, the government's particular commitment to a policy of community care entails a key role for the formal voluntary sector as well as the informal sector.

Implicit in any expansion of voluntary sector provision consequent upon these four factors is a move away from the traditional system of annual grants-in-aid to a more rigorous contractual relationship over a number of years. In Bromley for example Age Concern were awarded a three year £650000 contract in 1990 for the provision of meals, snacks, recreational activities and personal care services such as chiropody at five day centres in the borough. The creation of such relationships between the voluntary sector and local authorities could pose certain difficulties. Gutch and Young (1988) for example suggest that the very different natures of voluntary organisations and private companies might make it undesirable for the same sort of contract procedures to be applied to both the voluntary and the private sectors. Over and above that general consideration however, a number of specific issues present themselves in relation to the consequences for voluntary organisations of a contractual relationship with local authorities.

We have already seen the importance which some have attached to the experimental and innovative role of voluntary organisations, a role which implies a certain freedom of manoeuvre: 'voluntary organisations with a developmental function . . . who would act in an entrepreneurial way' (Hatch and Mocroft, 1983, p. 127) might well be constrained by the terms of contracts likely to be couched in terms of performance of specified and thus already familiar services. Moreover the 'first duty' of 'herald and forerunner', identified above, implies that voluntary organisations shall not only conduct experiments but shall also proclaim the results: the role of advocate and campaigner for new services or for newly identified needs has long been one cherished by the voluntary sector. Indeed the NCVO emphasised the importance of the advocacy role in its evidence to the Griffiths review of community care. The need to devise service contracts which safeguard, or allow the parallel continuance of, the experimental and advocacy roles may perhaps be one specific example of the need to go beyond the established form of contract. Alternatively it may require councils to discount or disregard the more radical activities or statements of voluntary bodies so long as they perform satisfactorily in the area of their contracted mainstream services: though some may find that a hard and self-denying ordinance.

A further issue is that of accountability, specifically the multiple accountability of a voluntary body linked by contract to a local authority. One problem is that cited by Leat (1988, p. 7): 'the voluntary sector is valued for its independence and flexibility . . . but how is greater accountability to be achieved without damaging independence and flexibility?' Moreover accountability to the local authority for contract performance sits alongside accountability to the members of the management committee of the voluntary organisation as well as to any other funding bodies or individuals. In addition the voluntary sector has moved away from a belief that 'users needed to be told what to do, to be educated and protected'; increasingly the emphasis has been on accountability to the users, at least as an aspiration even if it has 'created problems either in principle or practice or both' (idem, pp. 76 and 78). Certainly the NCVO concluded that it would be necessary 'to find new ways of giving the user a place in the contractual arrangements' between the voluntary sector and local government (Nathan, 1990, p. 23).

Some of these issues have been addressed by the NCVO in its call for the development of a 'voluntary sector strategy' between local authorities and the local voluntary sector.

> The strategy should ensure that the funding relationship does not jeopardise the independence of voluntary organisations, nor their ability to carry out research, campaign and lobby on behalf of their users. The strategy should highlight the innovative qualities of the voluntary sector, and encourage innovation (NCVO, 1990, p. 3).

Although the initiative for the development of such strategies has come largely from the voluntary sector, a small number of local authorities have taken up the challenge. Kingston-upon-Thames for example, on the initiative of its social services department, convened a meeting of councillors, officers and voluntary organisations in 1989 which established a working group of officers from the two sectors. The working group was hoping to produce an agreed joint report on a voluntary sector strategy by the autumn of 1990. From the point of view of voluntary sector organisations proposals to clarify and codify relationships between themselves and the local authorities have become increasingly relevant, especially in the context of likely voluntary sector involvement in community care. In London for example 'Local authority officers are making approaches to individual voluntary groups to offer service contracts. These approaches are nearly always made behind the scenes, without clear criteria being developed, and without wider consultation'. The London Voluntary Services Council has thus attempted to fill the gap by producing service contract guidelines emphasising amongst other things, 'equality of opportunity, user involvement in the planning of services, and a plurality of service provision as central aims' (Phaure, 1990).

Underlying many of the voluntary sector's concerns about taking over more service provision is the basic question of how far the sector can retain its essential character. Thus one participant at an NCVO seminar referred to the need for voluntary bodies to avoid becoming 'pale imitations of the statutory services they replace' (Thompson, 1989, p. 3) Local authorities too are aware of such problems, though not always from the same point of view as voluntary organisations. Arun District Council (1987b, p. 19) for example, as part of a four year plan for its relations with voluntary bodies, aimed 'to introduce a greater degree of professionalism into the sector, whilst retaining the voluntary spirit without which the sector will not survive'. Rather less tenderness perhaps was shown by Essex County Council (1990a, p. 2) when it observed that payments to the voluntary sector in future would be 'very much on a contractual basis, and certainly many voluntary organisations will need to review their way of working to suit the new situation'. If voluntary sector provision is to be justified on grounds of pluralism and diversity then clearly the more it becomes a 'pale imitation' of local government the more it may fail to fulfil the role assigned to it.

The private sector

There is a long and varied history of private sector involvement in the provision of local services. For example Sidney and Beatrice

Webb (1922, p. 326) recorded how at the turn of the eighteenth and nineteenth centuries there was a 'perpetual conflict in the minds of the Vestrymen between the desirability of clean streets on the one hand and the pecuniary saving to the parish on the other, of accepting the very lowest tender' from 'the new race of contractors who came forward as Scavengers and Rakers'. In some cases the nature of town refuse actually gave it a commercial value, whether for manuring or for mixing 'dust' with clay for brick making. In these happy circumstances private contractors actually paid the parish authorities for the privilege of cleaning the streets, though the market conditions which allowed for this had faded away by the 1840s so that thereafter 'scavenging gradually became once more a source of municipal expenses' (idem, p. 338).

The pattern of services in mid-nineteenth century towns could sometimes seem like a Victorian rehearsal of modern aspirations for a mixed economy of provision. In Colchester for example, at this time,

> Private enterprise provided gas, water and public baths . . . . The local traders and agriculturalists paid for the new Corn Exchange . . . . Those wanting the amenities of a reading room or a good-quality library had to pay to belong to the Mechanic's Institute, . . . or to the Literary Institute . . . . The parks then available were the Botanical Gardens . . . or 'Mr Jenkin's Pleasure Gardens' . . . but entrance to either place was open solely to those paying for it. The only publicly financed education until the 1860s was that provided in the Workhouse. The Hospital, built in 1820 by subscription, remained entirely voluntary (Brown, 1980, p. 46).

Private sector involvement in local government could also manifest itself in the form of official council positions being held by individuals who also remained in practice in the commercial sector. Thus in county government prior to 1914 'the leading officials frequently took in "county work" with the day to day running of a private practice'; indeed in the case of Cheshire 'the clerk's department of the county council continued to be part of the Potts family business' until 1931 (Lee, 1963, pp. 66–7). Such practices as this are perhaps best seen as hangovers from the days before local authorities became large bureaucratic organisations requiring full time commitment from their officers. Even then however, some small local authorities prior to local government reorganisation in the 1970s would rely on the services of private sector professionals for advice and expertise, especially perhaps on legal and financial matters, since they could not afford to employ the necessary staff on a permanent basis.

Apart from private sector professionals, private sector contractors have had a continuing role in local government right up to the present day. For most of the present century however this has been less in the context of the 'scavenging and raking' of two hundred years ago and more in that of public works. The use of private firms to undertake all manner of design and construction work, for housing, roads and schools for instance, has been commonplace: in some cases indeed such firms have had a major impact on the thinking that has underlain particular schemes, notably in the case of high-rise housing (Dunleavy, 1981). Whether they were professional firms or contractors, private companies in these roles were being used essentially to supplement the resources of the local authority itself, in a way not dissimilar to the use sometimes made of the voluntary and informal sectors in the welfare field. In the 1980s however, the role of the private sector ceased to be that of an optional supplement and became more that of a direct competitor as part of a process of privatisation.

The concept of privatisation has been defined in many ways. One of its earliest proponents in relation to local government saw it as 'the process by which a local authority service provided by its own employees (direct labour) is replaced by one contracted for by the authority, but provided by private businesses or occasionally, by voluntary effort' (Forsyth, n.d., p. 4). Here we will adopt a slightly broader definition, embracing also the transfer of assets out of the local public sector. Moves towards privatisation seek to secure value for money and to widen consumer choice. The aim is to combine public service 'with the private enterprise disciplines of efficiency, cost effectiveness and responsiveness to consumer requirements' (ibid.). It is the second goal, that of widening consumer choice, which concerns us here.

The use of asset transfers as a means of enlarging choice has been employed most ambitiously in the field of housing. During the 1980s over one million households took advantage of 'right to buy' legislation which allowed council tenants to acquire their homes on terms which provided for often substantial discounts from market value. For these households the opportunity to buy their existing home in this manner clearly afforded them a choice of tenure that had hitherto not been open to them. In due course it also allowed them to move fully into the private sector housing market through the sale of their own ex-council property and purchase of an 'off-estate' dwelling. It does however seem possible that this form of widening of choice may have been obtained at the expense of narrowing the choice of others. Given the parallel decline in council house building the transfer into private hands of a million dwellings, often the more desirable ones, must have curbed the choices open both to remaining tenants seeking transfers and to aspiring tenants on council waiting lists.

A second form of asset transfer in housing has been the 'tenants' choice' element in the Housing Act 1988, a development of the provisions in the Housing Act 1985 for transfer of council housing to housing associations. The choice involved here related to the possibility of tenants exchanging their local authority landlord for a private landlord or a housing association. This choice however depends upon an alternative landlord expressing an interest in acquiring a given estate: tenants cannot, as it were, demand a change of landlord in the absence of any transfer proposals. They can however express their views in a ballot if a prospective landlord puts forward a takeover scheme. This ballot though operates on the novel, some might say perverse, principle that the transfer can only be prevented if a majority of those eligible to vote actually vote against: abstentions are thus effectively counted as votes in favour. By the middle of 1990 some twenty two authorities had launched proposals for transfers, all but one of them to housing associations. In ten cases the ballots produced results favourable to transfer: in the remaining twelve cases the transfers were halted by tenant opposition expressed either through the formal ballot or through other consultations before the ballot stage. One noticeable by-product of the emergence of transfer proposals has been an escalation of activity by tenants' organisations, not merely in authorities where such proposals took concrete form but also in cases where 'pre-emptive ballots' were conducted in order to discourage would-be alternative landlords. In Hammersmith and Fulham for example the Federation of Tenants' and Residents' Associations conducted such ballots on twenty-five estates, each of them producing large majorities for retaining the council as landlord (Dwelly, 1989).

The transfer of assets involved under the right to buy and tenant's choice legislation entails a movement of property from the local authority sector to the private sector and, in the case of housing associations, the voluntary sector. A rather different form of transfer was introduced for English and Welsh schools under the Education Reform Act 1988. This allowed schools with more than 300 pupils to choose to opt out of the control of the local education authority and to seek grant maintained status, with funding coming direct from central governments. In Scotland such schools become known as self-governing rather than grant maintained schools, under the Self-governing Schools (Scotland) Act 1989. The actual assets of the schools, the land and the buildings are transferred into the trusteeship of the governors.

Moves towards grant-maintained status can be made either by the governors or by a parents' petition: in either case a ballot of parents is required with a simple majority of votes being cast in favour before proposals can be submitted to the Secretary of State for approval, modification or rejection. By the start of the 1990–91 academic year some 78 schools, out of 108 holding ballots, had opted to become grant-maintained for a variety of reasons including avoidance of closure, avoidance of merger, disagreement over selection procedures, hopes for greater financial flexibility and a belief that the new status would minimise bureaucratic interventions from above. On the last count it is certainly true that the running of such schools becomes the responsibility of the governors, including five parent governors. However they are in turn responsible to the Secretary of State and it remains unclear how far this will in practice give them more freedom of choice in running their schools than does the new local management of schools that remain with the education authority.

Turning now from transfers to contracting out, the links here with consumer choice are rather different. The right to buy, tenants' choice and opting out have all been designed to contain some mechanism whereby tenants and parents can exercise or express a choice, whether through individual purchase or through a ballot. In the case of contracting out the link is not so direct since individual service users do not participate in the process of awarding contracts. Instead, 'with different firms vying for local government service contracts, the authority can . . . pick out the best and most efficient for its citizens' (Forsyth, n.d. p. 5). Thus it is the local authority which exercises the choice on behalf of the public, on the firm assumption that the latter have made an implicit choice in favour of 'the cheapest and most efficient way of getting its work done' (Adam Smith Institute, 1985, p. 1).

The development of contracting out since the late 1970s represented a new departure from the traditional practice whereby private firms tendered in competition with one another for contracts for house building or road construction work for example. The competition now became designed to place existing local authority service providers in contention with the private sector. Ascher (1987) suggests that the initial motivation of some of the first councils to go down this route, such as Southend, lay in a desire to escape from industrial relations problems with their manual workers. However contracting out was soon being seen in more ambitious terms. The Local Government, Planning and Land Act 1980 sought to impose new disciplines on Direct Labour Organisations by requiring them to tender for specified areas of construction, maintenance and highways work and to earn a specified rate of return on capital employed. The Local Government Act 1988 went considerably further, by extending compulsory competitive tendering to six specific areas of local authority work, namely refuse collection, street cleaning, cleaning of buildings, vehicle maintenance, grounds maintenance and catering.

The outcome of the first round of compulsory tendering in 1988–9 was that 80 per cent of the 400 contracts at stake went to the 'in house' local authority work force rather than to private firms. Nonetheless the combination of pre-1988 voluntary tendering and post-1988 compulsory tendering has meant that some authorities have now accumulated a considerable portfolio of privatised services. In the case of Westminster City Council for example these now include catering, library and office cleaning, parks maintenance, street-lamp cleaning, architectural services, social services cleaning and transport, estates cleaning, leisure centre management, refuse collection, street cleaning, public convenience cleaning, printing, heating, community charge registration, food analysis and burial and cremations. With a total of eighteen services contracted out, Westminster was in 1989 at the head of the table, followed by Wandsworth. Over 200 other authorities had by then privatised at least one service, including seventeen English shire districts with four or more services contracted out: nearly 600 service contracts were in operation.

The introduction of such a number of contracts into local authority operations certainly suggests a diversification in the pattern of service provision: however the concentration of refuse and cleaning services into two major commercial groups (BET and the Hamley Group) operating through subsidiaries implies that this diversity may be more apparent than real. One commentator has accordingly suggested that 'it is clearly unrealistic to expect public monopolies to be replaced by a diverse market of small, locally owned, competing entrepreneurs' (Thomas, 1988, pp. 164–5). If that suggestion contains any truth then it raises an important question about the true significance for diversity and choice of the multi-sector or multi-agency provision of traditional local government services.

Municipal pluralism?

At the start of this chapter we set the debate about a greater role for the informal, voluntary and private sectors in the context of the wider debate about welfare pluralism, for both of them addressed the issues of diversity and choice. Those issues themselves can in turn be related to the emergence of a more diverse and more demanding public and to the shift away from the centralised, standardised modes of service provision characteristic of the Fordist era. The move towards multi-sector, multi-agency provision of local services is not exhausted by the examples discussed in the preceding pages. A full list of the agencies now engaged in contributing to the overall servicing of localities would also have to include urban development corporations, a variety of joint boards and joint committees, especially in Greater London and the metropolitan counties, city technology colleges, training and enterprise councils, public-private partnerships, arms-length companies and private developers. In so far as this pattern of a multiplicity of agencies tends to replace a system of municipal monopoly of service provision it is tempting to identify it as producing a local variant of welfare pluralism, a new municipal pluralism. Such a development could be interpreted as making

British local government more akin to the system found in the United States, with its more fragmented and pluralist pattern of service provision (see Hambleton, 1990). Alternatively it might be suggested that we are witnessing not the Americanisation but the Victorianisation of local government, as our earlier account of nineteenth century Colchester described it, producing not so much a post-Fordist as a pre-Fordist system. However, leaving such speculations aside, the form of municipal pluralism that has been emerging is one which raises some important questions about its significance for the enhancement of diversity and choice.

The mere existence of informal or voluntary sector provision alongside public sector provision does not in itself indicate the presence of diversity and choice. It may reflect simply the inability of some people to exercise a desired choice of public sector facilities because the latter are inadequate in terms of availability and must therefore be supplemented in some way. Thus a lack of nursery schools or of child care facilities may provoke some mothers to organise pre-school playgroups on a self-help basis. This however could be seen as a form of self-exploitation producing 'facilities on the cheap, incorporating the unpaid labour of mothers themselves' (Finch, 1984, p. 18) reflecting the urgency of need rather than the luxury of choice.

Nor does the replacement of a public sector monopoly by a private or a voluntary sector monopoly in a given locality thereby increase choice. For example, the transfer of the entire housing stock of Sevenoaks Borough Council to the West Kent Housing Association in 1989 may have made sense in terms of housing finance, or of fending off a private landlord, or of defending the stock by extinguishing the right to buy. Yet with the service still being administered by the same (transferred) staff from the same offices and with no local authority housing left in existence there seems little element of choice involved other than at the point of the tenants' ballot: the choice was a once and for all choice rather than one capable of being exercised on any continuing basis thereafter over a range of alternatives. For actual choice to be a continuing reality municipal pluralism requires a mixed economy of service provision to operate at the local point of consumption. In that sense it requires the other sectors to genuinely complement and compete with public sector provision of a particular service rather than totally displace it. Moreover it also presumably necessitates that each sector has something distinctive to offer in order to provide the diversity that enriches choice.

Here again there are straws in the wind which suggest that there are pressures working against such diversity. Reference was made earlier to the possibility that grants to self-help groups in the informal sector could transform such bodies into more formally organised elements of the voluntary sector, while moves towards contractually based funding could pressure the voluntary sector in turn to accommodate its ways of working to suit those of the public sector. Meanwhile the public sector finds itself increasingly under pressure to adopt the culture and practices of the private sector. In the context of compulsory competitive tendering for example it has been suggested that if local authorities are to bid successfully for service contracts then they 'need to adopt many of the attitudes and practices of their commercial rivals. A new style and culture are needed' (Audit Commission, 1989, p. 22). Such a new style and culture is also being promoted by pressures for value for money and for greater cost effectiveness in areas not affected by compulsory tendering. The encouragement of a more entrepreneurial approach and of the development of internal markets within local authorities bears witness to the realities of these pressures.

Another aspect of this matter is that the voluntary sector might also come to take on the characteristics of the private sector. For example Maxwell (1989, p. 8) speculates about 'market pressure for a convergence of structure and ethos between the voluntary sector and the private sector', partly in response to government encouragement to seek funding through private donations, corporate giving and business sponsorship but also from the market effect produced by competitive tendering. Similarly Holman (1990) claims to detect governmental 'pressure to make voluntary bodies a part of the market system' and fears that private corporations 'are gaining the power to shape much of the voluntary agenda' through their preferred patterns of grant giving. Gutch and Young (1988, pp. 32–3) quote the experience of an American voluntary agency which

> was being forced increasingly to look to more lucrative areas of work, and this meant turning away from the population in the inner cities and advertising services . . . in the wealthy suburbs . . . [An] emphasis on market forces, combined with public

spending cuts, means that grants have to be replaced with fees for service if the agency is to survive. Voluntary agencies look more and more like businesses.

Perhaps the first area of the voluntary sector to encounter these sorts of pressures may be that of the housing associations, which are now obliged by the Housing Act 1988 to supplement government grants by attracting funding from the private sector. Thus Maxwell (1989, p. 13) detects a 'tendency, already evident among housing associations . . . to try to strengthen their financial base by moving "up-market"'.

If the voluntary sector does come under pressure to adjust its operations to meet both the requirements of local government and the demands of the market place then the range of diversity of ethos, goals and practices potentially offered by municipal pluralism becomes somewhat limited. This limitation is of course even more pronounced if local government is itself at the same time accommodating its own ways of working to those of the private sector.

The question that may thus be asked is whether or not current developments towards a municipal pluralism of multi-agency service delivery may not be undermined as creators of diversity and choice by pressures for the universal adoption of the attitudes, practices, style and culture of the private sector in all the other sectors, whether directly or indirectly. Such a question will however seem exceptionally perverse to those for whom the private sector itself is by its very nature the best available mechanism for maximising choice. From that perspective neither welfare pluralism nor municipal pluralism are truly adequate to the tasks of providing diversity and choice. Instead a much more radical strategy is advocated, one which reshapes local government along private sector lines and which wherever possible ensures that 'Individuals and families . . . make choices themselves instead of being forced to accept the collective decision made by a local political body' (Adam Smith Institute, 1989, p. 60). Others however see the pre-requisites of choice in a different light and question the assumption 'that choice in itself leads to empowerment: we can all read the menu – so we can all eat in the restaurant' (Dowson, 1989, p. 10). As these two contrasting remarks suggest, the debate about modes of service provision is not solely one about devising appropriate mechanisms. It is not merely technical or organisational issues which are being addressed: there is also a broader agenda involving some fundamental perspectives on the proper role and nature of local government.

7 Models of Change

[T]he culture in which local government in Britain functions is itself changing in important ways. This is particularly true of the relationship between the individual and the state, through the development of 'consumerism' and the concept of the 'active citizen'. It is also reflected in the development of the 'enabling' authority.

Bogdanor et al., 1990, pp. 1–2.

In the previous four chapters we have encountered a wide range of initiatives adopted by local authorities in their attempts to get closer to their public. Some of them have developed out of earlier experiments; others have been more recent in origin. Taken together they provide a varied repertoire of innovations from which individual councils can draw in differing combinations to suit their own priorities.

However the adoption of these varying initiatives is not always a wholly random matter, of the 'pick and mix' variety. As we saw at the end of chapter 2 some attempt was made within the political parties and in management circles to develop rather more coherent local authority responses to the pressures from a more demanding public. One way of characterising these responses is that developed by Hambleton and Hoggett, based not so much on their partisan or managerial origins as on their differing modes of service provision. They suggest that during the 1980s those local authorities most determined to move away from a traditional mode of bureaucratic paternalism did so through the embrace of one of three reform strategies; these strategies were based respectively on an individual consumer responsive mode of public provision, on a democratised collectivism within the public sector and on market based and privatised provision (Hambleton and Hoggett, 1987; Hambleton 1990). Here it will be suggested that three similar strategies or models of change may also be identified, not in terms of their favoured mode of provision, but by reference to their differing models or perceptions of the proper role of the public and of the latter's relationship with local government. Two of these roles we have already encountered, those of the consumer and the citizen and it is they which have dominated much of the debate about local government and the public. There is however a third role, as yet waiting in the wings, but foreshadowed perhaps by some of the policies of the post-1979 Conservative government and commanding articulate support from some of that government's supporters. This role is that of the local shareholder.

Local shareholders

In 1988 Nicholas Ridley made his own considered contribution to the debate about local government in his Centre for Policy Studies pamphlet *The Local Right: enabling not providing*. He was clear about the need for local authorities to concentrate on what is really wanted and needed by local people, 'to improve accountability, to eliminate waste, duplication and unnecessary functions, and to improve value for money' (p. 7). To secure these ends he commended the introduction of the community charge but he also regretted that the private sector 'has not penetrated deeply enough into local government circles' (p. 26) and suggested that 'we should always question whether it is right for the public sector to do a job when private individuals or companies could and would compete to do the job themselves' (p. 29). If this strategy were to be followed then the emphasis would shift 'from the council as monopoly provider and manager to the council as enabler and monitor' (p. 21).

Ridley's pamphlet attracted some attention since he was at the time Secretary of State for the Environment with ultimate responsibility for local government, as well as being a known adherent of the Thatcherite New Right. However he was not really breaking new ground, for his general line of argument had been anticipated by others on the New Right in earlier years. Three years previously for example Butler, Pirie and Young (1985) had drawn on the work of over a hundred experts for *The Omega File* of the Adam Smith Institute, whose review of government functions included a section on local government. They saw 'no reason why any service should be exempted from the obligation to invite tenders . . . . The range of services which are potential candidates for alternative provision by contract is almost endless' (p. 350). They went on to identify twenty-nine such services in addition to advocating a mixture of private sector and market orientated arrangements for such major policy areas as education, housing, social services and town planning.

A belief in the strategy of privatisation does not necessarily stop at proposals to contract out services or to introduce charges or market relations. Mather (1989, pp. 231–2) goes so far as to contemplate what seems to be the virtual colonisation of local government by the private sector.

> [A]s local authorities become more businesslike the contribution of business itself is likely to increase. Business can be expected to strengthen its contribution across a range of fronts: as contractor for the direct provision of services . . . ; as model for the organisation and management of services remaining in direct provision by the public sector . . . ; through the secondment of staff and a developing interchange between the public sector, business and the academic world . . . ; through formal structures of consultation . . . . As local government becomes more businesslike, business will undoubtedly consider that the business of local government will require a strengthened determination by business to involve itself in both policy and delivery mechanisms, as part of a general contribution to social well being as well as directly as a contractor.

At the heart of this new relationship between local government and business would be a wide-ranging set of contractual arrangements including contracts

> with outside private sector providers . . . with authority officers, increasingly appointed on fixed term performance related agreements . . . [and] with customers, who will have strengthened rights to redress for unsatisfactory service – plus, increasingly,

the right to go elsewhere . . . . The future of local government should be seen in this sense of a series of contracts. (idem, p. 233).

A private sector oriented local government system based upon a series of contractual relationships would operate in a very different way from the traditionally established model. Support for such changes is found in the policy statements of councils which have contemplated taking the first steps down this road. Bradford, for example, during its period as a Thatcherite flagship from 1988 to 1990 committed itself to a role 'limited to the provision of those services which cannot be adequately provided by the private sector . . . . Bradford Council will revert from being primarily a direct provider of services to being an enabling authority'. This would entail the introduction of competitive tendering 'throughout the Authority' and a welcome for 'officer proposals for management buyouts of Council services'. Such moves would require that 'the structure of the organisation must be recast . . . [and] management processes must be redefined' (Bradford City Council, 1989).

The sorts of organisational and managerial changes which might be required under such circumstances would imply a considerable 'hollowing out' of the authority leaving it with a rather skeletal structure. Such changes were identified by another authority under Thatcherite leadership, Arun District Council, in advancing its four year strategy for the period 1987–91. The council was committed 'to continually press for action to push out more and more services into a competitive environment'; this would entail 'a deliberate diminution of the corporate organisation to a "core" structure backed by private sector support and a variable workforce periphery' (Arun District Council, 1988, p. 3 and 1987a, p. 22). This advocacy of a core and periphery structure followed an earlier 1985 commitment 'to produce a slimmer organisation moving away from traditional local government practices towards the best in the business field' (Arun District Council, 1987a, p. 4). This commitment finds a sympathetic echo in the claim of Nicholas Ridley (1988, p. 26) that 'inside every fat and bloated local authority there is a slim one struggling to get out'. Some go on to carry the arguments further and to argue that such a degree of slimming may well make it logical to amalgamate two-tier local government into a 'leaner, more efficient' system based on single tier all-purpose authorities (Mason, 1989a, p. 61). It is not, however, mere size which is at issue in any move towards a slimmer core and periphery structure.

The ultimate logic of such a structure would be one in which a core of programme directors, strategic policy advisers and contract managers stood in an arm's length relationship to contracted service providers, who might be in house or out of house and whose services might be provided for the public (for example refuse collection) or for the core organisation itself (for example computing facilities). The eventual result might be the emergence of 'an entirely new type of local government officer', no longer concerned with professional specialisms or with managing large departments but 'skilled in the arts of contract specifications, purchasing and supply, and quality control' (Mather, 1989, p. 222). Indeed even these officers might ultimately be dispensed with, for it is possible that 'the task of monitoring the contracts could itself be contracted out' (Butler, Pirie and Young, 1985, p. 350).

It is not only the nature and role of the local government officer which would change in this scenario; so too would that of the councillor. Freed of the task of detailed service management through committees 'the job of being a local councillor would, I believe, be more attractive to the leaders of local communities, not less so. It would take less of busy people's time' (Ridley, 1988, p. 35). The Adam Smith Institute (1989, p. 59) similarly looks for reforms which should attract 'some talented people . . . put off by . . . interminable meetings discussing the provision of council services in detail'. On this last point Mather (1989, p. 222) foresees the possibility that committee business, far from 'requiring fortnightly or monthly meetings, going on until late in the evening . . . could be despatched in one, two or three meetings a year'. The possible amalgamation of two-tier authorities into all-purpose authorities could also permit 'good local politicians . . . [to] spread their talents less thinly' and thus help to overcome the problem that 'too few high calibre people [are] attracted to local government' (Heffer, 1990).

The claim that a slimmed down, largely privatised form of local authority would prove more attractive to 'high calibre' and 'talented' people does of course re-open the recurring debate about councillor calibre. This debate is one which can be seen as having something of a hidden agenda, since it tends to conflate calibre or talent with social status or economic position. Dearlove (1979, pp. 104–5) argues that concerns over councillor calibre have embodied the 'bitter lament' of 'business groups' who are anxious 'to recapture the social relations, style of politics, and class of leadership, that existed before the franchise was extended and before the working class rose to some sort of position of local political power through the Labour Party'.

Running in parallel with this 'bitter lament' and with the wistful desire to recapture an earlier style of politics there also exists a profound distaste and disdain amongst many in the business community for the rough and ready realities of democratic local politics. Clements' study of the social and economic elite in Bristol, for example, uncovered the unwillingness of local notables to expose themselves to the rigours of a decision making system in which their views and assumptions could be the subject of debate, challenge and sustained opposition. They were more used to a world in which 'one speaks with authority, you don't have to argue' and where one was 'used to a position of responsibility and getting obeyed – I should be driven mad if I had to argue the toss with a lot of half-wits' (Clements, 1969, p. 186). In the light of these interpretations, the advocacy of a slimmer, largely privatised form of local government attracting a higher calibre of councillor suggests not only the intended colonisation of local government by the business community, it also implies a desire for a basically de-politicised local government within which members of that business community would feel at ease.

Such pressure for a depoliticised form of local government is not however solely attributable to the desire to make it more amenable to the sensitivities of business people. It also echoes the profound suspicion of the political process itself which is commonly encountered on the New Right. This suspicion embraces a general fear once expressed by Margaret Thatcher: 'The role of government is limited . . . if you extend democracy into every single sphere of life, you are denying personal liberty' (quoted in *The Independent*, 8 June 1989). There is also however a particular concern expressed for example in Hayek's belief that whereas 'the pursuit of the selfish aims of the individual will usually lead him to serve the general interest, the collective actions of organised groups are almost invariably contrary to the general interest'; indeed Hayek

fears that the working of traditional liberal democratic institutions
'necessarily leads to a gradual transformation of the spontaneous
order of a free society into a totalitarian system conducted in the
service of some coalition of organised interests' (Hayek, 1976, p.
138; 1973, p. 2).

Clear, if less apocalyptic, echoes of this concern over interest
group politics are evident in New Right analyses of local government. For example:

> In political life, councillors are subject to pressures from a variety
> of different sources from outside local interest groups demanding
> this or protesting against that; from the Council's own workforce
> and its Unions – very powerful lobbies: from the general public
> . . . what the general public 'wants' is difficult to judge from a
> pile of ballot papers. It can be difficult for the politician on the
> basis of the representations he gets from the public to assess what
> is in the public interest (Ridley, 1988 pp. 27–8).

In similar vein Mather (1989, p. 234) has argued that

> the politician's vote motive, its appeals to interest groups, its
> trade offs and opportunities for 'deals', its short-termism and
> organisational rigidities, the incentives it provides for building up
> alliances built on dependency, have together proved an ineffec-
> tive means of delivering local services to local customers.

Minford too has abhorred 'the traditional view of local authorities
as highly politicised mini-states . . . [with] a mandate to redistribute
income locally': in particular he condemned the old rates system as
one which provided

> incentives to local government to provide services to client voting
> groups at the expense of the minority of full personal ratepayers,
> the business ratepayer, and the general taxpayers elsewhere. The
> community charge [however] is designed to place the burden of
> financing *marginal* expenditure fully on those who benefit from it
> (Minford, 1988, p. 12; emphasis in original).

He therefore looked forward to 'the depoliticisation and privatisation of local authority activity under the reformed [i.e. community

charge] system' (idem, p. 13). Minford's enthusiasm for privatisation and depoliticisation and his particular concern with rate-payers, taxpayers and chargepayers not only reflects the general stance of the New Right, it also gives new and added emphasis to the longer established tradition of the Conservative Party as the party of the ratepayers.

The traditional concern for the interests of those who are taxed to finance service provision remains a strong Conservative characteristic and tends to outrank concern for those who consume the services. For example Kenneth Baker as Secretary of State for Education, dismissed the result of a ballot in which 94.3 per cent of parents in a 55 per cent poll had rejected the transfer of schools out of the control of the Inner London Education Authority on the grounds that 'it does not represent the wishes of the ratepayers who pay for the service' (quoted in Cave, 1989). Alternatively the notion of a consumer interest can simply be re-defined: 'Our customers are our ratepayers' was the formulation offered by one Conservative district councillor. Indeed a major purpose of the community charge is precisely that of making all (adult) service users also service funders. The logical conclusion of this combination of new strategy and old tradition is the search for a system of local government which is privatised, is depoliticised and is organised primarily on the basis of representing the interests of those who provide its finances. Such a system has been proposed by the Adam Smith Institute in the form of the 'community company'.

> The basic outline of the proposal is that . . . a community company would own and manage all the properties and assets of the former council, or those relating to particular services if it did not take over the entire functions, with its articles of incorporation spelling out its responsibilities towards local residents. Those residents would become shareholders in the new companies and would elect a board of directors (Adam Smith Institute, 1989, p. 52).

Such a scheme has as its initial exemplar the experience of Thamesmead Town Ltd, set up in 1987 after a ballot of tenants on the former GLC estate produced a majority in favour of the creation of a non-profit distributing limited company to run the estate. The company owns and manages some 5000 houses and 300 industrial and commercial properties, looks after 200 acres of recreational land and water areas and provides support for a number of local community organisations. The first chairman of the company, Clive Thornton, saw it as something of a prototype for local government: 'I want Thamesmead to move towards taking over all services from the local authorities' (quoted in Sanders, 1989).

Apart from the inherent advantages which its advocates see as intrinsic to a private sector model, the community company is seen as having two specific sets of merits. One advantage is that since the company would function under the provisions of company law it would escape the restrictions of traditional local government law: it would thus 'be able to operate commercially, offering services to other communities, to public bodies and of course, to private sector companies' (Mason, 1989a, p. 63). The other advantage would again accrue from company law, namely the provisions that 'directors are always answerable to their shareholders and can be dismissed by them' and that company general meetings would give shareholders 'a direct say in company policy' (Mason, 1989b, p. 27). Such aspirations, though indeed sustained by company law, might however be regarded as rather ambitious in the light of actual shareholder indifference to the exercise of their rights in most private sector companies. Be that as it may, the details of the share holding arrangements would require clarification: should they be based on a nominal share value of £1 for example, or should they be shares whose value reflected increases or decreases in the value of the community's assets? The mechanisms for electing the directors would also need to be specified: it could be on an 'at large' basis or on a ward basis.

Whatever the details might prove to be, the basic outline is clear – a structure based on the provisions of company law, operating on commercial rather than on political lines, and with the public cast in the role of local shareholders. A form of local government modelled upon a perception of the public as local shareholders can be seen as the natural corollary of much traditional and contemporary thinking on the political right. It reflects a particular preoccupation with protecting the interests of those who finance local services and is perhaps a logical development of that preoccupation. It is also perhaps a further step along the journey that began with the introduction of the community charge. The intention behind the community charge has been to make every adult feel as if they are in effect compulsory shareholders in the municipal enterprise, anxious to see their 'investment' used prudently and sparingly and to protect themselves against any excessive calls upon their purse.

The shareholder model of local government can thus be seen as one which envisages a more active protective role on behalf of those who are the funders of local government, in place of the rather more passive role of ratepayer. It is however a model which still conceives of shareholders 'owning' the local authority as a corporate body, even if the latter's own service functions are contracted out to other agencies. It does not therefore have quite such radical implications as the experiment conducted in the American city of Baltimore where 'a host of programs aimed at enhancing citizen ownership' and designed to ensure that 'communities, even destitute ones, buy into urban improvements' required neighbourhood groups for example to raise funds and buy the necessary equipment if they wanted a local playground (Peters and Austin, 1986, p. 225).

Taken together, the Baltimore experiment and the creation of Thamesmead Town have overtones of the recent growth in the United States of 'private residential government' in which residents individually own their own property but share ownership of common facilities. Known as 'common-interest housing developments' and run by elected boards of directors such ventures are ones in which

> residents privately support – and exclusively enjoy – a variety of services, ranging from police protection to swimming pools to local self-government, that were once the province of cities . . . and put more formerly public services into the private sector on a 'pay-for-your-own' basis . . . offering homogeneous population, physical security, stable housing values, local control and freedom from exposure to the social ills of the cities (McKenzie, 1989, p. 257).

Such a form of private residential government seems a recognisable variant of a local shareholder model of local government.

The local shareholder model draws on a pre-existing model, that of the company, the law relating to which provides us with a relatively specific set of definitions about the role and rights of shareholders. The same however cannot be said of the roles of consumer and of citizen which have tended to dominate much of the recent debate about local authority relations with the public. Indeed there are widely differing usages of the terms consumer and citizen in the latter context. Midwinter (1979, p. 134) for example refers to 'the consumers of local government, in both their user and ratepayer roles', which implies an elision of the user and funder or consumer and shareholder roles. Pollitt (1988b) suggests another elision, arguing that in the public sector one must talk of the 'consumer-citizen'. The private sector model of the consumer, he argues, is inadequate for the public sector, where consumers may have rights and/or obligations which are not encountered in private transactions and where services may be allocated according to need rather than according to willingness and ability to pay. Drawing on the work of Held, he also goes on to offer a means whereby we can draw some distinction between the consumer and the citizen elements of his joint model. He identifies an instrumental and a developmental approach to the political process. The instrumental approach is one which emphasises the importance of 'satisfying individuals' wants [and] . . . increasing provider sensitivity to consumer preferences'; the developmental approach by contrast is more concerned 'to develop civic consciousness and enhance individual and group autonomy' and to create 'an informed, committed and developing citizenry' (Pollitt, 1988b, p. 83; Held, 1987, p. 102). It is on the basis of this instrumental–developmental distinction that we now discuss models of local government based on the consumer and citizen roles respectively.

Local consumers

We have already encountered in earlier chapters a variety of initiatives designed to make life easier for service consumers: one stop shops, formal complaints procedures, improved reception arrangements and better communications are examples. However the period since the mid-1980s has seen the development of a school of thought arguing that greater responsiveness to the consumer must be more than a series of piecemeal measures: it must instead represent 'an actual shift in organisational cultures' (Pollitt, 1988a, p. 121). In similar terms consumerism has also been described as 'more a frame of mind than the existence of elaborate structures' (Kirkpatrick, 1988, p. 42) and as 'a state of mind' (Fenwick, 1989, p. 47).

This should not however lead us to conclude that a concern for local service consumers operates solely at the level of thinking helpful and beautiful thoughts. Potter (1988, p. 150) for example argues that it requires 'a structural underpinning' of five basic principles, namely those of 'access, choice, information, redress and representation'. Walsh (1990) suggests that the quality of service that users receive can be judged in terms of the match, or the gap, between consumer expectation and producer performance. Aspects of service provision such as reliability, responsiveness, competence, access, courtesy, communication, credibility, security, understanding and knowledge all therefore need to be handled in such a way as to minimise or if possible abolish any gap between expectation and performance. Moreover he offers the reminder that even the most technically competent service provision may fail to satisfy the consumer if there is any unpleasantness in the relationships or the surroundings which provide the context of provision.

Fenwick (1989) identifies seven specific consumerist strategies currently being followed. They are: direct collection of public views, through surveys for example; improved access to services, including decentralisation; improved access to information; the use of subjective performance indicators; active marketing and public relations; increased public participation and accountability; and changes in administrative and managerial style inspired by the notion of managerial 'excellence'. Even more specific, and certainly far more numerous, were the 232 ideas for improving customer care produced by the staff of East Dorset District Council in 1989. They included a five day target time for answering letters, an L-plate badge for new staff, a tea and coffee machine in the reception area, case officer identification on all correspondence, toys for children in the reception area, evening opening one day a week, a public open day, home visits for the disabled and a book for visitors' comments. East Dorset's efforts secured them victory in a management competition, the Tom Peters 90 Day Excellence Challenge, in 1989, which returns us to the question of organisational cultures and states of mind, for it was the work of Peters which encouraged the placing of a particular emphasis on such an approach to consumer or customer orientation.

Peters' and Waterman's book *In Search of Excellence*, with its sub-title *Lessons from America's Best-Run Companies*, was seen to convey a message which could be translated for use in British local authorities. A key part of that message was that 'top-performing' companies had 'a special way of being close to the customer' (p. 193), that they were characterised by 'the dominance and coherence of [a] culture' which focused on the customer (p. 75) and that even lip-service paid by staff to such a culture was useful because 'once they start talking the philosophy, they may start living it, even if, initially, the words have no meaning' (p. 260). The priority attached to customer orientation in these private sector companies was all the more significant for the fact that it outranked any 'desire to be the low-cost producer' and was the 'something besides cost [which] usually comes first' in such companies (pp. 159 and 193).

Wrekin District Council was one of the first councils to accept the Peters and Waterman message after its then chief executive had been introduced to the book by a friend in the United States. The notion of learning from the private sector was given added impetus by the chief executive's own exposure to private sector customer orientation at a course at Ashridge management centre and by the experience of one of the council's personnel officers who went on secondment to Marks and Spencer at about the same time. The outcome was a review of all aspects of council–customer relations in 1984–5 and the adoption of a series of initiatives some of which were later chronicled in a report titled, in respectful imitation, *In (re)Search of Customers* (1988). The overarching concern was to create a corporate culture based upon core values of 'Quality, Caring and Fairness', values to be reinforced through inductions, staff development, team briefings, an employee newsletter, training in customer care and communications and the setting of service targets and indicators. Within the context of that culture, specific initiatives related to service delivery were put under way including improved reception facilities, local service shops, residents' attitude surveys and area based working across all departments.

If Wrekin was in many ways a pathfinder, other authorities have also travelled in the same direction. We have for example already encountered Braintree District Council's use of opinion polling to formulate an Action Plan on issues concerning local residents and its establishment of a comprehensive complaints procedure for dissatisfied customers. These ventures have been part of a broader package of measures including the development of public relations and marketing capabilities, the publication of a council quarterly newspaper and a tenants' newsletter, the introduction of name badges for staff, improved access for disabled people to the council's headquarters and the production of a free *Quality Life Catalogue* listing a portfolio of the 64 separate services or facilities offered by the council, together with 33 services which people might think are run by the council but are in fact the responsibility of other identified bodies. In terms of a set of organisational values Braintree has committed itself to customer orientation and action orientation as well as to a belief in quality, in the abilities of individual staff and in the need to be both responsive and responsible (Braintree District Council, 1987).

York City Council began the production of an annual Citizen's Charter in 1989 to tell local residents in advance what the council was hoping to achieve in its various services; it also introduced customer contracts for street cleaning, specifying to all residents in two areas of the city the frequency, type, cost and standard of sweeping they could expect and detailing how residents could follow up any apparent shortcoming. Other councils have linked the contract idea with the payment of compensation for failure to perform. Thus Newcastle-Upon-Tyne City Council has a compensation scheme for tenants whose repair deadlines are not met, whilst Cambridge City Council allows tenants in that situation to get the work done and then to bill the council for the cost (Local Government Information Unit, 1990, p. 3). On a quite different tack other councils are reviewing their own internal committee arrangements to see whether there is a better way of enabling elected members to focus on customer requirements rather than on the details of service administration. Cambridgeshire County Council for example has abolished most sub-committees and reduced the role of main service committees. It has however created service advisory groups to advise chief officers by 'working with relevant client groups and other public and voluntary bodies in their service areas' and has set up select panels to look at individual issues with the aid of outside as well as inside expertise (Eales, 1990, p. viii; Kerr, 1990).

The interest which some councils have shown in a customer orientation cannot all be attributed to the inspiration of Tom Peters. A number of publications canvassing similar ideas appeared in the 1980s under the auspices of the Local Government Training Board (LGTB) (1987), the National Consumer Council (NCC) (1986) and the Audit Commission (1988). Bearing such titles as *Getting Closer to the Public, Learning from the Public, Measuring Up* and *The Competitive Council*, they converged on the need for services to perform to the satisfaction of those who consumed them.

It is fair to describe much of this literature, along of course with that of Peters and Waterman, as largely managerial rather than political in tone and content, reflecting a preoccupation with instrumental concerns for consumer satisfaction rather than with any concern for the development of citizenship. Two consequences seem to have followed from this apolitical managerialism. The first is the ability of a key officer, often a chief executive, to launch a customer orientation drive without appearing to court political trouble from members. Perhaps particularly in modest shire districts, still comparatively fresh from 1970s reorganisation, a chief executive has been able to do this without having to fear trouble from long entrenched traditions and practices or from large and powerful departments. Even so, any such initiative must require at least the acquiescence if not the eager support of the politicians if it is to succeed. In practice consumerism seems to prove acceptable to several shades of political opinion particularly perhaps those from moderate Conservative to moderate Labour. This can be seen as the second consequence of its managerialist origins – it is not politically tainted to any serious degree.

The broad political appeal of consumerism and customer orientation can be seen from considering the political nature of the authorities cited in the previous paragraphs during their embrace of these ideas. Wrekin has been moderate Labour; Braintree has swung from minority to majority to minority Conservative control; York, Newcastle-Upon-Tyne and Cambridge have been moderate Labour. Cambridgeshire has moved from being a hung authority into Conservative control; and East

Dorset, whilst Conservative, has disavowed privatisation with a commitment to 'retain in-house those services subject to competition' (East Dorset District Council, 1989), a stance similar to that adopted by Conservative Braintree.

In some ways it is perhaps the embrace of consumerist ideas by some Labour councils which has been the more surprising development: whilst being apolitical in origin these ideas could be interpreted as grounded more in the traditions of the market place than of public service. Moreover Labour often saw itself historically as committed to defending the interests of public service employees as much as, if not more than, consumers. Indeed for much of the 1980s Labour local government conference sessions on defending or improving local services tended to be dominated by issues of job protection rather than consumer responsiveness. Only towards the end of the decade did this begin to change, as Labour became increasingly concerned to improve both the image and the performance of a politically threatened public sector.

Simultaneously leading Labour councillors began to talk the language of consumerism. Margaret Hodge, chair of the Association of London Authorities, claimed that the priority of Labour councillors should be 'to serve the interests of the people for whom we provide services' and that this should 'take precedence over trades union interests, or even jobs' (*Local Government Chronicle*, 3 July 1987). Not long before, the Labour leader of Lewisham had expressed his debt to *In Search of Excellence* and his commitment to the idea of a council that was 'close to the customer' (Sullivan, 1987, p. 21). Labour's turn-of-decade policy review confirmed this new direction with its commitment to a 'quality programme for local government', embracing a Quality Commission to replace the Audit Commission and a proposal for widespread use of customer contracts (Labour Party 1989b and 1990).

The wide appeal of consumerism and customer orientation may not only reflect its apolitical, managerial origins; it may also be related to a certain diffuseness in the concepts themselves. We have referred above both to consumers and to customers as if the terms were wholly interchangeable. This in turn however reflects the approach of many in local government. In a survey conducted by Hague (1989, p. 16) he not only discovered a variety of terms being used to describe those who received council services – public, customers, users, consumers and clients – but also found 'evidence to suggest that all of these terms are used interchangeably by many respondents with scant regard for nuances of meaning'. Such nuances include the professional dependency relationship implied by 'client', whilst as we have seen earlier in the context of education and social services the term 'user' is not always wholly explicit. The term 'consumer' at least embraces the notion of receipt of service without prejudging the terms on which that receipt takes place: the use of the term 'customer' is largely an import from the language of private sector management and could be taken to imply an exchange relationship of payment for services.

A consumer may however be seen either as an individual with rights which need to be defended or as part of a market or audience to be captured and therefore the object of persuasive attention. More generally the term 'consumerism' can embrace not only the vigorous defence of consumer interests but also the celebration of the virtues of high levels of consumption, the notion of 'consumer capitalism vindicated' (Jones, 1965, p. 354) and even the claim proudly voiced by Home Office Minister John Patten, that 'I consume, therefore I am' (quoted in *The Guardian*, 11 October 1988). Local authorities may not see themselves as part of the machinery of consumer capitalism, yet their embrace of public relations, market research and marketing in the name of consumer-ism or customer orientation can sometimes make them appear keener to 'sell their wares' than to stir up issues of consumer rights. Essex County Council (1990b) for example produced a corporate Action Plan in 1990 which included a section under the title *Closer to the Public* which acknowledged the need to 'listen to what people say'. However, the emphasis in the action items that followed was very much on the need 'To raise awareness of the County Council', 'To establish and promote the identity and the image of the County Council', 'To increase public use of County Council premises' and 'To market Essex at home and abroad'. In themselves these are unexceptional aspirations but they do reflect more the 'hard sell' approach than a concern for establishing and defending the rights of the public as service consumers. The temptation to approach consumers in this way may be all the stronger in an era when local authorities like to think of themselves as proactive rather than reactive, as initiators rather than responders.

In the final analysis there is perhaps something rather limited in the concept of the local consumer. Consumption is an act of receipt rather than of creation and no matter how much their complaints are listened to or their interests are taken into account consumers are ultimately a means to the wider ends of their providers, be they in the public or private sectors, be they political or financial. America's best run companies did not get close to the customer just for the sake of a warm, cosy feeling: the ultimate purpose was bound up with the interests of the companies. Similarly local government in Britain has discovered the consumer not for wholly altruistic reasons but as part of its defensive response to pressures from central government and from the public for more effective and accountable performance. Consumers may be increasingly the object of local authorities' attention but they can still all too easily be the object of a subject–object relationship with those authorities, benign though it may be.

For some commentators a concern for consumers is thus a necessary but inadequate step. Approaches which are laudable in so far as 'the individual consumer can be brought more into the picture' nevertheless 'speak the language of "consumer" and "choice" rather than the language of "power" and "control"' (Hoggett, 1990, p. 70). Similarly, Potter (1988, pp. 157 and 156) suggests that 'Consumerism is fine as far as it goes, but it does not go far enough to affect a radical shift in the distribution of power'; nor does it 'encourage consumers to take account of the preference of others'. With this latter point she takes up Rhodes' (1987) argument on the need to promote amongst the public a wider concern than for their own individual consumer preferences and to have regard to notions of citizenship which embrace a recognition of the rights of others and of the importance of duties as well as rights.

The need thus to move from an instrumental focus on the consumer to a more developmental focus on the citizen can be seen also in the work of Clarke and Stewart. Their advocacy of a 'public service orientation' represented a variant of customer orientation with its emphasis on the obligation to provide high quality public services, an obligation which demanded closeness to the customer. Initially their argument was couched in terms of 'putting value . . . on the public as customer' (Clarke and Stewart, 1985, p. 2) but it soon came to take a wider view, recognising that 'the customer is also citizen . . . [and] that there are citizens other than customers' (Clarke and Stewart, 1986, p. 10). 'Concern for the citizen as well as the customer distinguishes the *public* service orientation from the concern for the customer that should mark any service organisation . . . . Thus the public service organisation is *not merely consumerism*' (Stewart and Clarke, 1987, p. 170; first italics mine, second italics in original).

We thus find ourselves offered a third model for the relationship between local government and the public, one based not on the protective role of the local shareholder nor on the instrumental role of the local consumer but on the developmental role of the local citizen.

Local citizens

The concept of the citizen is one which provides us with as much debate as it does definition. Moreover the debate has been particularly lively in recent years for it has not been confined to arguments about perceptions of the local public as encountered in the remarks of Rhodes or Stewart and Clarke. There has been a wider political debate taking place about the nature and role of the citizen, a debate often summarised as being concerned with the 'active citizen'.

In January 1988 the *New Statesman* settled on the idea of citizenship as its radical theme for the year: in the following month the then Home Secretary, Douglas Hurd, introduced the notion of the active citizen in a speech at Tamworth, the town where Robert Peel had produced his famous Manifesto in 1835. The *New Statesman* initiative culminated in the launching of Charter 88, which described itself as 'a citizen's movement for constitutional change' seeking to establish political, civil and human rights in constitutional form. Mr Hurd's own Tamworth Manifesto was endorsed enthusiastically by the 1988 Conservative annual conference which embraced the idea of the active citizen as a key theme for Conservative politics for the 1990s. As we have seen, in the following year, 1989, Mrs. Thatcher gave the role of the citizen a central place in her address to the Conservative local government conference.

This shared enthusiasm for the citizen by both right and left did not necessarily however focus upon the same object, for the two wings of politics had rather different ideas about the true role of the citizen and the nature of citizenship. The fundamental distinction between the two approaches is well captured by Luntley (1989) who recognises two models of citizenship, the individual and the social.

In the former the source of the bonds that tie people together arises from the individual. The only condition is that individuals have the imaginative resources to reach out to embrace others with their charity . . . . On the individual model individuals empower themselves into citizenship . . . . On the individual model society does not really exist . . . . The onus is squarely on the individual to come up with the moral stamina to reach out to others (p. 133).

In the social model of citizenship however, the bonds that tie people together

arise from the community which collectively acts to ensure that certain conditions for citizenship are properly met . . . that society be organised in the appropriate way . . . The social model recognises . . . that individuals need to be empowered by the sort of economic and social arrangements in which they find themselves . . . . Meeting the conditions of citizenship . . . is not done to enable success for individuals but to enable success for citizens, people with a moral and social role within a larger framework, a civil polity (pp. 133 and 154).

Luntley's references to charity in the case of the individual model and to the polity in the case of the social model suggest that we may also understand the two models as commending respectively philanthropic and political involvements as the true mark of the active citizen. The philanthropically active citizen is the one whom Douglas Hurd was particularly anxious to prompt: 'We've got to say to those people doing quite well, look, there's a community to which you belong – be an active citizen within it' (quoted in *Sunday Times*, 16 October 1988). In similar vein John Patten encouraged 'the enterprising individual . . . someone who cares' and urged such people 'to work for the benefit of others': however he warned of 'those whose only aim is to cause a stir' (*Sunday Times*, 11 December 1988).

We have referred earlier to the notion of the citizen as being a developmental rather than an instrumental role, one which embraces ideas of a wider civic consciousness rather than the satisfaction of personal wants. In the individual, philanthropically oriented model of citizenship the emphasis is primarily on developing a recognition of private citizenship obligations performed especially through voluntary service and charitable giving. The social, politically oriented model however is one which argues that private obligations, though important, are not enough to constitute an adequate conception of a genuinely public citizenship. The latter must extend rights and the power to exercise them as well as identify obligations and must embrace political participation as well as good works (cf. Lister, 1990).

The response from the left to right wing advocacy of the philanthropically active citizen has thus been to argue for the virtue of political activity. It has been suggested that philanthropy is necessarily inadequate since 'Altruism . . . is inherently discretionary. We choose the people towards whom we wish to be charitable, and a necessary consequence of that is that some are not chosen' (Plant, 1989). Opposing both the discretionary and therefore discriminatory implications of philanthropic citizenship and Hurd's 'privatised conception of citizenship that intends to whisk away the notion of political community' the left have placed their emphasis on a citizenship which 'embodies a concept of the common good' (Plant, 1988, p. 3) and which embraces ideas of 'civic activity, public spiritedness and political participation in a community of equals' (Mouffe, 1988, pp. 30 and 29). Such a belief in 'equalized opportunities for effective participation in matters to be decided collectively' reflects a particular strand of concern with citizenship which can be found in that brand of ethical socialism associated with Hobhouse, Marshall and Tawney (Dennis and Halsey, 1988, p. 208). However it also represents one element of a broader enthusiasm on the left for political, rather than philanthropic or market based decision making.

Two rather different reasons are to be found for this emphasis on the virtue of politics, which of course stands diametrically in opposition to the distrust of politics which we have encountered amongst the New Right. Rustin (1985, p. 38) argues that 'A preference for political mechanisms over all others should . . . be a signal mark of socialist values' on the grounds that politics 'uniquely equalizes the formal powers of individuals in society, in contrast to the greater inequality of resources which derives from the market or from the claims of technical competence'. Here we see politics as an equalising mechanism: others on the left also stress its developmental function as a means of creating the necessary pre-conditions of socialism. Kitching for example lays stress on the need to 'encourage any and all activities which involve *turning a passive citizenry into an active one* . . . since without it the construction of *democratic* socialism is impossible': such a socialism would require 'a citizenry of the greatest knowledge, sophistication and self-discipline' (Kitching, 1983, pp. 14 and 44; emphasis in original).

Much of the writing on citizenship and local government has tended, if sometimes only implicitly, to focus on the political rather than the philanthropic model of citizenship. The consequences of adopting the political rather than the philanthropic model for example are evident in the discussion by Ranson and Stewart of citizenship and management in the public domain. First, 'just systems of distribution' are needed lest poverty, ignorance and unemployment conspire to 'disable citizens from contributing to the life and quality of the public domain'; and second, citizens need to be seen not solely as individuals 'but also, intrinsically, [as] "individuals as a member of" the public as a political community'. This latter role as a member of the political community in turn requires the development of 'a necessary balance in the institutions of participatory and representative government' which recognises that 'the institutions of participatory democracy must be strengthened' (Ranson and Stewart, 1989, pp. 13,14,16 and 18).

If a participatory citizens' democracy is to be developed in the public domain then it is likely that it is at the local level that experiments need to be undertaken, since for most people the realities of domestic and work commitments make this the most accessible arena in terms of geographical and organisational scale. We have already encountered both the recent efforts made by some local authorities to increase participation by various service users and the moves towards decentralisation designed to make services more accessible and responsive. In a few cases the scale or ambition of such ventures have also reflected political, usually Labour but sometimes Liberal, aspirations to expand representative democracy in a participatory direction.

We have already referred in other contexts to some schemes with modest participatory elements in them. Basildon's area committees for example provide for tenant and community representation alongside the councillors who make up the bulk of the membership. Stirling's version of participation has been of the very active 'hands-on' type combining the traditions of self-help and community development. Other authorities have recently experimented with other arrangements for enhancing greater participation by local residents in the decision making process. Middlesbrough District Council established eleven community councils between 1984 and 1986, each with the right to be consulted by the local authority before decisions are made relating to its area. The community councils hold open meetings chaired by a ward councillor at four to six weekly intervals and are themselves composed partly of elected residents and representatives of local voluntary organisations. Although essentially consultative bodies they each have a very modest four figure budget expendable on items within the council's overall powers and policy.

The London borough of Tower Hamlets, under the influence of Liberal community politics rather than Labour's local socialism, set up seven neighbourhood committees with executive powers in 1986 to replace most of the former borough-wide service committees. The new committees were composed of ward based councillors, which involved the ruling Liberals ceding control to Labour in three neighbourhoods, but were also to be shadowed by consultative arrangements, which vary amongst the neighbourhoods, to provide a grassroots input. Despite the latter element the Tower Hamlets venture has been ambitious mainly in terms of its internal reorganisation in the direction of localised decision making by councillors. Glasgow and Islington by way of contrast provide instances of Labour authorities, the former of a traditional cast, the latter more oriented to the New Left, grappling with the 'development of an urban grassroots democracy' (Duncan, 1990) in the sense of enabling external participants to bring their views to bear on councillors and officers.

In the case of Glasgow the vehicle for such a development has been the system of community councils provided for by the Local Government (Scotland) Act 1973, whose provisions the city council put into effect in 1976–7 rather more eagerly than did some other Scottish authorities. The city now has 104 community councils with a membership that may consist both of those directly elected and those nominated by local organisations: the lower age limit for both voting and membership is sixteen and three per cent of the nearly 2000 community councillors in Glasgow are from this age group, which remains disenfranchised south of the border. The activities of the councils, which are grant aided by the city council, have developed in a number of directions. From an initial concern with establishing or preserving local community identities through galas and festivals they have moved on to such activities as campaigning on local issues in order to influence the city council, the health authority, British Rail and other public bodies, the provision of certain welfare services such as lunch clubs for pensioners, and participation in the city council's eight area management committees. These area bodies, established in 1980, allowed for co-option of community council representatives in 1983, allowing them to join with district and regional councillors in monitoring local service provision, advising the central Policy and Resources Committee on local issues and controlling a six figure area budget for environmental improvements and projects.

Duncan (idem, p. 12) suggests that the involvement of community council representatives 'has made area management [in Glasgow] less prone to the marginalisation suffered by area systems elsewhere in Britain'. He also goes on to argue that

> The main lesson from Glasgow for other urban authorities considering increasing local participation by infusing representative with direct democracy, is that establishing the decision-making structure in itself is insufficient. In order for grassroots or direct democracy to make a substantive contribution to decision-making, and to sustain this input, it is crucial that they have access to a support system, which can provide them with a wide range of services and information (idem, p. 15).

In Glasgow's case the necessary support is provided by a Community Councils Resource Centre funded by the city council and staffed by the University of Strathclyde. The centre provides such facilities or resources as training, a library, stationery, photocopying, information on both substantive local issues (such as planning) and on questions of organisation and procedure and advice on new and proposed legislation.

If Glasgow's democratisation initiative had its origins in the 1970s, that of Islington emerged a decade later, as part of a wider enthusiasm in the 1980s for the decentralisation of council services, especially, though not exclusively, amongst left Labour local authorities. An earlier wave of interest in localised forms of management and service delivery in the 1960s and 1970s, such as the Department of the Environment's trials of area or neighbourhood management schemes in Dudley, Haringey, Kirklees, Liverpool, Newcastle-upon-Tyne and Stockport, stemmed mainly from managerial and professional concerns, particularly in the context of addressing what were seen as the area-specific problems of inner city communities. The more radical decentralisation initiatives of the 1980s by contrast had clear political sources, in Islington's case for example, a Labour manifesto commitment to security the 'effective involvement of the community' in decision making (Islington Labour Party Local Government Committee, 1981, p. 3).

Having decentralised much, though not all, of its service delivery, on the basis of twenty four neighbourhoods, each with its own neighbourhood office, Islington moved in 1986 towards the setting up of neighbourhood forums as the democratisation element in its decentralisation scheme. The forums were given the formal status of advisory committees of the council with terms of reference which included the following: to comment on planning and licensing applications; to draw up programmes for the spending of neighbourhood office budgets; to help integrate the local community; to act as a sounding board for local views; and to operate within an equal opportunities framework. The council produced a model constitution for the forums, though they could develop their own subject to council approval. Membership of the forums was based on election, nomination by local organisations or a mixture of the two. In practice two forums opted for an elected body, six for representation from organisations and the remaining sixteen for a mixture of the two mechanisms. Whatever the mode chosen the approved constitutions required a minimum of two places on each forum to be reserved for each of five normally under-represented sections of the community – people under 21, elderly people, disabled people, women with caring responsibilities and people from ethnic minorities.

The experience of the neighbourhood forums in operation was the subject of a comprehensive review carried out by the council in

1989 which identified a number of problems that had arisen as the forums were established and set to work. It may be of more than coincidental interest that some of these problems were similar to those identified by Glasgow community council representatives at a conference that took place whilst the Islington review was under way (Islington London Borough Council, 1989; University of Strathclyde and City of Glasgow, 1989). Both the Islington review and the Glasgow conference regarded their respective initiatives as fundamentally worthwhile but they did identify some key problems to be addressed.

The Islington review found that councillors who are forum members were thought to be ambivalent about the forums, with frequent complaints 'that councillors arrive late for forum meetings or leave early or do not attend at all' and that they had conflicting loyalties 'to the departments and committees they have a lead role in and to their political party' (para. 13.6). Community councillors in Glasgow complained similarly of 'councillors flitting in and out' of area management committee meetings and of district councillors giving priority to their own policy preferences: 'political pressures [were] taking precedence over the needs of the communities' so that 'if then decisions were made that did not suit the elected members, these decisions were overturned at later meetings' (pp. 16, 4 and 7). There were problems too with departments and their officers: in Islington there was a 'clear feeling' among forum members that some central departments and even some neighbourhood officers 'are not interested in forums and see them as irrelevant' whilst there was a 'lack of accountability of officers to forums' leading to 'buck-passing, letters being ignored, responses being delayed . . . and the absence of information' (paras. 9.3 and 13.3). The latter concerns found an echo at the Glasgow conference: 'There is a widespread problem over the failure of departments of both District and Regional Councils to acknowledge, let alone reply to, requests for information from community councils' (p. 3). In Islington there was concern over confusion arising from 'parallel consultation' on housing issues with the neighbourhood forums and the separate tenant liaison forums (para. 9.8): the Glasgow conference likewise heard regrets that the city council 'consults solely with the Glasgow Council of Tenants' Associations, ignoring the right of community councils' and a call that steps be taken 'to involve community councils in these deliberations' (p. 4).

Both in Islington and in Glasgow there was a desire to see more contested elections, which had so far been 'geared to encourage people to stand rather than resolving competition for places' (para. 17.1); it was felt that 'contested elections would improve the standing of the community council both within its own area and in the eyes of the local authority' (p. 10). There was also a concern over the issue of true representativeness. At the Glasgow conference the question was raised as to how far voting could produce a 'fully representative' community council 'for every age/area/ employment type' (p. 12). The Islington review found that despite the special provision for under represented sections of the community the forums were still not fully representative of these sections, especially the under 21s and the Afro-Caribbeans: progress had certainly been made but there was still some way to go in achieving proper representation (para. 20.3).

One issue which the Islington review referred to almost in passing and which the Glasgow conference did not take up was the possibility that' Only a limited number of people are attracted to the idea of spending their evenings discussing council/community affairs' (para. 20.5). This topic was examined by Khan in his study of neighbourhood forums in Islington and Sheffield: he was led to conclude that 'forums consist largely of activists', that is to say those who were already members of one or more other organisations as well as the forum. In Islington 60 per cent of respondents to a survey of forum members were also members of another local organisation and 40 per cent were members of a national organisation: tenants' associations, trades unions and political parties loomed large amongst these involvements. Such activists were not themselves a cross section of the local population since they came from 'the more settled and secure elements of the community'; moreover 'being experienced in the running of meetings, they can exclude the inexperienced from fully participating in meetings' in the absence of 'effort put into trying to help new and inexperienced participants' (Khan, 1989, pp. 15 and 17).

The possible domination of neighbourhood forums and similar bodies by activists calls up a fundamental debate concerning the notion of the participating citizen. It relates to a far more basic issue than questions of the relations between forums and politicians or parties or departments, or of the best electoral or representative procedures. The debate is centred around the belief which one element of the New Left in 1960s America encapsulated in the slogan: 'Freedom is an endless meeting' (quoted in Miller, J., 1987, p. 215): to which came the riposte that:

A very precious part of human freedom is *not* to make decisions. What would life be like if it were necessary to attend a meeting every day to decide at which hour the street lights should go on [or] on which side [cars] . . . would pass each other? (Moore, 1972, p. 69).

This issue was addressed by Michael Walzer in his essay *A Day in the Life of a Socialist Citizen*, where he observed that 'self-government is a very demanding and time-consuming business . . . and when the organs of government are decentralised so as to maximise participation, it will inevitably become more demanding still'. The problem that this presents is not only that some people fail to participate because of their inability to do so, because they are 'afraid, uneducated, lacking confidence and skills'. There are also those who fail to participate because of their inclination to do other things with their time, to 'take long walks, play with their children, paint pictures, make love and watch television'. The inabilities can be overcome perhaps by various measures of encouragement and support; but it remains debatable how far non-participatory inclinations can be legitimately challenged or discounted. If the equal worth of all human beings is assumed then the interests of both participants and non-participants need to be protected.

The alternative is 'the sharing of power among the activists . . . the rule of the people with the most evenings to spare' (Walzer, 1980, pp. 130,136,133 and 134). Of course it may be true that although for most people the practice of participatory citizenship 'may not be a natural one for human beings, in the sense that they would not spontaneously engage in it . . . it is not thereby inconsistent with what their nature can become' (Oldfield, 1990, p. 187). Meanwhile however, it may be necessary to recognise that whereas activists 'represent themselves . . . the others must *be represented* . . . participatory democracy has to be paralleled by representative democracy' (Walzer, 1980, p. 136; emphasis in original).

The need for Walzer's cautionary note may seem rather remote from the very modest efforts to introduce elements of participatory democracy into local authorities, though even there, as we have seen, the presence of the activist has already been identified. However, as we are reminded by J. Miller (1987, p. 95) in his account of the origins of pressures for participatory democracy in the 1960s, it was seen by its early advocates as 'an essential complement to representative institutions. It did not replace them'. In practice that seems the likely outcome of attempts to build a new model of local government around the concept of the participating citizen.

An enabling politics?

At the start of this chapter we referred to Hambleton and Hoggett's identification of three coherent reform strategies within local government. These three strategies were based on differing modes of provision, one market-based and privatised, one responsive to individual public sector consumers and one based on a collectivist and democratised public sector. We then went on to discuss three possible models of local government built around the roles of members of the public as local shareholders, as local consumers and as local citizens. These three roles we may see as active replacements for the traditional and more passive roles of rate-payer, client and voter and as having respectively a protective, an instrumental and a developmental character.

The three modes of provision and the models based upon the three active roles would appear to match one another quite closely. This correspondence allows us to see the local shareholder as being the key public role under a marketised and privatised mode of provision; similarly the local consumer has the key role under the individual consumer responsive mode and the local citizen has the key role under the collectivist democratic mode. All these various relationships are portrayed in diagrammatic form in Table 1, which also attempts to link these relationships with the most appropriate types of initiatives and thus to suggest how the recent conceptual and operational reappraisals within local government might correspond with one another.

TABLE 1   Three models of change

1 Traditional passive roles	2 New active roles	3 Character of active roles	4 Mode of provision	5 Nature of related initiatives
Ratepayer	Shareholder	Protective	Market based and privatised	Municipal pluralism with a private sector leading edge
Client	Consumer	Instrumental	Individual consumer responsive	Informative and consultative
Voter	Citizen	Developmental	Democratic and collectivist	Participative and consultative

Whatever model is adopted in the case of any given local authority its adoption is likely to be advocated and justified largely on the grounds that it will ultimately benefit the public, however defined. Such claims raise two major questions about the actual nature of such beneficiaries. The first concerns the extent to which the introduction of such models may also serve to benefit certain service providers as well as service users. To introduce elements of these models into existing organisations inevitably entails a degree of turbulence and chaos. Indeed followers of Tom Peters have often relished the title as well as the contents of his 1987 book *Thriving on Chaos: Handbook for a Management Revolution*. Introducing new models of provision can well provide an opportunity, indeed a need, to promote a more widespread reform, if not revolution, in the internal management of the authority.

Such a venture can provide the occasion for attempts at redefining the roles, for example, of councillors and of officers. Thus in Tower Hamlets the move towards a radical decentralisation of service delivery and decision making to the neighbourhood level within the authority was based on the principle of 'active councillors', able to focus on the communities that elected them and to get things done in that arena rather than dissipating their energies across the borough. The intention was to empower councillors more effectively, as well as to make them more accountable to their public (Lowndes, 1990).

Clearly however other strategies could be devised in the name of more efficient and responsive management which in effect narrowed the role of councillors by redefining their functions to those dealing with broad strategy and performance monitoring whilst 'allowing the managers to manage'. Indeed given a full programme of market research and opinion polling and with better face-to-face relations between council staff and service users the two latter groups could in some scenarios emerge as the key actors, with the councillors' intermediary role dwindling away into superfluity: the demands in some quarters for fewer (and better) councillors perhaps echoes this possibility. Certainly the arguments of the Audit Commission in their paper *We Can't Go On Meeting Like This* (1990) gave distinct support to such efforts to redefine the role of the councillor, though with little evidence that councillors themselves actually wanted to see their role redefined in the strategic and monitoring directions being suggested.

Whether or not councillors' roles are re-defined as a by-product of new initiatives there is clearly also scope for the development of new careers for officers implicit in the implementation of some of these initiatives. Public relations, marketing, contract management and quality control are all obvious examples. The increasing importance attached to managerial skills as a tool for implementing new initiatives may also widen the aspirations of those professional officers who acquire them, more of whom may come to see themselves as potential chief executives or as capable of employment in a wider range of posts than in local government alone.

For senior officers the particular prospects of municipal pluralism might also offer the opportunity for some 'bureau-shaping'. Thus Dunleavy argues that the contracting out of service provision to private firms or voluntary groups may allow senior officers to ensure their continued functioning 'in small, elite and centrally placed staff agencies . . . not in large budget but routine, troublesome and conflict-prone line agencies'. So long as there is a policy level role to perform at the top

> why should a Director of Technical Services in a local authority care if refuse collection is privatized, thereby removing the need for her to manage some of the best-organized and most militant public service workers as well as listening to endless debates amongst councillors on the timing of refuse collection runs? (Dunleavy, 1986, pp. 20–1).

From that perspective contracting out offers the opportunity to senior officers of 'advancing their class (and frequently gender) interests against those of rank and file state workers and service consumers' (ibid., p. 30). If there are indeed new careers to be made or more agreeable elite agencies to be created then one further question which arises is whether we may not then begin to witness the triumph of Laffin's techno-bureaucrats over the frontline public service professionals, thereby creating a very different organisational culture from one dominated by those engaged in regular service delivery to the public.

Dunleavy's reference above to class and gender interests has a relevance beyond that of characterising the nature of senior local government officers. It can be related also to our second major question about the nature of the beneficiaries of new initiatives in local government, namely the question of the relationship between individual roles and social groups. As we have seen, much of the recent discussion of local government's dealings with the public has focused on devising appropriate responses to a public defined in terms of particular roles. This certainly helps to clarify such discussions and to concentrate local authority efforts more clearly on how to relate to their public. Nonetheless a pre-occupation with individual roles, whilst an advance on the notion of some vague general public, does have one major drawback, which is that identified by Bottomore (1975, pp. 114–15):

> the emphasis on individual actors enacting roles . . . tends to produce an excessively individualistic conception of social behaviour, in which society is viewed as an aggregate of individuals related only through the complex role system of the society as a whole, while the social groups within the society are

neglected . . . and the relations of competition and conflict between them receive little attention.

As we saw in our opening chapter, local government's reappraisal of its public has involved a recognition of the importance both of social groups and of individual roles. It is perhaps true however that whereas a concern for social groups and for issues of equity between groups was a particular feature of the 1970s and early 1980s, in more recent times that concern has been overtaken, though by no means wholly displaced, by a preoccupation with the treatment received by individuals, in their various roles, at the hands of local government. Thus the merging of race and women's committees and of their respective support units in some authorities has been seen as indicative of their reduced status since the late 1980s (Hill, 1989). An interest in substantive outcomes for particular social groups has receded, though again not vanished, in the face of a new interest in the procedural experience of individuals.

Such a concern for individuals could be altruistic but it could also have certain attractions for those in positions of power in local authorities if it had the effect of somehow delegitimating the political claims of social groups. The public confined to individual roles may be easier to handle than the public as actual or potential groups making organised demands and intruding as a political force into the policy making process. No doubt it was such a possibility which attracted Mirabeau when, at the time of the French Revolution, he advised Louis XVI that 'The idea of creating a single class of citizens would have pleased Richelieu: so smooth a surface must ease the exercise of power' (quoted in Avril, 1969, p. 130). The public acting as private individuals, rather than as organised groups, may be less threatening to established centres of power, even if they do require the expenditure of extra time and effort to respond to their demands.

The deliberate 'construction' of the public as individuals may also make them more amenable to managerial rather than to political treatment. If the early and middle 1980s saw the assertion of political priorities in local government, arising out of the demands of social groups, perhaps since the late 1980s we have been witnessing the reassertion of managerial priorities couched in terms of a response to the public as individuals, a response which might be described as a form of managerial individualism. It would nevertheless obviously be wrong to discount the importance of individuals and their experience, since in the last analysis it is people as individuals who actually experience satisfaction, frustration or disappointment in their dealings with local government and who have to live within the consequences of those dealings. However, a concentration on individuals and their roles at the expense of social groups risks overlooking two significant problems.

The first such problem is that identified by Lustgarten and by Young in the context of equal opportunities policy. Thus Lustgarten (1989, p. 18) argues that not only is discrimination 'both a major element and a continuing long-term cause of disadvantage' but that the essence of discrimination is that someone 'is ill-treated or shares some social circumstances, because of his involuntary membership of a group'. Similarly, Young (1989, p. 108) sees debates about disadvantage as being based on 'the relative distribution between groups of valued attributes' with a consequent need 'to consider the individual's life-chances and deserts in a group context'. In the context of local authority policy making, recognition of the relevance of such a group perspective can sometimes be affected by 'the disjuncture between group conceptions of equality on which equal opportunity policies are based and the individualistic terms in which rights are commonly construed' (idem, p. 107). To translate this general point into the more specific terms used previously in this book, local authorities in concentrating on the procedural rights of individuals in their roles as local citizens, consumers or shareholders might be in danger of overlooking the substantive disadvantages experienced by members of social groups defined by class, race, gender, age, disability or sexual orientation.

Moreover, and this is our second problem, the ability to perform effectively the active individual roles of citizen, consumer or shareholder may be significantly affected by membership of a disadvantaged social group. Thus Lister (1990, p. 2) argues that

> the meaning of citizenship rights and obligations cannot be understood in isolation from the inequalities of power, status and resources (reflecting the dimensions of gender, race and disability as well as social class) that structure them.

One corollary of a concern with such inequalities would be a belief that

> if we are going to have universal citizenship, in a political sense, for our society, then . . . we should set about the task of giving [people] the economic security which . . . is the necessary pre-condition for good citizenship (King and Waldron, 1988, p. 431).

Now it may well be beyond the capacity of local government to make major advances towards economic security for all. Nevertheless it may still be possible for local authorities to supply some elements of an 'infrastructure for citizenship' which would facilitate the playing of 'a full and active role in the public political community' (Lister, 1990, p. 46).

In previous chapters we have encountered various instances, in Newham, in Sheffield, in Glasgow, in Stirling and in Greenwich for example and in the case of school governors under LMS, where there has been recognition of the need to facilitate public involvement with training and support rather than simply expect it to happen. Ventures of this type have been commended by the Association of Metropolitan Authorities (1989, pp. 20 and 15) which has urged the importance of 'enabling people to achieve things for themselves – through suggestion, education, organisation-building and providing information and advice' and suggested that 'such an enabling orientation should become part of the culture of local government as a whole'.

Such an enabling orientation differs from the enabling model associated with Nicholas Ridley's 'enabling not providing' formula, which focuses rather narrowly on a council's role in enabling services to be supplied from other sources rather than providing them itself. It also differs from a second model canvassed by Clarke and Stewart. They argue for a broader enabling role defined not in relation to service provision but in terms of 'enabling the community to meet the needs, opportunities and problems faced in the most effective way' (Clarke and Stewart, 1989, p. 1) as a form of community government based on a power of general competence rather than one confined to service delivery.

A third model, that of a local authority with an enabling role as a support service, training agency and resource centre for potentially active citizens – or indeed consumers or shareholders – could of course complement the idea of groups of such people taking an increasing share of local service delivery, as in Ridley's first narrow model of the enabling council. It could also facilitate the identification and articulation of local 'needs, opportunities and problems' as envisaged in Clarke and Stewart's second, broader enabling model of community government. This third enabling model might thus be regarded not as a 'broad' or a 'narrow' version but perhaps one taking a 'deeper' view, addressing itself to the grass roots of politics as much as to service provision and community government. Its aim would be to offer such assistance and encouragement as might be necessary to enable those who might otherwise be prevented from doing so to play whatever active role they wished in the local 'public political community'. In that sense local government would be involved in the creation of an enabling politics within which questions both of the procedural rights of individuals and of the substantive outcomes for social groups could be publicly addressed.

Bibliography

ABRAMS, P., ABRAMS, S., HUMPHREY, R. and SNAITH, R. (1989) *Neighbourhood Care and Social Policy* (London: HMSO).

ADAM SMITH INSTITUTE (1983) *The Omega File: Local Government Policy* (London: Adam Smith Institute).

ADAM SMITH INSTITUTE (1985) *Contracting the Council Empires* (London: Adam Smith Institute).

ADAM SMITH INSTITUTE (1989) *Wiser Counsels: The Reform of Local Government* (London: Adam Smith Institute).

ALLEN, R. (1988) 'Local Authority Publicity: Advice', Local Government Information Unit *Briefing* no. 25, pp. i–v.

ALLISON, L. (1986) 'Spirit of the Eighties', *New Society*, 25 April, p. 24.

ALMOND, G. and VERBA, S. (1963) *The Civic Culture: Political Attitudes and Democracy in Five Nations* (Princeton University Press).

ALTY, R. and DARKE, R. (1987) 'A City Centre for People: Involving the Community in Planning for Sheffield's Central Area', *Planning Practice and Research*, no. 3, pp. 7–12.

AMBROSE, P. (1986) *Whatever Happened to Planning?* (London: Methuen).

ARENDT, H. (1979) 'On Hannah Arendt', in M. A. Hill (ed.) *Hannah Arendt: The Recovery of the Public World* (New York: St. Martin's Press) pp. 301–39.

ARNOLD, P. and COLE, I. (1987) 'The Decentralisation of Local Services: Rhetoric and Reality', in P. Hoggett and R. Hambleton (eds) *Decentralisation and Democracy*, Occasional Paper 28, School for Advanced Urban Studies, University of Bristol, pp. 133–55.

ARNSTEIN, S. (1971) 'A ladder of citizen participation in the USA', *Journal of the Royal Town Planning Institute*, vol. 57, no. 4, pp. 176–82.

ARUN DISTRICT COUNCIL (1987a) *Strategy Papers 1987–1991* (Littlehampton: Arun District Council).

ARUN DISTRICT COUNCIL (1987b) *Programme Plans 1987–1991: Housing and Community Care Programme Plan* (Littlehampton: Arun District Council).

ARUN DISTRICT COUNCIL (1987c) *Working for the Public: An Action Plan for Getting Closer to the Customer* (Littlehampton: Arun District Council).

ARUN DISTRICT COUNCIL (1988) *Four Year Strategy*, a position statement from the retiring Chief Executive, December 1988.

ASCHER, K. (1987) *The Politics of Privatisation* (London: Macmillan).

ASSOCIATION OF METROPOLITAN AUTHORITIES (1989) *Community Development: the Local Authority Role* (London: Association of Metropolitan Authorities).

AUDIT COMMISSION (1988) *The Competitive Council*, Management Paper No. 1 (London: HMSO).

AUDIT COMMISSION (1989) *Preparing for Compulsory Competition*, Occasional Paper No. 7 (London: HMSO).

AUDIT COMMISSION (1990) *We Can't Go On Meeting Like This: The Changing Role of Local Authority Members*, Management Paper No. 8 (London: HMSO).

AUDIT COMMISSION, LOCAL GOVERNMENT TRAINING BOARD AND INSTITUTE FOR LOCAL GOVERNMENT STUDIES (1985) *Good management in local government* (Luton: Local Government Training Board).

AVRIL, P. (1969) *Politics in France* (Harmondsworth: Penguin).

BACON, W. (1978) *Public Accountability and the Schooling System* (London: Harper and Row).

BAINE, S. (1975) *Community Action and Local Government*, Occasional Papers on Social Administration No. 59 (London School of Economics).

BALL, M. (1989) 'Trade and Industry', in M. Ball, F. Gray and L. McDowell, *The Transformation of Britain* (London: Fontana) pp. 71–95.

BAMFORD, T. (1990) *The Future of Social Work* (London: Macmillan).

BARBER, B.R. (1984) *Strong Democracy: Participatory Politics for a New Age* (Berkeley: University of California Press).

BARCLAY, P. M. (1982) *Social Workers: Their Role and Tasks* (London: Bedford Square Press).

BARNES, J. (1988) 'The Social Service Inspectorate's Work on Using Social Services', in I. Allen (ed.) *Hearing the Voice of the Consumer* (London: Policy Studies Institute) pp. 29–36.

BARRY, N. (1987) *The New Right* (London: Croom Helm).

BARTRAM, M. (1988) *Consulting Tenants: Council Initiatives in the late 1980s* (London: Community Rights Project).

BEER, S.H. (1982) *Britain Against Itself: The Political Contradictions of Collectivism* (London: Faber and Faber).

BENJAMIN, R.W. (1977) 'Local Government in Postindustrial Britain: Studies of the British Royal Commission on Local Government', in V. Ostrom and F. P. Bish (eds) *Comparing Urban Service Delivery Systems* (Beverly Hills: Sage) pp. 149–72.

BEN-TOVIM, G., GABRIEL, J., LAW, I. and STREDDER, K. (1986) *The Local Politics of Race* (London: Macmillan).

BENTWICH, H. (1962) *Our Councils: The Story of Local Government* (London: Routledge and Kegan Paul).

BERESFORD, PAUL (1987) *'Good Council Guide': Wandsworth 1978–87* (London: Centre for Policy Studies).

BERESFORD, PETER (1988) 'Consumer Views: Data Collection or Democracy', in I. Allen (ed.) *Hearing the Voice of the Consumer* (London: Policy Studies Institute) pp. 37–51.

BEST, J. and BOWSER, L. (1986) 'A People's Plan for Central Newham', *The Planner*, November 1986, pp. 21–5.

BEVERIDGE, LORD (1948) *Voluntary Action* (London: Allen and Unwin).

BHADURI, R. (1988) 'Race and Culture: the "invisible" Consumer', in I. Allen (ed.) *Hearing the Voice of the Consumer* (London: Policy Studies Institute) pp. 21–7.

BIRCHALL, J. (1988) *Building Communities the Cooperative Way* (London: Routledge and Kegan Paul).

BIRKINSHAW, P. (1985) *Grievances, Remedies and the State* (London: Sweet and Maxwell).

BIRKINSHAW, P. (1987) 'Consumers and Ratepayers', in M. Parkinson (ed.) *Reshaping Local Government* (Oxford: Policy Journals) pp. 154–64.

BLAU, P.M. and SCOTT, W.R. (1963) *Formal Organizations: A Comparative Approach* (London: Routledge and Kegan Paul).

BLUNKETT, D. and GREEN, G. (1984) *Building from the Bottom* (London: Fabian Society).

BLUNKETT, D. and JACKSON, K. (1987) *Democracy in Crisis: The Town Halls Respond* (London: The Hogarth Press).

BOADEN, N., GOLDSMITH, M., HAMPTON, W. and STRINGER, P. (1982) *Public Participation in Local Services* (London: Longman).

BOGDANOR, V., GRANT, M., HEPWORTH, N., HODGSON, R., TRAVERS, T. and WENDT, R. (1990) *Enhancing Local Government*, a discussion paper, published by the authors.

BOTTOMORE, T.B. (1975) *Sociology: a Guide to Problems and Literature* (London: Allen and Unwin).

BRADFORD CITY COUNCIL (1988) *Report of the Director of Employment and Environment Services to the Policy and Resources Committee*, 5 December 1988.

BRADFORD CITY COUNCIL (1989) *A Model for the 1990s*, a policy document approved by the Council on 18 July 1989.

BRAINTREE DISTRICT COUNCIL (1987) *Public Service Orientation: The Action Plan* (Braintree: Braintree District Council).

BRIGGS, A. (1968) *Victorian Cities* (Harmondsworth: Penguin).

BRISTOW, S.R. (1982) 'Rates and Votes – The 1980 District Council Elections', *Policy and Politics*, vol. 10, no. 2, pp. 163–80.

BRITTAN, S. (1976) 'The economic contradictions of democracy', in A. King (ed.) *Why is Britain becoming harder to govern?* (London: BBC Publications) pp. 96–137.

BROWN, A.F.J. (1980) *Colchester 1815–1914* (Chelmsford: Essex Record Office).

BROWNILL, S. (1987) *The Politics of Local Change: A Case Study of the People's Plan for Newham's Docklands*, unpublished Ph.D. Thesis, University of Birmingham.

BROWNILL, S. (1988) 'The People's Plan for the Royal Docks: Some Contradictions in Popular Planning', *Planning Practice and Research*, no. 4, pp. 15–21.

BUCKINGHAMSHIRE COUNTY COUNCIL (1989) *Complaints: A Review of the Procedure for Handling Complaints* (Aylesbury: Buckingamshire County Council).

BUDGE, I., BRAND, J.A., MARGOLIS, M. and SMITH, A.L.M. (1972) *Political Stratification and Democracy* (London: Macmillan).

BULLER, H. and LOWE, P. (1982) 'Politics and Class in rural preservation: a study of the Suffolk Preservation Society', in M.J. Moseley (ed.) *Power, Planning and People in Rural East Anglia* (Norwich: Centre of East Anglian Studies, University of East Anglia) pp. 21–41.

BULMER, M. (1989) 'Introduction' to Part IV in M. Bulmer, J. Lewis and D. Piachaud (eds) *The Goals of Social Policy* (London: Unwin Hyman) pp. 189–98.

BURGESS, T. (1986) 'Cambridgeshire's Financial Management Initiative for Schools', *Public Money*, June 1986, pp. 21–4.

BUTLER, E., PIRIE, M. and YOUNG, P. (1985) *The Omega File: A Comprehensive Review of Government Functions* (London: Adam Smith Institute).

BUTTON, S. (1984) *Women's Committees*, Working Paper 45, School for Advanced Urban Studies, University of Bristol.

CASTELLS, M. (1977) *The Urban Question* (London: Edward Arnold).

CASTELLS, M. (1983) *The City and the Grassroots* (London: Edward Arnold).

CAVE, E. (1989) 'Consumerism in Education', *Public Money and Management*, vol. 9, no. 1, pp. 29–33.

CHESHIRE COUNTY COUNCIL (1987) *Service Attitude Survey* (Chester: Cheshire County Council).

CLAPHAM, D. (1990) 'Housing', in N. Deakin and A. Wright (eds) *Consuming Public Services* (London: Routledge) pp. 56–82.

CLARKE, C. and GRIFFITHS, D. (1982) *Labour and Mass Politics* (London: Labour Co-ordinating Committee).

CLARKE, M. and STEWART, J. (1985) *Local Government and the Public Service Orientation: or does a public service provide for the public?*, Local Government and Public Services Working Paper no. 1 (Luton: Local Government Training Board).

CLARKE, M. and STEWART, J. (1986) *The Public Service Orientation: Issues and Dilemmas to be faced*, Local Government and Public Services Working Paper no. 4 (Luton: Local Government Training Board).

CLARKE, M. and STEWART, J. (1989) *Challenging Old Assumptions: the enabling Council takes shape* (Luton: Local Government Training Board).

CLARKE, M. and STEWART, J. (1990) *Developing Effective Public Service Management* (Luton: Local Government Training Board).

CLAY, M. (1985) *Liberals and Community* (Hebden Bridge: Hebden Royd Publications).

CLEMENTS, R. (1969) *Local Notables and the City Council* (London: Macmillan).

CLIPSOM, A. (1987) 'Bradford's: "Open Government" Experience', in R.A. Chapman and M. Hunt (eds) *Open Government* (London: Croom Helm) pp. 123–33.

COCHRANE, A. and ANDERSON, J. (eds) (1989) *Politics in Transition* (London: Sage).

COLE, I. (1987) 'The Delivery of Housing Services', in P. Willmott (ed.)

Local Government Decentralisation and Community (London: Policy Studies Institute) pp. 37–48.

COMMUNITY DEVELOPMENT PROJECT (1977) *The Costs of Industrial Change* (London: Inter-Project Editorial Team).

COMMUNITY RIGHTS PROJECT (1986a) *In Decisions 2: Tenant Participation in Housing* (London: Community Rights Project and Community Advisory Group).

COMMUNITY RIGHTS PROJECT (1986b) *Public Involvement in Council/ Committee Meetings* (London: Community Rights Project).

CONSUMERS' ASSOCIATION (1989) 'Town Hall Ratings', *Which?*, March, pp. 130–2.

COUSINS, P. (1982) 'Quasi-Official Bodies in Local Government', in A. Barker (ed.) *Quangos in Britain* (London: Macmillan) pp. 152–63.

COX, W.H. and LAVER, M. (1979) 'Local and National Voting in British Elections: Lessons from the Synchro-polls of 1979', *Parliamentary Affairs*, vol. XXXII, no. 4, pp. 383–93.

CROUCH, S. (1986) 'Marketing Can Improve Your Economic Health – The Portsmouth Experience', *Local Government Policy Making*, June 1986, pp. 75–9.

DALLEY, G. (1988) *Ideologies of Caring: Rethinking Community and Collectivism* (London: Macmillan).

DAY, P. and KLEIN, R. (1987) *Accountabilities: five public services* (London: Tavistock).

DEAKIN, N. and WRIGHT, A. (1990) 'Introduction', in N. Deakin and A. Wright (eds) *Consuming Public Services* (London: Routledge) pp. 1–16.

DEARLOVE, J. (1973) *The Politics of Policy in Local Government* (Cambridge University Press).

DENNIS, N. (1970) *People and Planning* (London: Faber and Faber).

DEARLOVE, J. (1979) *The reorganisation of British local government* (Cambridge University Press).

DENNIS, N. and HALSEY, A.H. (1988) *English Ethical Socialism* (Oxford University Press).

DEPARTMENT OF HEALTH (1979) *Caring for People* (London: HMSO).

DEPARTMENT OF THE ENVIRONMENT (1981) *Ministerial Guidelines on Inner City Programmes* (London: HMSO).

DEPARTMENT OF THE ENVIRONMENT (1986) *Paying for local government* (London: HMSO).

DEPARTMENT OF THE ENVIRONMENT (1989) *Tenants in the lead: the Housing Cooperatives Review* (London: HMSO).

DOWSON, S. (1989) 'Innovation and Advocacy: A Vision for the Future', in NCVO *Should Voluntary Organisations Provide More Services?*, Contracts for Care Conference Report no. 2 (London: NCVO) pp. 8–11.

DUBS, A. (1990) *The voluntary sector – what should Labour's approach be?*, background paper for Labour Party local government conference (London: Labour Party).

DUNCAN, S. and GOODWIN, M. (1988) *The Local State and Uneven Development* (Cambridge: Polity Press).

DUNCAN, T. (1990) 'Community Councils in Glasgow – The Development of an Urban Grassroots Democracy', *Local Government Studies*, vol. 16, no. 2, pp. 8–16.

DUNLEAVY, P. (1980) *Urban Political Analysis* (London: Macmillan).

DUNLEAVY, P. (1981) *The Politics of Mass Housing in Britain, 1945–1975* (Oxford University Press).

DUNLEAVY, P. (1986) 'Explaining the Privatization Boom: Public Choice Versus Radical Approaches', *Public Administration*, vol. 64, no. 1, pp. 13–34.

DUNLEAVY, P. (1989) 'The end of class politics?', in A. Cochrane and J. Anderson (eds) *Politics in Transition* (London: Sage) pp. 172–210.

DUTTA, R. and TAYLOR, G. (1989) *Housing Equality: an action guide* (London: CHAR).

DWELLY, T. (1989) 'Better the devil you know', *New Statesman and Society*, 13 January 1989.

DYER, J. (1988) 'Voting on the Buses', *Local Government Administrator*, October 1988, pp. v-vi.

EALES, K. (1990) 'Preparing for the new decade', *Local Government Administrator*, February 1990, pp. vii-ix.

EAST DORSET DISTRICT COUNCIL (1989) *Statement of Management Priorities* (Wimborne: East Dorset District Council).

EDWARDS, J. (1988) 'Local Government Women's Committees', *Local Government Studies*, vol. 14, no. 4, pp. 39–52.

ELKIN, S. (1974) *Politics and Land Use Planning* (Cambridge University Press).

ENTEZARI, M. (1988) *Funding the Voluntary Sector in London* (London: London Voluntary Service Council).

ESSEX COUNTY COUNCIL (1989) *Meals on Wheels in Essex* (Chelmsford: Essex County Council).

ESSEX COUNTY COUNCIL (1990a) *Minutes of the Policy and Resources Subcommittee of the Social Services Committee*, 7 March 1990.

ESSEX COUNTY COUNCIL (1990b) *The Essex County Council Action Plan* (Chelmsford: Essex County Council).

EVANS, S. M. and BOYTE, H. C. (1986) *Free Spaces: The Sources of Democratic Change in America* (New York: Harper and Row).

FAGENCE, M. (1977) *Citizen Participation in Planning* (Oxford: Pergamon Press).

FENWICK, J. (1989) 'Consumerism and Local Government', *Local Government Studies*, vol. 16, no. 1, pp. 45–52.

FINCH, J. (1984) 'The Deceit of Self-Help: Pre-school Playgroups and Working Class Mothers', *Journal of Social Policy*, vol. 13, no. 1, pp. 1–20.

FINCH, J. and GROVES, D. (1980) 'Community Care and the Family: A case for Equal Opportunities?', *Journal of Social Policy*, vol. 9, no. 4, pp. 487–511.

FINER, H. (1933) *English Local Government* (London: Methuen).

FORSYTH, M. (n.d.) *Re-servicing Britain* (London: Adam Smith Institute).

FRANKLIN, B. (1988a) *Public Relations Activities in Local Government: a Research Report* (Croydon: Charles Knight Publishing).

FRANKLIN, B. (1988b) *Civic Free Newspapers: Propaganda on the Rates?*, paper presented to the Political Studies Association annual conference, April 1988, at Plymouth Polytechnic.

FRASER, D. (1979) *Power and Authority in the Victorian City* (Oxford: Basil Blackwell).

FREEMAN, J. (1983) 'Introduction' in J. Freeman (ed.) *Social Movements of the Sixties and Seventies* (New York: Longman) pp. 1–5.

GAME, C. (1981) 'Local Elections', *Local Government Studies*, vol. 7, March–April, pp. 63–8.

GARVIN, J. L. (1932) *The Life of Joseph Chamberlain, Volume One 1836–1885* (London: Macmillan).

GAY, P. and YOUNG, K. (1988) *Community Relations Councils* (London: Policy Studies Institute).

GERTH, H. H. and MILLS, C. W. (1969) *Character and Social Structure* (London: Routledge and Kegan Paul).

GLASSBERG, A. (1981) *Representation and Urban Community* (London: Macmillan).

GOODWIN, M. (1989) 'The Politics of Locality', in A. Cochrane and J. Anderson (eds) *Politics in Transition* (London: Sage) pp. 141–71.

GOSS, S. (1984) 'Women's initiatives in local government', in M. Boddy and C. Fudge (eds) *Local Socialism?* (London: Macmillan) pp. 109–32.

GOSS, S. (1988) *Local Labour and Local Government* (Edinburgh University Press).

GOWER DAVIES, J. (1972) *The Evangelistic Bureaucrat* (London: Tavistock).

GRANT, W. (1983) *Chambers of Commerce in the UK System of Business Interest Representation*, Working Paper No. 32, Department of Politics, University of Warwick.

GREGOR, A. (1990) 'Advocacy at planning committees', letter in *The Planner*, 28 September 1990.

GRICE, A. (1989) 'Council Chiefs learn to put the public first', *Sunday Times*, 19 March 1989.

GRIFFITHS, SIR R. (1988) *Community Care: Agenda for Action* (London: HMSO).

GUTCH, R. and YOUNG, K. (1988) *Partners or rivals? Developing the relationship between voluntary organisations and local government* (Luton: Local Government Training Board).

GUTTRIDGE, P. (1987) 'Public Relations: a mistrusted profession', *Local Government Chronicle*, 2 October, p. 20.

GYFORD, J. (1984) *Local Politics in Britain* (London: Croom Helm).

GYFORD, J. (1985a) 'The Politicization of Local Government', in M. Loughlin, M. D. Gelfand and K. Young (eds) *Half a Century of Municipal Decline 1935–1985* (London: Allen and Unwin) pp. 77–97.

GYFORD, J. (1985b) *The Politics of Local Socialism* (London: Allen and Unwin).

GYFORD, J. (1988) 'A Councillor's Case-work', *Local Government Studies*, vol. 14, no. 3, pp. 9–12.

GYFORD, J. and JAMES, M. (1983) *National Parties and Local Politics* (London: Allen and Unwin).

GYFORD, J., LEACH, S. and GAME, C. (1989) *The Changing Politics of Local Government* (London: Unwin Hyman).

HACKNEY LONDON BOROUGH COUNCIL (1988) *Working Together* (Hackney: Hackney London Borough Council).

HADFIELD, E.C.R. and MACCOLL, J. (1949) *British Local Government* (London: Hutchinson).

HADLEY, R. and HATCH, S. (1981) *Social Welfare and the Failure of the State* (London: Allen and Unwin).

HAGUE, B. (1989) *Local Authorities and a Public Service Orientation: Ideas into Action*, Local Authority Management Unit Discussion Paper 89/3 (Newcastle upon Tyne: Newcastle-upon-Tyne Polytechnic).

HAGUE, B. (1990) 'Implementing a Public Service Orientation in Local Government: The Process of Change', in K. Harrop and J. Fenwick (eds) *Consumerism and the Public Services*, Local Authority Management Unit Discussion Paper 90/1, Newcastle-upon-Tyne Polytechnic, pp. 32–49.

HAGUE, C. (1988) *The Development of Tenant Participation*, Research Paper no. 24, Department of Town and Country Planning, Edinburgh College of Art/Heriot-Watt University.

HAIN, P. (1980) *Neighbourhood Participation* (London: Temple Smith).

HALL, P. (1988) 'The Industrial Revolution in Reverse?', *The Planner*, January 1988, pp. 15–19.

HALL, S., WILLIAMS, R. and THOMPSON, E. (1969) 'The May Day Manifesto', in C. Oglesby (ed.) *The New Left Reader* (New York: Grove Press) pp. 111–43.

HALSEY, A.H. (1987) 'Social Trends Since World War II', in Central Statistical Office *Social Trends 17* (London: HMSO).

HAMBLETON, R. (1989) 'Local communities and the 1989 Act', *Going Local*, no. 14, pp. 17–19.

HAMBLETON, R. (1990) *Urban Government in the 1990s: Lessons from the USA*, Occasional Paper 35, School for Advanced Urban Studies, University of Bristol.

HAMBLETON, R. and HOGGETT, P. (1987) 'Beyond Bureaucratic Paternalism', in P. Hoggett and R. Hambleton (eds) *Decentralisation and Democracy: Localising Public Services*, Occasional Paper 28, School for Advanced Urban Studies, University of Bristol, pp. 9–28.

HAMBLETON, R., HOGGETT, P. and TOLAN, F. (1989) 'The Decentralisation of Public Services: A Research Agenda', *Local Government Studies*, vol. 15, no. 1, pp. 39–56.

HAMILTON, M.A. (1933) *John Stuart Mill* (London: Hamish Hamilton).

HAMPTON, W. (1987) *Local Government and Urban Politics* (London: Longman).

HAMPTON, W. (1990) 'Planning', in N. Deakin and A. Wright (eds) *Consuming Public Services* (London: Routledge) pp. 17–34.

HARLOW DISTRICT COUNCIL (1990) *A Consultation Guide to Good Practice* (Harlow: Policy and Planning Division, Harlow District Council).

HARRIS, R. and SELDON, A. (1979) *Over-ruled on Welfare* (London: Institute of Economic Affairs).

HARRISON, P. (1983) *Inside the Inner City* (Harmondsworth: Penguin).

HASLUCK, E. L. (1936) *Local Government in England* (Cambridge University Press).

HATCH, S. and MOCROFT, I. (1983) *Components of Welfare* (London: Bedford Square Press).

HATTON, D. (1988) *Inside Left: The Story So far* . . . (London: Bloomsbury).

HAYEK, F. (1973) *Law, Legislation and Liberty: Vol. 1, Rules and Order* (London: Routledge and Kegan Paul).

HAYEK, F. (1976) *Law, Legislation and Liberty: Vol. 2, The Mirage of Social Justice* (London: Routledge and Kegan Paul).

HELD, D. (1987) *Models of Democracy* (Oxford: Polity Press).

HEFFER, S. (1990) 'A clean sweep to end our town hall torpor', *Daily Telegraph*, 23 May 1990.

HILL, B. (1989) 'More equal than others', *New Statesman and Society*, 24 March 1989.

HIRST, P. (1989) 'After Henry', *New Statesman and Society*, 21 July, pp. 18–19.

HOBSBAWM, E. (1981) *The Forward March of Labour Halted?* (London: Verso).

HOGGETT, P. (1987) 'A farewell to mass production? Decentralisation as an emergent private and public sector paradigm', in P. Hoggett and R. Hambleton (eds) *Decentralisation and Democracy*, Occasional Paper 28, School for Advanced Urban Studies, University of Bristol, pp. 215–32.

HOGGETT, P. (1990) 'Reflections on Local Socialism', in Lawson, N. (ed.) *New Maps for the Nineties* (London: Clause 4 Publications and Chartist Publications) pp. 62–76.

HOLLIS, P. (1987) *Ladies Elect* (Oxford University Press).

HOLMAN, B. (1990) 'Charity begins in the office', *The Guardian*, 23 May 1990.

INGLEHART, R. (1977) *The Silent Revolution: Changing Values and Political Styles Among Western Publics* (Princeton University Press).

INSTITUTE OF PUBLIC RELATIONS (1986) *Public Relations in Local Government* (London: Institute of Public Relations)

ISLINGTON LABOUR PARTY LOCAL GOVERNMENT COMMITTEE (1981) *A Socialist Programme for Islington 1982*.

ISLINGTON LONDON BOROUGH COUNCIL (1989) *Review of Neighbourhood Forums*, report of the Chief Executive to the Neighbourhood Services Sub-committee, 11 September 1989.

JOHNSON, N. (1987) *The Welfare State in Transition: The Theory and Practice of Welfare Pluralism* (Brighton: Wheatsheaf Books).

JOHNSTON, R. J. and PATTIE, C. J. (1989) 'The Changing Electoral Geography of Great Britain', in J. Mohan (ed.) *The Political Geography of Contemporary Britain* (London: Macmillan) pp. 51–68.

JONES, A. (1988) 'Collaboration with Consumers: Learning How to Listen', in I. Allen (ed.) *Hearing the Voice of the Consumer* (London: Policy Studies Institute) pp. 53–61.

JONES, G.W. and STEWART, J.D. (1982) 'The Local Factor in a Local Election', *Local Government Chronicle*, 18 June.

JONES, P. d'A. (1965) *The Consumer Society* (Harmondsworth: Penguin).

JORDAN, A.E. and RICHARDSON, J.J. (1987) *Government and Pressure Groups in Britain* (Oxford University Press).

KATEB, G. (1984) *Hannah Arendt: Politics, Conscience, Evil* (Oxford: Martin Robertson).

KAVANAGH, D. (1980) 'Political Culture in Great Britain. The Decline of the Civic Culture', in G. A. Almond and S. Verba (eds) *The Civic Culture Revisited* (Boston: Little, Brown).

KEITH-LUCAS, B. (1952) *The English Local Government Franchise* (Oxford: Basil Blackwell).

KERR, D. (1990) 'Client Focus: An Appraisal by a Member Panel of What Public Service Orientation means to Cambridgeshire', in K. Harrop and J. Fenwick (eds) *Consumerism and the Public Services*, Local Authority Management Unit Discussion Paper 90/1, Newcastle-upon-Tyne Polytechnic, pp. 11–21.

KHAN, U. (1989) *Neighbourhood Forums and the 'New Left': Representation Beyond Tokenism?*, paper presented to the Political Studies Association annual conference, University of Warwick, April 1989.

KING, D.S. and WALDRON, J. (1988) 'Citizenship, Social Citizenship and the Defence of Welfare Provision', *British Journal of Political Science*, vol. 18, no. 4, pp. 415–43.

KING, R. (1985) 'Corporatism and the Local Economy', in W. Grant (ed.) *The Political Economy of Corporatism* (London: Macmillan) pp. 202–28.

KINGSMILL JONES, M.L. (1951) 'The Relationship between Voluntary Associations and the Local Authorities', *The Councillor*, vol. 4, no. 2, pp. 3–8.

KIRKPATRICK, J. (1988) 'Consumer Strategy in the Public Sector: are you being served?', *Public Money and Management*, vol. 8, nos. 1/2, pp. 41–3.

KITCHING, G. (1983) *Rethinking Socialism* (London: Methuen).

KRIEGER, J. (1986) *Reagan, Thatcher and the Politics of Decline* (Cambridge: Polity Press).

LABOUR COORDINATING COMMITTEE (1984) *Go Local to Survive: Decentralisation in Local Government* (London: Labour Coordinating Committee).

LABOUR PARTY (1988) *Consumers and the Community* (London: Labour Party).

LABOUR PARTY (1989a) *Meet the challenge, make the change* (London: Labour Party).

LABOUR PARTY (1989b) *Quality Street: Labour's quality programme for local government* (London: Labour Party).

LABOUR PARTY (1990) *A good deal: developing customer contracts in local government* (London: Labour Party).

LAFFIN, M. (1986) *Professionalism and Policy: The Role of the Professions in the Central-Local Government Relationship* (Aldershot: Gower).

LANSLEY, S., GOSS, S. and WOLMAR, C. (1989) *Councils in Conflict: The Rise and Fall of the Municipal Left* (London: Macmillan).

LASKI, H.J. (1935) 'The Committee System in Local Government', in H.J. Laski, W. Ivor Jennings and W.A. Robson (eds) *A Century of Municipal Progress, 1835–1935* (London: Allen and Unwin) pp. 82–108.

LAWRENCE, R. (1990) 'Birmingham's Community Care Special Action Project', *Local Government Administrator*, vol. 9, no. 4, pp. 20–1.

LEADBEATER, C. (1988) 'Power to the person', *Marxism Today*, October, pp. 14–19.

LEAT, D. (1988) *Voluntary Organisations and Accountability* (London: NCVO).

LEE, J.M. (1963) *Social Leaders and Public Persons* (Oxford University Press).

LEES, R. and MAYO, M. (1984) *Community Action for Change* (London: Routledge and Kegan Paul).

LEICESTER CITY COUNCIL (n.d.) *Customer Care Code: Guide to a Better Service for Housing Staff* (Leicester: Leicester City Council).

LEONARD, P. (1973) 'Professionalism, Community Action and the Growth of Social Service Bureaucracies', in P. Halmos (ed.) *Professionalisation and Social Change*, Sociological Review Monograph no. 20, pp. 103–17.

LEWIS, N., SENEVIRATNE, M. and CRACKNELL, S. (1988) *Complaints Procedures in Local Government* (Sheffield: Centre for Criminological and Socio-legal Studies, University of Sheffield).

LINDSAY, R. (1986) 'Different Approaches to "Going Local": Cunninghame District Council', in Institute of Housing, *Going Local in Scotland* (Edinburgh: Institute of Housing Scottish Training Unit) pp. 18–26.

LISTER, P. (1990) *The Exclusive Society: Citizenship and the Poor* (London: Child Poverty Action Group).

LIVERPOOL BLACK CAUCUS (1986) *The Racial Politics of Militant in Liverpool* (London: Runnymede Trust and Liverpool: Merseyside Area Profile Group).

LIVINGSTONE, K. (1981) Interview in *Marxism Today*, November, pp. 16–20.

LOCAL GOVERNMENT INFORMATION UNIT (1990) *New Directions in local government: going for quality* (London: Local Government Information Unit).

LOCAL GOVERNMENT TRAINING BOARD (1987) *Getting Closer to the Public* (Luton: Local Government Training Board).

LOCAL GOVERNMENT TRAINING BOARD (1988) *Learning from the Public* (Luton: Local Government Training Board).

LOUGHLIN, M. (1986) *Local Government in the Modern State* (London: Sweet and Maxwell).

LOWE, P. and GOYDER, J. (1983) *Environmental Groups in Politics* (London: Allen and Unwin).

LOWE, S. (1986) *Urban Social Movements* (London: Macmillan).

LOWNDES, V. (1990) *Thriving on Chaos? Experiences of Decentralisation in an East London Borough*, paper presented to the annual conference of the Political Studies Association, University of Durham, April 1990.

LUNTLEY, M. (1989) *The Meaning of Socialism* (London: Duckworth).

LUSTGARTEN, L. (1989) 'Racial inequality and the limits of the law', in R. Jenkins and J. Solomos (eds) *Racism and equal opportunity policies in the 1980s* (Cambridge University Press) pp. 14–29.

MACKINTOSH, M. and WAINWRIGHT, H. (eds) (1987) *A Taste of Power: The Politics of Local Economics* (London: Verso).

MANCHESTER CITY COUNCIL (1986) *Report of the Consultation and Participation Officer's Working Party*, Neighbourhood Services Committee, 15 July 1986.

MARSHALL, G., NEWBY, H. and ROSE, D. (1989) *Social Class in Modern Britain* (London: Hutchinson).

MARWICK, A. (1982) *British Society Since 1945* (Harmondsworth: Penguin).

MASON, D. (1989a) 'Local Government', in M. Pirie (ed.) *A Decade of Revolution: The Thatcher Years* (London: Adam Smith Institute) pp. 45–63.

MASON, D. (1989b) 'Private Reasons . . .', *Local Government News*, April 1989, pp. 26–7.

MATHER, G. (1989) 'Thatcherism and Local Government: An Evaluation', in J. Stewart and G. Stoker (eds) *The Future of Local Government* (London: Macmillan) pp. 212–35.

MATHEWS, J. (1989) *Age of Democracy: the Politics of post-Fordism* (Oxford University Press).

MAUD, J. (1937) *Local Government in Modern England* (London: Thornton Butterworth).

MAUD, SIR J., Chairman (1967a) *Management of Local Government, Volume 1, Report of the Committee on the Management of Local Government* (London: HMSO).

MAUD, SIR J., Chairman (1967b) *Management of Local Government, Volume 2, The Local Government Councillor* (London: HMSO).

MAUD, SIR J., Chairman (1967c) *Management of Local Government, Volume 3, The Local Government Elector* (London: HMSO).

MAXWELL, S. (1989) *Riding the Tiger: The Scottish Voluntary Sector in the Market Economy* (Edinburgh: Scottish Council for Voluntary Organisations).

MAYER, J. E. and TIMMS, N. (1970) *The client speaks* (London: Routledge and Kegan Paul).

MCCAFFERTY, P. and RILEY, D. (1989) *A Study of Cooperative Housing* (London: HMSO).

MCDOWELL, L. (1989) 'In Work', in M. Ball, F. Gray and L. McDowell, *The Transformation of Britain* (London: Fontana) pp. 137–80.

MCKAY, D. H. and COX, A. W. (1979) *The Politics of Urban Change* (London: Croom Helm).

MCKENZIE, E. (1989) 'Morning in Privatopia', *Dissent*, Spring 1989, pp. 257–60.

MCKIE, D. (1973) *A Sadly Mismanaged Affair* (London: Croom Helm).

MIDWINTER, E. (1979) 'To spend or not to spend: the consumer's neglected viewpoint', in M. Minogue, (ed.) *The Consumer's Guide to Local Government* (London: Macmillan) pp. 134–37.

MILL, J.S. (1947) *Utilitarianism, Liberty and Representative Government* (London: J. M. Dent and Sons).

MILLER, G. (1987) 'The Industrialists' View – George Miller', in D. Englefield (ed.) *Local Government and Business: A Practice Guide* (London: Municipal Journal Ltd) pp. 88–92.

MILLER, J. (1987) *"Democracy is in the Streets": From Port Huron to the Siege of Chicago* (New York: Simon and Schuster).

MILLER, W. (1988) *Irrelevant Elections? The Quality of Local Democracy in Britain* (Oxford University Press).

MINFORD, P. (1988) 'How to De-politicise Local Government', *Economic Affairs*, vol. 9, no. 1, pp. 12–16.

MOORE JNR., B. (1972) *Reflections on the Causes of Human Misery and upon Certain Proposals to Eliminate Them* (London: Allen Lane The Penguin Press).

MORI (1989) *Residents' Attitude Survey* conducted for Braintree District Council (London: MORI).

MORTON, J. (1989) 'Under new management', *Local Government News*, October 1989.

MOUFFE, C. (1988) 'The civics lesson', *New Statesman and Society*, 7 October 1988, pp. 28–31.

NAIRN, I. (1982) *The Break-up of Britain* (London: New Left Books).

NATHAN, LORD (1990) *Effectiveness and the Voluntary Sector* (London: NCVO).

NATIONAL CONSUMER COUNCIL (1986) *Measuring Up: Consumer Assessment of Local Authority Services* (London: National Consumer Council).

NCVO (1988) *NCVO Annual Review 1987–88* (London: NCVO).

NCVO (1989) *Voluntary Agencies Directory* (London: NCVO).

NCVO (1990) *Planning for Partnership: A Framework for Local Authorities and Voluntary Organisations* (London: NCVO).

NCVO (n.d.) *Supporting Local Voluntary Action* (London: NCVO).

NEWCASTLE-UPON-TYNE CITY COUNCIL (1985) *West City Consumer Survey 1985: Report by Head of Policy Services to Performance Review and Efficiency Committee*, 4 October 1985.

NEWHAM DOCKLANDS FORUM (1983) *The People's Plan for the Royal Docks* (West Ham: Newham Docklands Forum).

NEWHAM LONDON BOROUGH COUNCIL (1989) *Central Newham: Adopted Local Plan* (East Ham: Newham London Borough Council).

NEW SOCIETY (1988) *Grassroots Initiatives* (London: Bedford Square Press).

NEWTON, K. (1976) *Second City Politics* (Oxford University Press).

NORWICH CITY COUNCIL (1987) *Report of the City Treasurer, on the Public Opinion Survey of Environmental Services, to the Planning Committee*, 18 June 1987.

NORWICH CITY COUNCIL (1988) *Norwich Advice Services and the Advice Arcade: Second Report* (Norwich: Norwich City Council).

OLDFIELD, A. (1990) 'Citizenship: an Unnatural Practice?', *Political Quarterly*, vol. 61, no. 2, pp. 177–87.

OUSELEY, H. (1984) 'Local Authority Race Initiatives', in M. Boddy and C. Fudge (eds) *Local Socialism?* (London: Macmillan) pp. 133–59.

PALMER, J.A.D. (1972) 'Introduction to the British Edition', in R. Goodman, *After the Planners* (Harmondsworth: Penguin) pp. 9–50.

PERKIN, H. (1973) 'Public Participation in Government Decision-making: The Historical Experience', *Proceedings of the Town and Country Planning Summer School 1973* (London: Royal Town Planning Institute) pp. 6–9.

PETERS, T.J. (1987) *Thriving on Chaos: Handbook for a Management Revolution* (London: Pan).

PETERS, T.J. and AUSTIN, N. (1986) *A Passion for Excellence: The Leadership Difference* (London: Fontana/Collins).

PETERS, T.J. and WATERMAN, R.H. JR. (1982) *In Search of Excellence: Lessons from America's Best-run Companies* (London: Harper and Row).

PHAURE, S. (1990) 'London Community Care Alliance', *Voluntary Voice*, issue 45, p. 24.

PINKNEY, R. (1984) 'An Alternative Political Strategy? Liberals in Power in English Local Government', *Local Government Studies*, vol. 10, no. 3, pp. 69–84.

PLANT, R. (1988) *Citizenship, rights and socialism*, Fabian Tract No. 531 (London: Fabian Society).

PLANT, R. (1989) 'Trinity of Concern', *The Times*, 13 February 1989.

POLLITT, C. (1988a) 'Editorial: consumerism and beyond', *Public Administration*, vol. 66, no. 2, pp. 121–4.

POLLITT, C. (1988b) 'Bringing consumers into performance measurement: concepts, consequences and constraints', *Policy and Politics*, vol. 16, no. 2, pp. 77–87.

POTTER, J. (1988) 'Consumerism and the public sector: how well does the coat fit?', *Public Administration*, vol. 66, no. 2, pp. 149–64.

POWER, A. (1988) *Under New Management* (London: Priority Estates Project).

PRASHAR, U. and NICHOLAS, S. (1986) *Routes or Roadblocks? Consulting Minority Communities in London Boroughs* (London: Runnymede Trust).

PRIOR, D., JOWELL, T. and LAWRENCE, R. (1989) 'Carer Consultation: towards a strategy for consumer-led change', *Local Government Policy Making*, vol. 16, no. 2, pp. 17–25.

PROFILE PUBLIC RELATIONS (1988) *A Communications Audit for Norfolk County Council* (London: Profile Public Relations).

RANSON, S. (1990) 'Education', in N. Deakin and A. Wright (eds) *Consuming Public Services* (London: Routledge) pp. 182–200.

RANSON, S. and STEWART, J. (1989) 'Citizenship and Government: The Challenge for Management in the Public Domain', *Political Studies*, vol. xxxvii, no. 1, pp. 5–24.

REDCLIFFE-MAUD, LORD, Chairman (1969) *Royal Commission on Local Government in England 1966–1969, Volume 1, Report* (London: HMSO).

REDLICH, J. and HIRST, F.W. (1970) *The History of Local Government in England* (London: Macmillan).

REGAN, D.E. (1980) *A Headless State: The Unaccountable Executive in British Local Government*, an inaugural lecture (University of Nottingham).

RHODES, R.A.W. (1987) 'Developing the public service orientation, or let's add a *soupcon* of political theory', *Local Government Studies*, vol. 13, no. 3, pp. 63–73.

RICHARDSON, T.R. (1988) *Public Relations in Local Government* (London: Heinemann).

RIDLEY, N. (1988) *The Local Right: enabling not providing* (London: Centre for Policy Studies).

ROCHDALE METROPOLITAN BOROUGH COUNCIL (1987) *Community Based Action Areas*, Annual Review of Policies and Progress 1986–7.

ROSE, E.J.B. et al. (1969) *Colour and Citizenship* (Oxford University Press).

ROXBURGH DISTRICT COUNCIL (1989) *Report of the Chief Executive, Development of Tourism and Publicity Committee*, 12 January.

RUSTIN, M. (1985) *For a Pluralist Socialism* (London: Verso).

RYAN, A. (1990) 'State and citizen: a mutual respect', *The Times*, 12 September 1990.

SAFE NEIGHBOURHOODS UNIT (1987) *Your Views for a Change: A Survey of Residents' Views on Borough Services* (London: Safe Neighbourhoods Unit).

SAMUEL, R. (1985) 'Breaking up is very hard to do', *The Guardian*, 2 December.

SANDERS, C. (1989) 'Blueprint for the future?', *New Statesman and Society*, 5 May 1989, pp. 26–7.

SAUNDERS, P. (1980) *Urban Politics: A Sociological Interpretation* (Harmondsworth: Penguin).

SEABROOK, J. (1984) *The Idea of Neighbourhood* (London: Pluto Press).

SELDON, A. (1982) 'Preface', in D. Green, *Welfare State: For Rich or For Poor?* (London: Institute of Economic Affairs) pp. 5–7.

SENEVIRATNE, M. and CRACKNELL, S. (1988) 'Consumer complaints in public sector services', *Public Administration*, vol. 66, no. 2, pp. 181–93.

SHERMAN, A. (1970) *Local Government Reorganisation and Industry* (London: Aims of Industry).

SHORT, J. (1989) *The Humane City* (Oxford: Basil Blackwell).

SIMON, E.D. (1926) *A City Council from Within* (London: Longman).

SKEFFINGTON, A., Chairman, (1969) *People and Planning, Report of the Committee on Public Participation in Planning*, (London: HMSO).

SMITH, B.C. (1967) 'Torquay', in L.J. Sharpe (ed.) *Voting in Cities* (London: Macmillan) pp. 209–31.

SMITH, G. (1988) 'Applying Marketing to the Public Sector: the Case of Local Authority Leisure Centres', *International Journal of Public Sector Management*, vol. 1, no. 3, pp. 36–45.

SMITH, J. (1987) 'Social Services', in D. Clode, C. Parker and S. Etherington (eds) *Towards the Sensitive Bureaucracy* (Aldershot: Gower) pp. 75–85.

SMITH, R.W. and PRESTON, F.W. (1977) *Sociology: an introduction* (New York: St. Martin's Press).

STEVENSON, J. (1984) *British Society 1914–45* (Harmondsworth: Penguin).

STEWART, J. (1986) *Has Marketing a Role in Local Government?*, Discussion Paper no. 6 (Luton: Local Government Training Board).

STEWART, J. and CLARKE, M. (1987) 'The public service orientation: issues and dilemmas', *Public Administration*, vol 69, no. 2, pp. 161–77.

STEWART, J. and STOKER, G. (1988) *From local administration to community government*, Fabian Research Series 351 (London: Fabian Society).

STEWART, M. (1984) *Talking to Local Business: The involvement of Chambers of Commerce in local affairs*, Working Paper 38, School for Advanced Urban Studies, University of Bristol.

STIRLING DISTRICT COUNCIL (1988) *Partnership with the People* (Stirling: Stirling District Council).

STOKER, G. (1988) *The Politics of Local Government* (London: Macmillan).

STOKER, G. (1989) 'Creating a Local Government for a Post-Fordist Society: The Thatcherite Project?', in J. Stewart and G. Stoker (eds) *The Future of Local Government* (London: Macmillan) pp. 141–70.

STOREY, K. (1986) 'Getting along with the planners', *Local Council Review*, vol. 37, no. 1, p. 9.

SULLIVAN, D. (1987) 'Indigestion and the Radish', *Chartist*, May–June 1987, pp. 20–21.

TAAFFE, P. and MULHEARN, T. (1988) *Liverpool: A City that Dared to Fight* (London: Fortress Books).

TAM, H. (1989) 'Marketing has a distinct function with wider scope than selling', *Local Government Chronicle*, 18 August 1989, p. 27.

THOMAS, C. (1988) 'Contracting-Out: Managerial Strategy or Political Dogma?', in V. V. Ramanadham (ed.) *Privatisation in the UK* (London: Routledge) pp. 153–70.

THOMPSON, C. (1989) 'Dilemmas for Voluntary Groups', in NCVO, *Should Voluntary Organisations Provide More Services?*, Contracts for Care Conference Report No. 2 (London: NCVO) pp. 1–3.

THORNLEY, A. (1989) *What Happened to Participation in Planning? The British Experience under Thatcherism*, paper presented to the Third Annual Congress of the Association of European Schools of Planning, Tours, France, November 1989.

UNIVERSITY OF STRATHCLYDE AND CITY OF GLASGOW DISTRICT COUNCIL (1989) *Community Councils Conference 1989: Report of Proceedings* (Glasgow: Community Councils Resource Centre).

VIELBA, C. (1986) 'Marketing and Local Government: A Contradiction in Terms?', *Local Government Studies*, vol. 12, no. 6, pp. 14–19.

WALLER, R. (1980) 'The 1979 Local and General Elections in England and Wales: Is there a Local/National Differential?', *Political Studies*, vol. XXVIII, no. 3, pp. 443–50.

WALSH, K. (1989) *Marketing in Local Government* (Harlow: Longman).

WALSH, K. (1990) 'Duality of Service in Housing Management', in K. Harrop and J. Fenwick (eds) *Consumerism and the Public Services*, Local Authority Management Unit Discussion Paper 90/1, Newcastle-upon-Tyne Polytechnic, pp. 22–31.

WALZER, M. (1980) *Radical Principles* (New York: Basic Books).

WANDSWORTH LONDON BOROUGH COUNCIL (1988) *It's your home . . . your estate . . . You decide!*, an information pack about management co-ops in Wandsworth.

WARDE, A. (1989) 'The Future of Work', *Social Studies Review*, September, pp. 11–15.

WARREN, J. H. (1948) *Municipal Administration* (London: Pitman).

WEBB, S. (1891) *The London Programme* (London: Swan, Sonnenschein and Co.).

WEBB, S. (1910) 'Social movements', in A. W. Ward, G. W. Prothero and S. Leathes (eds) *The Cambridge Modern History*, Vol. XII (Cambridge University Press) pp. 730–65.

WEBB, S. and B. (1922) *English Local Government: Statutory Authorities for Special Purposes* (London: Longman, Green and Co.).

WEBSTER, K. (1988) 'Hampshire Strengthens Its Marketing', *County Councils Gazette*, July 1988, pp. 110–12.

WEST LANCASHIRE DISTRICT COUNCIL (1989) *Local Control for Council Tenants in Digmoor*, an information sheet for residents.

WHITE, I. (1988) 'Consumer Influences: Challenge for the Future', in I. Allen (ed.) *Hearing the Voice of the Consumer* (London: Policy Studies Institute) pp. 1–12.

WHITEHEAD, P. (1985) *The Writing on the Wall* (London: Michael Joseph).

WIDDICOMBE, D., Chairman (1985) *Local Authority Publicity, Interim Report of the Committee of Inquiry into the Conduct of Local Authority Business* (London: HMSO).

WIDDICOMBE, D., Chairman (1986a) *The Conduct of Local Authority Business, Report of the Committee of Inquiry into the Conduct of Local Authority Business* (London: HMSO).

WIDDICOMBE, D., Chairman (1986b) *Research Volume I: The Political Organisation of Local Authorities* (London: HMSO).

WIDDICOMBE, D., Chairman (1986c) *Research Volume II: The Local Government Councillor* (London: HMSO).

WIDDICOMBE, D., Chairman (1986d) *Research Volume III: The Local Government Elector* (London: HMSO).

WIDDICOMBE, D., Chairman (1986e) *Research Volume IV: Aspects of Local Democracy* (London: HMSO).

WILKINSON, B. (1988) 'Brighton Womens' Committee', National Association of Local Government Womens' Committees *News Bulletin*, no. 3, pp. 9–11.

WILLMOTT, P. (1986) *Social Networks, Informal Care and Public Policy* (London: Policy Studies Institute).

WILLMOTT, P. (1987) *Friendship Networks and Social Support* (London: Policy Studies Institute).

WILLMOTT, P. (1989) *Community Initiatives: Patterns and Prospects* (London: Policy Studies Institute).

WISTRICH, E. (1972) *Local Government Reorganisation: the first years of Camden* (London: Camden London Borough Council).

WOLFENDEN, LORD (1978) *The Future of Voluntary Organisations* (London: Croom Helm).

WOMEN'S NATIONAL COMMISSION (1989) *Womens' Organisations in Great Britain 1987/88* (London: Cabinet Office).

WREKIN DISTRICT COUNCIL (1987) *Report of the Chief Executive, on Customer Services: Local Shops, to the Policy and Resources Committee*, 15 October.

WREKIN DISTRICT COUNCIL (1988) *In (re)Search of Customers* (Telford: Wrekin District Council).

YOUNG, K. (1985) 'Shades of Opinion', in R. Jowell and S. Witherspoon (eds) *British Social Attitudes: the 1985 Report* (Aldershot: Gower) pp. 1–32.

YOUNG, K. (1989) 'The space between words: local authorities and the concept of equal opportunities', in R. Jenkins and J. Solomos (eds) *Racism and equal opportunity policies in the 1980s* (Cambridge University Press) pp. 93–109.

YOUNG, M. and WILLMOTT, P. (1957) *Family and Kinship in East London* (London: Routledge and Kegan Paul).

ZIPFEL, T. (1989) *Estate Management Boards: An Introduction* (London: Priority Estates Projects).

ZUBAIDA, S. (ed.) (1970) *Race and Racialism* (London: Tavistock).

Index

Index

Heffer, S. 156
Held, D. 162
Hill, B. 184
Hirst, F.W. 55
Hirst, P. 30
Hobsbawm, E. 33
Hobson, J.A. 25
Hodge, M. 167
Hoggett, P. 31, 113, 169
  reform strategies 152–3, 180
Hollis, P. 10
  Edwardian local
    government 15–16
  women 5, 55–6
Holman, B. 149
House of Lords 55
housing
  asset transfers 143–5
  building industry and diverse
    forms 35
  user participation 59, 60–6
Housing Act (1980) 60
Housing Act (1985) 60–1, 144
Housing Act (1988) 144, 150
housing associations 144, 150
housing co-operatives 63
Housing and Planning Act
  (1986) 65
Hurd, D. 170, 171

individual roles 8–20
  enabling politics 183–7
  social groups and 21, 183–4
  see also citizens; clients;
    consumers; customers;
    ratepayers; shareholders;
    voters
industrialisation 24–6
  de-industrialisation 27–32
industry
  attracting 120–1
  local and consultation 86–8
informal sector 127–8, 128–35
information 53–4, 106–24
  improving access 107–15
  marketing 120–4
  public relations 115–20
information technology 113

Inglehart, R. 40
Inner London Education
  Authority 35, 159
Institute of Marketing 120
Institute of Public Relations 115,
  123
Ipswich Angle 118
Islington 102, 112
  neighbourhood forums 176–8
  race relations committee 84
  tenant management co-ops 64

Jackson, K. 19
James, M. 10
Jenkin, P. 57, 119
Johnson, N. 126, 129
Jones, A. 131, 131–2
Jones, G.W. 14
Jones, P. 168
Jordan, A.E. 42
Jowell, T. 131

Kateb, G. 20
Kavanagh, D. 38–9
Keith-Lucas, B. 9, 10, 12
Kerr, D. 166
Khan, U. 178
King, D.S. 186
King, R. 88
Kingsmill Jones, M.L. 136
Kingston-upon-Thames 140–1
Kinnock, N. 18
Kirkpatrick, J. 163
Kitching, G. 173
Krieger, J. 39

Labour Coordinating
  Committee 49
Labour Party
  consumerism 167; and
    citizenship 18, 19–20
  council newspapers 118–19
  multi-cultural education 35
  pressure groups 45, 48–9
  voluntary sector 136
ladder of citizen
  participation 52–3
Laffin, M. 15